Communications in Computer and Information Science   1477

More information about this series at http://www.springer.com/series/7899

Aurona Gerber · Knut Hinkelmann (Eds.)

Society 5.0

First International Conference, Society 5.0 2021
Virtual Event, June 22–24, 2021
Revised Selected Papers

Editors
Aurona Gerber 🆔
University of Pretoria
Pretoria, South Africa

Knut Hinkelmann
FHNW University of Applied Sciences
and Arts Northwestern Switzerland
Windisch, Switzerland

ISSN 1865-0929   ISSN 1865-0937 (electronic)
Communications in Computer and Information Science
ISBN 978-3-030-86760-7   ISBN 978-3-030-86761-4 (eBook)
https://doi.org/10.1007/978-3-030-86761-4

This Springer imprint is published by the registered company Springer Nature Switzerland AG
The registered company address is: Gewerbestrasse 11, 6330 Cham, Switzerland

Preface

This volume of Springer, CCIS 1477, contains the revised accepted papers of Society 5.0 2021, the 1st International Conference on Society 5.0[1].

It is with great pleasure that we write this preface to the proceedings of the First International Conference on Society 5.0 (Society 5.0 2021), held as a virtual forum during June 22–24, 2021. In 2022, we hope the Society 5.0 conference will take place in Switzerland and, given the support for our first conference, we are confident that this multi- and interdisciplinary conference will grow into a premier conference series.

The annual conference series is jointly organized by the Universidad EAFIT (Colombia), the University of Pretoria (South Africa), University of Camerino (Italy), the Business School of the Shenzhen Technology University (China), the Universiti Malaysia Kelantan (Malaysia), Putra Business School (Malaysia), and the FHNW University of Applied Sciences and Arts Northwestern Switzerland.

Society 5.0 can be defined as a human-centered society that balances economic advancement with the resolution of social problems by a system that highly integrates cyberspace (virtual space) and physical (real) space. The aim of Society 5.0 is to create a society where social challenges are resolved by incorporating the innovations of the fourth industrial revolution (e.g., Internet of Things, big data, artificial intelligence (AI), and the sharing economy) into industry and social life. The term originated in Japan from the government's Council for Science, Technology, and Innovation, and it tackles many aspects of society like healthcare, mobility, infrastructure, politics, government, economy, and industry.

Society 5.0 also involves the enormous opportunities and challenges of the 21st century. Problems such as climate change, migration, and resource consumption must be solved jointly and globally. Sustainable Development Goals (SDGs), such as poverty and education, require international efforts. Lessons learned from the COVID-19 pandemic can have an important impact on dealing with global challenges and crisis situations. Technological advancements and trends for digital transformation should assist us in addressing these global problems. Convergence of cyberspace and physical space can foster new forms of global cooperation. People, things, and systems are all connected in cyberspace. Results obtained by AI can exceed the capabilities of humans and are fed back to physical space.

The Society 5.0 conference series's plan is to include the entire range of high-quality research about these opportunities and challenges as well as showcase solutions. The theme for Society 5.0 2021 was "Integrating Digital World and Real World to Resolve Challenges in Business and Society."

We sincerely thank all our organizers, partners, authors, and reviewers without whom this conference could not have been realized.

---

[1] https://www.conference-society5.org/.

This volume of Springer's CCIS series contains the revised accepted papers of Society 5.0 2021, the First International Conference on Society 5.0[2]. We are thankful that our first annual Society 5.0 conference elicited the support it did during this challenging year with all the uncertainties due to the COVID-19 pandemic.

We received 54 submissions, which were sent out for review to our Society 5.0 Program Committee (PC). The PC was comprised of more than 60 members from across the world. Each paper was reviewed by at least three PC members in a rigorous, blind review process where the following criteria were taken into consideration: relevance to society 5.0, significance, technical quality, scholarship, and presentation that included quality and clarity of writing. For this Society 5.0 CCIS volume, 15 full research papers were selected, which translates to an acceptance rate of 28%.

Thank you to all the authors and PC members, and congratulations to the authors whose work was accepted for publication in this Springer volume. We wish our readers a fruitful reading experience with these proceedings!

June 2021   Aurona Gerber
                                                                                        Knut Hinkelmann

---

[2] https://www.conference-society5.org/.

Organization

The annual conference series is jointly organized by the Universidad EAFIT (Colombia), the University of Pretoria (South Africa), University of Camerino (Italy), the Business School of the Shenzhen Technology University (China), the Universiti Malaysia Kelantan (Malaysia), Putra Business School (Malaysia), and the FHNW University of Applied Sciences and Arts Northwestern Switzerland.

  University of Applied Sciences Northwestern Switzerland

Steering Committee

Patrick Renz (Chair)	FHNW University of Applied Sciences and Arts Northwestern Switzerland, Switzerland
Roselina Ahmad Saufi	Universiti Malaysia Kelantan, Malaysia
Ahmad Shaharudin Abdul Latiff	Putra Business School, Malaysiä
Marc Aeschbacher	FHNW University of Applied Sciences and Arts Northwestern Switzerland, Switzerland
Sara Aguilar-Barrientos	Universidad EAFIT, Colombia
Carolina Ardila-López	Universidad EAFIT, Colombia
Noorshella Che Nawi	Universiti Malaysia Kelantan, Malaysia
Flavio Corradini	University of Camerino, Italy
Zhuoqi Ding	Shenzhen Technology University, SZTU Business School, China
Wan Fadzilah Wan Yusoff	Putra Business School, Malaysia
Aurona Gerber	University of Pretoria, South Africa
Knut Hinkelmannn	FHNW University of Applied Sciences and Arts Northwestern Switzerland, Switzerland
Stephan Jüngling	FHNW University of Applied Sciences and Arts Northwestern Switzerland, Switzerland
Gordana Kierans	Shenzhen Technology University, SZTU Business School, China
Hanlie Smuts	University of Pretoria, South Africa
Arie Hans Verkuil	FHNW University of Applied Sciences and Arts Northwestern Switzerland, Switzerland

Program Committee Chairs

Aurona Gerber   University of Pretoria, South Africa, and Centre of
                                 AI Research (CAIR), South Africa
Knut Hinkelmann   FHNW University of Applied Sciences and Arts
                                 Northwestern Switzerland, Switzerland

Organizing Committee

Marc Aeschbacher   FHNW University of Applied Sciences and Arts
                                 Northwestern Switzerland, Switzerland
Devid Montecchiari   FHNW University of Applied Sciences and Arts
                                 Northwestern Switzerland, Switzerland

Program Committee

Aurona Gerber (Chair)   University of Pretoria, South Africa
Knut Hinkelmann (Chair)   FHNW University of Applied Sciences and Arts
                                 Northwestern Switzerland, Switzerland

Ahmad Shaharudin Abdul Latiff   Putra Business School, Malaysia
Andreas Abecker   Disy Informationssysteme GmbH, Germany
Marc Aeschbacher   FHNW University of Applied Sciences and Arts
                                 Northwestern Switzerland, Switzerland
Sara Aguilar-Barrientos   Universidad EAFIT, Colombia
Roselina Ahmad Saufi   Universiti Malaysia Kelantan, Malaysia
Luis Alvarez Sabucedo   Universidade de Vigo, Spain
Luis Anido Rifon   Universidade de Vigo, Spain
Dimitris Apostolou   University of Piraeus, Greece
Carolina Ardila-López   Universidad EAFIT, Colombia
Dominik Bork   Technical University of Vienna, Austria
Flavio Corradini   University of Camerino, Italy
Noorshella Che Nawi   Universiti Malaysia Kelantan, Malaysia
Zhuoqi Ding   Shenzhen Technology University, SZTU Business
                                 School, China
Said Easa   Ryerson University, Canada
Sunet Eybers   University of South Africa, South Africa
Wan Fadzilah   Putra Business School, Malaysia
Hans-Georg Fill   University of Fribourg, Switzerland
Stella Gatziu Grivas   FHNW University of Applied Sciences and Arts
                                 Northwestern Switzerland, Switzerland
Marie Hattingh   University of Pretoria, South Africa
Dikki Indrawan   IPB University, Indonesia
Mohammad Ismail   Universiti Malaysia Kelantan, Malaysia
Stephan Jüngling   FHNW University of Applied Sciences and Arts
                                 Northwestern Switzerland, Switzerland

Hans Friedrich Witschel   FHNW University of Applied Sciences and Arts
                                    Northwestern Switzerland, Switzerland
Noor Raihani Zainol   Universiti Malaysia Kelantan, Malaysia

Contents

Blockchain and IoT Integration
for Society 5.0

Diletta Cacciagrano, Flavio Corradini, and Leonardo Mostarda

Computer Science Department, University of Camerino,
62032 Camerino, Macerata, Italy
{diletta.cacciagrano,flavio.corradini,leonardo.mostarda}@unicam.it

Abstract. The integration of Blockchain and Internet of Things (IoT) will have many implications in the Society 5.0. Blockchain technology has the potential to deal with issues that are related to data ownership, data integrity and data market monopolies. Public blockchains support the implementation of the data democratisation vision where everybody has access to data and there are no gatekeepers that make use of isolated data silos. Smart contracts can be used to provide contract transparency and allow citizens to manage their own data and the deriving economic value. This paper describes a novel blockchain-based security protocol that has been applied to a bicycle rental case study. This has been designed and implemented with the Society 5.0 vision in mind. Users store their own rental data by using a public blockchain. This eliminates the need of a centralised authority, provides data immutability and allows users to agree on transparent smart contract to manage their insurance, their payments and their own rental data. The smart lock protocol has been implemented in a real industrial product that uses the Ethereum public blockchain.

Keywords: Society 5.0 · Blockchain · Internet of Things · Smart lock · Smart contracts

1 Introduction

We are living in an era where the innovation of enabling technologies such as Internet of Things (IoT), Artificial Intelligence (AI) [16] and robotics will play a major role and bring new changes to economy and society. This view complies with the 5th Science and Technology Basic Plan, that was adopted by the Japanese Cabinet in 2016. This introduces Society 5.0 [4, 12], a Japan's vision for the next step in human evolution after hunter-gather, agrarian, industrial and information society stages. It aims at enhancing industrial competitiveness and helping with the establishment of a society more attuned to individual needs. The focus is on the vast potential of accumulating data, and new technologies of the fourth industrial revolution, in order to find solutions to social issues such as the declining birth rate, an ageing population, and environmental and energy issues.

© Springer Nature Switzerland AG 2021
A. Gerber and K. Hinkelmann (Eds.): Society 5.0 2021, CCIS 1477, pp. 1–12, 2021.
https://doi.org/10.1007/978-3-030-86761-4_1

Essentially, Society 5.0 is an integrated human-centred ecosystem where people, IoT devices and systems are seamlessly connected. Data from IoT devices are analysed by AI and injected back into the society.

The vision of Society 5.0 cannot be realised unless problems of data monopoly, data abuse and data ownership are overcome [21]. To date GAFA companies (i.e., Google, Apple, Facebook, and Amazon) concentrate most of the data which worries about data monopoly and abuse. Data monopoly prevents small and medium enterprise the use of data for innovation. Data should be shared to the society for an effective use in the digital age. The effective use of data also requires the definition of its ownership. In the Society 5.0 vision [7] data should be controlled by its originator or available to everyone when there are no privacy concerns. Monopoly, abuse and ownership of data issues need to be solved in order to avoid the Society 5.0 to turn into a dark one [6].

Public blockchain technology [9,13,20] can be a viable solution for the aforementioned problems. Blockchain implements a distributed ledger where any participant can maintain secure transaction records, ownerships, and promises. Records can be kept immutable and secure by using distributed algorithms and cryptographic primitives without the need of a central trusted authority. Ownership is assigned to each account holder by using wallets. Modern blockchains such as Ethereum [2] also allow the definition of digital smart contracts. These allow users to execute, control and document legally important events and actions according to the contract terms or the agreement. Public blockchain data are available to everyone thus data monopoly is avoided. Smart contracts are public and can be used to make the users aware of the information they are exposing. This tames the problem of data abuse and create user awareness. Furthermore, the research community is also proposing new techniques to deal with privacy and confidentiality issues on blockchain [18]. Although Blockchain technology is a promising solution its applicability to IoT needs also to deal with some challenges. Smart contracts are run by miners which can result in slow execution time (e.g., 10 min to mine a Bitcoin block while 20 s to mine an Ethereum one) and expensive fees [5,9,11].

This paper presents a novel secure protocol which integrates users, blockchain, two or more contractors and IoT devices that are constrained in terms of CPU and memory. The protocol allows authorised users to perform operations on the IoT devices. Operations are securely logged on the public blockchain which provides immutability and allows the execution of smart contracts. These can be used for billing and data analysis purposes. Our protocol also deals with issues of blockchain scalability (in terms of transaction per seconds and fees) and user privacy. More precisely, the protocol allows real-time IoT device operations since it is not bound to the transaction speed of the main blockchain. User privacy is guaranteed since it is not possible to understand which users performed which operation from the public blockchain data. The protocol have been applied to an electrical bicycle (in the following referred to as ebike) rental industrial case study [10] which includes IoT smart locks, two contractors (i.e., Insurance and Service provider), the Ethereum public Blockchain and citizens. The rental service is a human-centred one which complies with the Society 5.0 vision. Our secure protocol allows users to rent and pay securely ebikes. Smart contracts are used by the user, insurance and service provider to define an immutable and transparent smart contract which defines the rental and insurance price and the user data that will be publicly released. Thus, the user has a clear understanding of which data are made public. The use of blockchain also solves the need of a trusted party between service provider and insurance that is needed to bill the user per hourly use. Public blockchain data can be used by any specialised data analysis companies (i.e., data monopoly is avoided) to inject back into the society useful information such as fuel saved, reduced carbon emission and other customised information.

The novelty of this paper can be summarised as follow: (i) a novel blockchain-based protocol securely controlling IoT devices, running on small embedded devices, scaling in terms of transaction per seconds and having low fees; (ii) a real Society 5.0 case study where data are transparently stored and processed, and information is fed back into the society for social purposes.

The rest of the article is organised as follows: Sect. 2 provides some background on Ethereum; Sect. 3 introduces the requirements of the smart lock application; Sect. 4 details the secure protocol and the overall system architecture; Sect. 5 discusses the security of the protocol and its compliance with the Society 5.0 vision; Sect. 6 describes the related work; finally, Sect. 7 concludes the article and outlines future work.

2   Ethereum Background

A **blockchain** is a ledger that records transactions amongst parties in a verifiable and permanent way. The ledger is implemented in a distributed fashion by a network of nodes (often referred to as miners) that interact to write new transactions via a distributed consensus protocol [15]. This allows transactions to be replicated across several nodes thus making some attacks (e.g., modification) difficult. We focus on Ethereum [19] which allows the transfer of currency and the execution of **smart contracts**. These can be written by using a Turing-complete language. Smart contracts are applications that are run by the blockchain network. Ethereum contracts are written by using the Ethereum Virtual Machine (EVM) code that is a low-level, stack-based bytecode language. The instructions of this language are often translated into a human readable form that is referred to as **opcode** (see [19] for a complete list of EVM bytecodes). High-level programming languages are also available to define smart contracts. These can be compiled into EVM bytecode and executed in the blockchain. One of the most prominent language to define smart contracts is **Solidity**. The Ethereum platform is also used for implementing the Ether cryptocurrency. This can be exchanged between accounts. A wallet keeps a couple of public/private keys (that is the address). These are used to get and spend Ether.

The Ethereum blockchain forms a increasing list of blocks. Figure 1 shows all data that are contained in a block. A State of Ethereum is defined as a Merkle

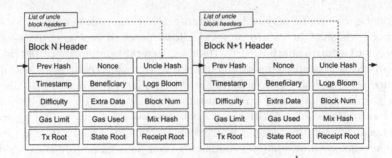

Fig. 1. Block data of the Ethereum blockchain

tree [8] and describes all current account balances and some additional data. The *state root* field is the hash of the root node of the state tree after all transactions are executed and finalised. The *tx root* field is the root of the Merkle tree which has all validated transactions. A transaction can be related to the transfer of Ether, the definition of a smart contract, the running of a smart contract or a token management. The *timestamp* and *Block num* are the block addition time and its a unique block identifier, respectively. The state after the transaction execution is kept in a transaction receipt store. All receipts are stored inside an index-keyed trie [14]. The hash of its root is placed in the block header as the *receipt root*.

The bloom filter [3] is created by using transaction log information. This is reduced to 256 bytes hash and all hashes are in the block header as the *logs bloom*. Each block also includes the hash of the prior block in the blockchain, *prev hash*, linking the two. This ensures the integrity of the previous block, all the way down to the first block. The hash is calculated on the header fields by using the Ethash [19] algorithm. More precisely, every time a new hash block is calculated, the Ethereum nodes perform a mining process (also referred to as proof-of-work) where they must find a nonce value that produces a desired hash[1]. When a node find the nonce (i.e., the block is solved), the consensus is used to spread the solution to other nodes. These verify the solution proposed and add the block to the blockchain. Sometimes separate blocks can be produced concurrently. This creates a temporary fork of branches. The Ghost protocol [17] is used in order to select one of the branches leaving the others as orphan ones (the orphan branches are stored in the *uncle hash* field). All Ethereum transactions cost a certain amount of **gas** [17], which corresponds to a tiny fee required by the blockchain infrastructure to process the transaction. The *gas limit* is the maximum amount of units of gas a user is willing to spend on a transaction. The block gas limit sets an upper limit to the *gas used* block field. This is the sum of all gas spent by the transactions of the block.

---

[1] This is a hash that contains a certain amount of initial zeros. The number of zeros, defined by the *difficulty* field, establishes the computational effort that is needed to find the hash.

3   Smart Lock Application Requirements

Figure 2 shows all entities that are involved in our smart lock system. Citizens can rent ebikes that are deployed in a smart city. Each ebike is equipped with a smart lock that can be opened and closed for renting purposes by using a mobile device. A service provider manages the user subscriptions and user rental authorisations while an insurance company provides liability, comprehensive, and collision coverage. Finally, companies such as data analysis ones can make use of publicly available data in order to perform analysis whose results are fed back into the society. The main functional and non-functional requirements of the smart lock system can be described as follows:

(R1) only users that are registered at the service provider can lock/unlock ebikes;

(R2) a user is charged per hourly use by using transparent contractual terms;

(R3) the profit is shared between the insurance and the service provider by using transparent contractual terms that cannot be changed unless they agree to do so;

(R4) rental contract and user data are stored in a trusted location and can be accessed at any time;

(R5) the lock and user device software should be suitable to run in a small embedded device that is constrained in terms of memory and CPU processing power (e.g., arduino [1]);

(R6) users privacy should be ensured (i.e., it should not be possible to understand which ebike is rent by which user);

(R7) the lock/unlock operations should take few seconds.

The first version of the smart lock application would store all lock and unlock user requests at the service provider. This would compute the user rental time at the end of each month in order to charge the user and pay the insurance fees. This solution was considered inappropriate by the insurance since they lack of mutual trust thus requirement R4 would be violated. As we are going to see in the next section a blockchain-based solution was implemented in order to ensure data immutability and avoid the need of a third trusted part.

4   A Blockchain-Based Smart Lock System

Figure 2 shows the smart lock protocol at a glance in the case the lock is open. For the sake of simplicity the protocol is not described by using a formal cryptographic notation (e.g., protocol narrations) and the focus is on the open/close rental operations (although any other operation is possible). We assume that all messages are confidential, messages are authenticated and timeliness is ensured. To this ending, encryption keys, timestamps and nonces are used. We use the notation || in order to denote the concatenation of data.

Figure 2 does not include the initial setup where the insurance and the service provider define and store a smart contract inside the Ethereum blockchain. This defines the hourly cost of the ebike renting, the insurance and service provider

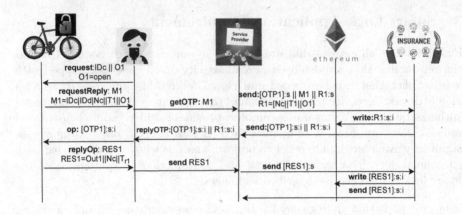

Fig. 2. Smart protocol opening scenario.

profit share, and all rental data that will be exposed. A user needs to register on the service provider website in order to use the rental service. At any time the user can use the rental contract from the Ethereum blockchain in order to view its terms, its fees, check his payment history, his rental data and other useful information.

An ebike rental always starts when the user sends his identity and an *open* operation to an ebike lock (message REQUEST:$ID_c||O_1$ of Fig. 2). The lock replies with a message M_1 that contains the identities of the device and the lock, a nonce N_c that uniquely identifies the user-device session and the time T_1 at which the operation was requested. The message M_1 is used by the user in order to interact with the service provider and get a one-time password (OTP) that is a password valid for one operation. A user can obtain the OTP by sending a request GETOTP:M_1 to the service provider. This receives the request and verifies the user subscription data and his balance. When the user is allowed to perform the operation a receipt $R_1 = [N_c||T_1||O_1]$ is generated and signed cooperatively by the service provider and the insurance company. This contains the operation OPEN that was granted to the user, the time T_1 at which the operation was requested and the user-device session identifier N_c. The signature is denoted with a colon followed by the signer. For instance in Fig. 2 $R_1 : s : i$ denotes the receipt R_1 signed by S and R. The signed receipt $R_1 : s : i$ is written on the Ethereum blockchain by the insurance company which also returns it to the service provider. The service provider and the insurance also generate and sign a one time password (i.e., $OTP_1 : s : i$ in Fig. 2). This is sent back to the user together with the receipt R_1 (message REPLYOTP : $OTP_1 : s : i||R_1 : s : i$ of Fig. 2). The OTP can be used to open the lock and the receipt R_1 can be kept locally by the user device for checking the fees to be paid or to solve any payment dispute that arises with the service provider.

The lock can now receive the OTP_1 and reply back to the user with the result of the operation (i.e., REPLYOP:RES_1 in Fig. 2). The data RES_1 contains the result of the operation (i.e., error or ok), the user-device session (i.e., N_c) and the time T_{r1} at with the result was generated. The result is always forwarded by the user to the service provider. The service provider and the Insurance cooperatively sign the result and write it on the blockchain. Error results are stored in the Ethereum blockchain in order to avoid the user is charged unfairly.

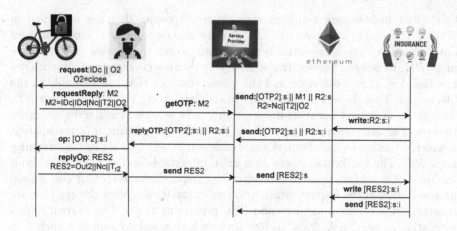

Fig. 3. Smart protocol closing scenario.

Figure 3 shows the closing scenario. The flow of the operations and their content are almost identical to the open operation. The only difference is the timestamp of the operation and the result (i.e., T_2 and T_{r2}), the generation of a new password (i.e., $OTP2$ in Fig. 3) and a new result content.

4.1 User and Insurance Fees Calculation

At the end of each month the service provider uses the smart contract and the public data in order to perform the following operations: (i) charge the users per hourly use; (ii) pay the insurance by considering the monthly bicycle rental time.

Suppose that a user session N_c is used to open the lock of a bicycle at time t_1 and the lock is closed at time t_2, then we denote with $t(N_c, t_1, t_2) = t_2 - t_1$ the time between a lock and an unlock operations (i.e., the time the bicycle was used). We denote with $T(u, a)$ the amount of hours the user u rents bicycles in a day a. This can be defined as $T(u, a) = \sum_i t(N_c, t_i, t_{i+1})$ where all t_i belongs to the same day a and N_c are all sessions of the user u in the day a. The user will be billed monthly by considering the monthly user bicycle rental time. This is calculated as follows: $T(u, m) = \sum_{a \in m} T(u, a)$ where u is the user and a is a day of the month m.

The service provider will pay the insurance company monthly by considering the monthly bicycle rental time. This can be calculated as follows $T(m) = \sum_{N_c \in m} t(N_c, t_i, t_{i+1})$ where N_c is a user session that is performed in the month m. The payment is done by using the blockchain as established by the registered contract.

5   Discussion and Results

Our smart lock system complies with all requirements that are described in Sect. 3. The one-time password OTP is only generated after a successful user authentication thus only authorised user can access the service (i.e., requirement $R1$). Ethereum ensures transparency and allows citizens to recompute the fees based on the public data and the public contract that are available at the blockchain. This ensures high integrity of the data stored (i.e., requirement $R2$). The profit is shared between the insurance and service provider by using an Ethereum smart contract. This defines the contractual terms in a transparent manner. Changes cannot be performed unless they agree to do so (i.e., requirement $R3$). The blockchain stores data in an immutable and secure way without the need of a central trusted authority (i.e., requirement $R4$). Our customised protocol allowed the implementation to run in small embedded devices that are constrained in terms of memory and CPU processing power. Our current implementation runs in an Arduino [1] like device where standard approach such TLS would not run (i.e., requirement $R5$). The public blockchain shows anonymous data that are the user random session identifier and the time of rental thus it is not possible to understand which ebike is rent by which user (i.e., requirement $R6$).

Our public blockchain-based implementation supports the data democratisation vision where everybody has access to data and there are no gatekeepers that make use of isolated data silos. To date data are used by third-party companies in order to calculate various statistics such as reduction in carbon emission and rental time. These statistics are fed back to the users in order to encourage a greener society.

OCM	RDA	SAT
10	634876	222607
20	1269688	416244
30	1904628	610379
40	2539952	803924
50	3206367	998992
60	3809896	1193854
70	4444836	1388638
80	5079584	1584176
90	5714780	1780853
100	6349208	1976492

Fig. 4. Gas consumption for the lock case study

We have simulated the smart lock protocol in order to calculate the fees that must be paid to write the user operations (i.e., open and close) on the public Ethereum Blockckain. We have used a scenario where each smart lock sends messages related to its opening and closing to a BESU Ethereum-based blockchain. A process generates 10 artificially generated datasets. The first dataset contains data for 10 opening and 10 closing messages in a month. Each subsequent dataset contains ten opening and closing operations more. The last dataset (the tenth) contains 100 opening and closing messages.

The insurance write the transaction on the blockchain according to the following two different strategies:

(RDA) this simulation is complaint with the protocol that is described in Sect. 4. Each opening and closing message is written by using a separate Ethereum transaction;

(SAT) this simulation stores at the end of each month all opening and closing operations in a single transaction.

Figure 4 shows our simulation results. We denote with OCM the amount opening operations in a month. For both RDA and SAT scenarions the gas consumption has a linear growth with respect to the number of OCM. The SAT approach saves around 64% gas consumption when compared with the RDA one. In fact, while the RDA solution writes an Ethereum transaction for each opening/close, the SAT solution only store an Ethereum transaction at end of each month (this has all opening and closing transactions). At the time of writing this paper, the RDA based solution for 100 opening and 100 closing operations would have a GAS consumption of 6349208 that is 1.7650798 ETH (about 2.524 euro). The SAT based solution would have a GAS consumption of 1976492 that is 0.5494648 ETH (about 785 euro). This account for 3.9 euro per operation. When off-chain approaches (see [5] for details) are considered, GAS consumption decreases to 23952 that is 0.0066587 (about 9.5 euro). This account for 0.04 euro per operations. The time that is need for the operations is acceptable since it always takes few seconds. In fact, our protocol is not bound to the transaction speed of the Ethereum main chain. The receipt is returned to the user by the service provider without waiting the Ethereum mining process (see Sect. 4 for details).

6   Related Work

Japan, where the Society 5.0 concept was born, represented some of the earliest adopter of Blockchain technology. Back in 2016, Japan's Ministry of Economy (METI) published a report about the impact of Blockchain technology with policy recommendations: the Japanese government followed this statement and we have seen numerous initiatives, as for example developing clear and fair laws to regulate cryptocurrency exchanges, or legally clarifying that Bitcoin is now considered an asset and a payment method.

At the beginning of 2018 Japan's biggest energy firm, TEPCO, invested in a British Blockchain startup. Other companies like SBI, Rakuten, Nomura and Daiwa are just a few of the brokerages spearheading the venture into new cutting-edge technologies like the Blockchain. Additionally, SBI launched its Ripple blockchain-based payments app for consumers. Is easy to see both the tech-savvy population and the government engaging in and encouraging Blockchain technology in Japan, again putting the country at the forefront of international technological development.

Sixteen Japanese virtual currency exchanges registered with the Financial Services Agency (FSA) joined forces in April 2018 to establish the Japan Virtual Currency Exchange Association.

Launched in 2018, the Virtual Currency Governance Task Force (VCGAF) is a study group established to develop safety measures for consumer protection. As they say "virtual currency perception has increased rapidly so in order to avoid large incidents consumer protection is an urgent task".

In May 2016, METI released a report on Blockchain technology, providing an overview of the technology, from detailing the step-by-step workings of a bitcoin transaction to outlining how the mechanics of the protocol could create stresses if applied to existing business practices. Use cases cited in the report included asset management, authentication, commercial distribution management, communication, content, crowdfunding, finance, IoT, loyalty points and rewards, medical services, prediction markets, public elections, sharing and storage.

Some cases of the Japanese government using Blockchain technology are: (i) Ministries of Justice and Land's Blockchain-based central repository of land and property registration; (ii) METI's Blockchain-based platform for trade; (iii) Japanese city of Tsukuba voting system using Blockchain.

Finally, METI also published "Japan's FinTech Vision", a comprehensive range of policy initiatives to nurture innovative FinTech services and create a dynamic market environment aimed at attracting entrepreneurs and companies from around the world.

In 2017, Tokio Marine and Nichido Fire Insurance and NTT DATA Corporation completed testing the first Blockchain-based insurance policy for marine cargo insurance certificates. Tokio Marine created a "data" bill of lading, letter of credit and a commercial invoice on a Blockchain, and tested this from the perspective of a shipper that needs a certificate of insurance in order to satisfy the insurance requirement on the letter of credit.

Organic Farm Aya, in Miyazaki Prefecture, together with Information Services International-Dentsu (ISID) and Sivira, worked on a pioneering blockchain pilot that will see organic vegetables grown in the prefecture logged on a distributed ledger. The system allows all parties to ensure the quality of organic produce from field to table. The pilot scheme also involves an Italian restaurant in Tokyo, which will begin sourcing its ingredients from farmers via the new platform.

Fujitsu launched "Blockchain Asset Service," and leverages user transaction data to promote regional revitalization. The Blockchain-based data storage system tokenizes traditional retail promotional strategies such as coupons and loyalty points, which the company claims will revitalize local economies by increasing consumers' willingness to buy, as well as improving data analysis methods in retail industries. With this service, users can collect digital points or stamps reading QR codes located in specific areas with smart devices, and then exchange them for coupons and other benefits that can be used in stores and shopping centers within the specified area. In addition, collection and usage data for the points, stamps, and coupons, which are recorded on the Blockchain distributed ledger, can be linked with user information for analysis.

7   Conclusions and Future Work

This paper presents a novel secure protocol which integrates users, blockchain, two or more contractors and IoT devices that are constrained in terms of CPU and memory. The protocol allows authorised users to perform operations on the IoT devices. Operations are securely logged on the public blockchain which provides immutability and allows the execution of smart contracts. We have applied our protocol to an ebike rental system that combines IoT devices (i.e., smart locks), companies (i.e., service provider and insurance) and the Ethereum blockchain. Our novel blockchain-based protocol is used to securely control the open and close operations of smart locks, bill the users and share the profit between service provider and insurance. The protocol runs on small embedded devices, reduces blockchain fees and has a good performance in terms of operation response time. In fact, the secure protocol is not bound to the Ethereum transaction validation time which would take around 20 s to complete. The use of the blockchain avoids data monopoly. Smart contracts are public and can be used to make the users aware of the economical terms and the information they are exposing. Blockchain also solves the need of a trusted party between service provider and insurance that is needed to store the user rental data and share the profit. Public blockchain data are used by specialised data analysis companies to inject back into the society useful information such as fuel saved, reduced carbon emission and other customised information. Our protocol only exposes a random number and the rental time. Thus, it is not possible to understand which ebike is rent by which user. As future work we are planning to apply the protocol to other application scenarios.

References

1. Badamasi, Y.A.: The working principle of an Arduino. In: 2014 11th International Conference on Electronics, Computer and Computation (ICECCO), pp. 1–4 (2014). https://doi.org/10.1109/ICECCO.2014.6997578
2. Bistarelli, S., Mazzante, G., Micheletti, M., Mostarda, L., Sestili, D., Tiezzi, F.: Ethereum smart contracts: analysis and statistics of their source code and opcodes. Internet Things **11**, 100198 (2020)
3. Bloom, B.H.: Space/time trade-offs in hash coding with allowable errors. Commun. ACM **13**(7), 422–426 (1970)

4. Deguchi, A., et al.: What is society 5.0? In: Hitachi-UTokyo Laboratory(H-UTokyo Lab.) (eds.) Society 5.0, pp. 1–23. Springer, Singapore (2020). https://doi.org/10.1007/978-981-15-2989-4_1

5. Cacciagrano, D., Corradini, F., Mazzante, G., Mostarda, L., Sestili, D.: Off-chain execution of IoT smart contracts. In: Barolli, L., Woungang, I., Enokido, T. (eds.) AINA 2021. LNNS, vol. 226, pp. 608–619. Springer, Cham (2021). https://doi.org/10.1007/978-3-030-75075-6_50

6. Economist: How to tame the tech titans – the dominance of Google, Facebook and Amazon is bad for consumers and competition (2018)

7. Radinsky, K.: Data monopolists like Google are threatening the economy. In: Competitive Strategy. Harvard Business Review (2015)

8. Merkle, R.C.: A digital signature based on a conventional encryption function. In: Pomerance, C. (ed.) CRYPTO 1987. LNCS, vol. 293, pp. 369–378. Springer, Heidelberg (1988). https://doi.org/10.1007/3-540-48184-2_32

9. Nakamoto, S.: Bitcoin: a peer-to-peer electronic cash system. Technical report, Manubot (2019)

10. Mondo Novo: 360lock smart padlock. iT Patent (2021). www.4-storm.com

11. Poon, J., Dryja, T.: The bitcoin lightning network: scalable off-chain instant payments (2016)

12. Salgues, B.: Society 5.0. Wiley, Hoboken (2018)

13. Sekaran, R., Patan, R., Raveendran, A., Al-Turjman, F., Ramachandran, M., Mostarda, L.: Survival study on blockchain based 6g-enabled mobile edge computation for IoT automation. IEEE Access 8, 143453–143463 (2020). https://doi.org/10.1109/ACCESS.2020.3013946

14. Singhal, B., Dhameja, G., Panda, P.S.: How Ethereum works, pp. 219–266. Apress, Berkeley (2018)

15. Swan, M.: Blockchain. O'Reilly Media, Sebastopol (2015)

16. Ullah, Z., Al-Turjman, F., Mostarda, L., Gagliardi, R.: Applications of artificial intelligence and machine learning in smart cities. Comput. Commun. 154, 313–323 (2020)

17. Vitalik, B.: Ethereum: a next generation smart contract and decentralized application platform (2018). Accessed 08 Dec 2018

18. Wang, S., Zhang, Y., Zhang, Y.: A blockchain-based framework for data sharing with fine-grained access control in decentralized storage systems. IEEE Access 6, 38437–38450 (2018). https://doi.org/10.1109/ACCESS.2018.2851611

19. Wood, G.: Ethereum: a secure decentralised generalised transaction ledger (2018). https://ethereum.github.io/yellowpaper/paper.pdf. Accessed 08 Dec 2018

20. Wood, G., et al.: Ethereum: a secure decentralised generalised transaction ledger. Ethereum Project Yellow Paper 151(2014), 1–32 (2014)

21. Yano, M., Dai, C., Masuda, K., Kishimoto, Y.: Creation of blockchain and a new ecosystem. In: Yano, M., Dai, C., Masuda, K., Kishimoto, Y. (eds.) Blockchain and Crypto Currency. ELIAP, pp. 1–19. Springer, Singapore (2020). https://doi.org/10.1007/978-981-15-3376-1_1

Modelling Transformation of Corporate Communications in the Digital Age

Susan Göldi[1] iD, Corin Kraft[2] iD, and Jacqueline Vitacco[3]([⊠]) iD

[1] Institute for Competitiveness and Communication ICC, School of Business, University of Applied Sciences and Arts Northwestern Switzerland FHNW, Olten, Switzerland
susan.goeldi@fhnw.ch
[2] Institute of Humanities and Social Science, School of Engineering, University of Applied Sciences and Arts Northwestern Switzerland FHNW, Windisch, Switzerland
corin.kraft@fhnw.ch
[3] School of Business, University of Applied Sciences and Arts Northwestern Switzerland FHNW, Olten, Switzerland
jacqueline.vitacco@fhnw.ch

Abstract. This article provides a brief overview on transformative trends in corporate communications based on a literature review. Furthermore, it presents a framework model on how to transform corporate communications in the digital age. The model is based on a grounded theory approach derived in a field study completed in 2015, which claims that more heterarchical structures in corporate communications are needed. In a subsequent project, the model is tested in an ongoing exploratory study. Based on the learnings from the two studies, we suggest a new model on how to organize corporate communications in the digital age. At the centre of the new model are written and audio-visual content, created by associates in a collaborative process and supported by the organisation.

Keywords: Corporate communications · Digital transformation · Heterarchical structures · Exploratory study · Field study

1 Introduction

Back in 2005, in a book on corporate communications Göldi claimed along with others [e.g. 1] that the field of corporate communications does not exclusively belong to communications experts, but to every single associate within the company. Through their behavior (e.g. customer contact, negotiations with suppliers, their appearance in public) associates contribute to (informal) corporate communications and represent their company due to the "constitutive capacity of communication" [2]. However, in contemporary theories of corporate communications, as well as in practice, communication is still seen as a managerial task. Since corporate communications reflects corporate policy, identity, reputation and image, it is mainly left to management and experts and not to employees in general for fear of "fragmentation" as opposed to an "orchestrated" or integrated communication approach [e.g. 3–7].

A. Gerber and K. Hinkelmann (Eds.): Society 5.0 2021, CCIS 1477, pp. 13–25, 2021.
https://doi.org/10.1007/978-3-030-86761-4_2

However, the integrated, unitary approach may no longer be as feasible as many would like it to be. In their review of perspectives on corporate communications, Christensen and Cornelissen [8] identify two different mindsets in corporate communications research and practice. On the one hand, a mindset that promotes the integrated approach, i.e., managing "all communication under one banner", which involves addressing different audiences at once with mainly one-way communication. On the other side of the equation lies a more participatory mindset that sees corporate communications as a more fragmented set of less uniform identities. They attribute this radical difference in perspectives to a "metonymic compression" [8]: "Communication" in corporate communications stands for a unitary actor while, in fact, by its very nature it also applies to many actors engaging in diverse communication activities. In any case, to date it does not seem that research in corporate communications has been able to resolve the discussion on whether, or when and why, corporate communications should be a centralized or decentralized business function.

Nevertheless, in practice, individual employees are still expected to align themselves with a unified corporate image or brand when communicating as members of an organization. The rise of digital channels poses a clear threat to this mindset and, thus, might finally change this. With the increasing pace of communication and need to be present and interact on digital channels, the one-person-speaks-for-the-firm-policy may eventually become obsolete. Social media, for example, which allow companies to have two-way conversations with individuals rather than with an abstract "audience" or stakeholder group, reduces the control companies have on messaging and agenda-setting as well as the public's interpretation of their messages. Employees sharing information on social media, either professionally or privately, are influencing corporate image although they might not always be aware of it [9], thus necessitating social media guidelines or policies to prevent unfavorable interpretations or fragmented messaging. These may be counterproductive. By its very nature, communication on social media channels should be authentic, transparent, immediate, collaborative, and it should represent the exact opposite of "centralized authority" [10–12]. In a similar way, communication on social media has also been described as "democratic" [e.g. 13]. Therefore, if the medium shapes the message, then the medium an organization chooses to communicate on may even be more important for corporate image and reputation than the message itself. However, many organizations continue to perceive these channels primarily as an additional venue to disseminate their one-way messages and are quasi-paralyzed for example when individual readers leave comments, thus turning it into a two-way communication.

Kaak [14] suggests that "new technologies may encourage new forms of communication" as technological advances have created new opportunities to communicate with stakeholders on an increased number of public-facing channels. As a consequence, the communications team alone cannot generate content effectively anymore which means that companies need new content generation workflows.

With more channels, new media and digital platforms, we expect that new digital opportunities in corporate communications will create an ever-increasing demand of communication content and dialogue. In order to produce more content, especially more authentic content, and interact fast on multiple channels, companies need to develop new concepts for producing, managing and publishing communication content. Implementing these new concepts will require new structures in the organization as a whole as well as new roles and processes for its communicators and content managers. These changes go along with digital transformation encompassing economic, social as well as political elements determined by new technology and reshaping business structures, roles and processes [15]. Up to now corporate communications remains "a neglected perspective in discussions on the digital transformation" [16]. Digital transformation might partly drive changes in corporate communication or be driven by the transformation of traditional corporate communications management [17].

This article provides a brief overview on transformative trends in corporate communications based on a literature review and the authors' experience with digital trends in Swiss SMEs as well as international companies (Sect. 2). Furthermore, it presents a framework model on how to transform corporate communications in the digital age. The model is based on a grounded theory approach derived from a field study completed in 2015 by Göldi and Waldau [18] claiming that more heterarchical structures in corporate communications are needed (Sect. 3). In a subsequent project, the model is tested and refined in an ongoing exploratory study that is briefly described (Sect. 4). Based on the learnings from the two studies, we suggest in the conclusions a new model on how to organize corporate communications in the digital age (Sect. 5).

2 Transformative Trends in Corporate Communications

One option to cope with the increased demand for content with limited resources is by streamlining content distribution. For example, a number of low-cost applications allow social media managers to curate content in multiple accounts and channels simultaneously. Single-source, multi-channel content management systems represent solutions with a more sophisticated set-up consisting of a repository of content. They enable content repurposing for multiple channels and audiences. Associated with the "create once, publish everywhere" approach (COPE), these solutions require that content is broken down into smaller semantic units which are tagged and stored in the repository, allowing the content manager to retrieve and combine content modules to produce a new whole.

Apart from saving resources which could be put to better use for content creation, a possible reason for the quick adoption of these solutions could be that, to a certain extent, they guarantee consistency in customer or user experience across channels. However, while representing a cost-effective way of repurposing and distributing content to digital channels, this approach often still requires editorial involvement for content to resonate with different audiences and contexts. Repurposing content may also result in a loss of authenticity.

Another option may be to change planning processes. A predominantly linear workflow, in which an approval process is instigated once content is created, could be transformed towards an iterative and situation-oriented collaborative approach [14], in which responsibility for creating and approving content is shared as required by the nature, topic or audience of content. However, managing alternating workflow as well as mapping it in a system can be difficult, which may at least partly explain the reluctance in adopting this approach. However, a trend towards less linear workflow may be emerging.

As Klewes, Popp and Rost-Hein [19] predict, "communicators will become curators of networks in which content takes shape in a more or less chaotic form". They observe three organizational trends within digital transformation in corporate communications:

- more creativity through breaking traditional systems and rules.
- a new form of employment identity that is coined by constant change and a "liquid" workforce.
- more connection through platforms that enhance collaboration and facilitate new production communities.

These communities are not limited to the workforce. Empowering customer groups or jointly producing content with customers is another content strategy that breaks with traditional approaches due to increased digital range. Described as customers assuming a new role of content co-creators and innovation drivers, Rumpold-Preining [20] concludes that more expertise in co-creation is needed in communication teams as it generates more customer focus. For example, incorporating customer feedback into a content strategy enables a data-driven and personalized approach towards content creation.

Among others, Kaak [14] and Shin, Picken and Dess [21] ascribe to empowering principles that lead, for example, to self-organization as well as to employees who take responsibility for their actions. In other words, instead of building structures to plan and control corporate communications, a company needs to empower its employees to communicate. This also involves structural empowerment, which ranks as a sufficient condition for innovation in many organizations [22] and as a necessary condition to empower individual employees [23].

There is extensive literature on empowerment. Nevertheless, Lee and Edmondson [24], for example, who review the literature on less hierarchical organizations and identify research categories, conclude that the scholarly understanding of decentralized authority remains limited. They also state that managerial hierarchy does not only persist because of a gap between 'a belief in its effectiveness and its actual effectiveness', but also because there are no well-known alternatives [24]. In the past decade, several companies have explored new ways of organizing themselves and have adopted less hierarchical structures as a result. For example, the online retailer *Zappos* adopted holacracy, an organizational system based on the principle of self-management [25]. Another example is the tomato processing company *Morning Star* that fosters a radical form of decentralization where employees enter bilateral contracts with their colleagues [26]. A third example is the computer game producer *Valve* that allows employees to choose which project they want to work on and, moreover, where the employee handbook explains that no one reports to anyone [27]. In Switzerland, *Swisscom*, the largest telecom services provider, started experimenting with holacracy; the internationally active textile producer *Freitag* changed its organizational structure to holacracy as well as the software developer *Liip*.

Clearly, empowerment is as closely connected to a change in structures, roles and processes as digital transformation itself. Managerial hierarchy works well as long as conditions are stable and tasks are well known. As soon as dynamic and novel situations arise, such as the challenges posed by new technologies, managerial hierarchy faces its limitations, ranging from the inhibition of "solving complex non-routine problems" to rigidity [24]. Attempts to avoid these consequences often finally lead to "numerous and varied efforts to organize less hierarchically" [24]. Huq's *Model A* [23] shows that core elements of empowerment such as power-sharing, participative decision-making, devolution of responsibility and people-oriented leadership style change traditional roles and accelerate processes. Spreitzer [28] claims that there are mainly two kinds of empowerment: structural and psychological empowerment. Whereas the former focuses on empowering structures, policies and practices, the latter focuses on "perceptions of empowerment" [28]. Structural and psychological aspects also seem closely linked as the responsibility for changing structures and roles lies with a company's leadership. However, top-level leaders and chief executives often feel threatened by the idea of empowering employees since they fear the loss of control and their own power. They have to be willing to let go of some of their responsibility and control in order to empower their employees and to allow space for action. Wilson [cited in 23] points out that finding a balance "between a democratic and an authoritative approach" is one of the main challenges for leaders. This means that leaders have to take on a new identity and shift their tasks towards enabling, encouraging and supporting employees. In order to empower employees, new approaches in corporate culture are also required, especially in dealing with failures and critical thinking. Otherwise, employees might want to avoid the consequences of making a wrong decision within a participative decision-making framework and therefore refrain from adopting a leading part in corporate communications.

3 Conception and Reflection of the Transformation Framework

In a field study, Göldi and Waldau [18] embarked on firstly, modelling, and, secondly, explaining the passive behavior of employees after collaborative platforms, equipped with the same functionalities as social media platforms, were introduced to their organization. Because a main premise of their study was that fundamental team transformation processes were required before the benefits of these platforms, such as knowledge transfer or peer learning, can be harvested by organizations, they decided to model and measure success of these processes within teams. However, finding an appropriate model turned out to be difficult, especially since most transformation models do not focus on employees and their actions. As Göldi and Waldau discuss [18], there are mainly two models that describe a change towards web-based communication: the DOI-model (Diffusion of Innovation) and the TOE model (Technology-Organization-Environment). Whereas the individual does not play a great role in the TOE, the more comprehensive DOI theory includes the individual attitudes of managers towards innovation. With distinction of the tow concepts of innovation and diffusion, the DOI theory contributes significantly to the differentiation of processes. However, neither model is suitable, in the context of communication and empowerment as they barely involve actors and actions.

3.1 Starting with the Actor-Type Model

Thus, the authors reverted to Dolata and Schrape's [29] actor-type model, which specifically categorizes user groups according to the purpose of their actions. The field study's main research question was to discover how approximately 300 employees and other stakeholder groups working directly or indirectly in corporate communications could be motivated to use a newly provided digital communication platform, which allows them to retrieve information, collaborate and share experience.

However, the Dolata and Schrape [29] model required extending for it to be able to map the transformational processes at play in this particular organization. Figure 1 shows Göldi and Waldau's [18] application (red square) and extension (green square) of Dolata and Schrape's [29] actor type model. Dolata and Schrape's model originally juxtaposes two categories of action types in a virtual room: "individual actions" (by individuals or individuals in swarms) and "collective actions" (by communities or organizations).

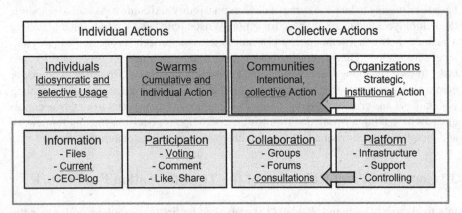

Fig. 1. Göldi and Waldau's [15] extension of Dolata and Schrape's [15] model (Color figure online)

Categorized along the original types of individual and collective actions, the model was first extended by the four areas of "information", "participation", "collaboration" and "platform" (Fig. 1, green square) in order to represent the four areas of action given by the new tool to enable digital corporate communication. Secondly, the model was revised by reading it from right to left (Fig. 1, red square), starting with "collective actions" and leading to "individual actions". This reversion makes sense in a conceptual (opposed to an analytical) scenario, when trying to fuel action and provide structure for digital corporate communications. In this application the corporate actor plays the role of enabler, providing resources and shaping infrastructure according to strategic goals.

In this new setting—which likely represents many corporate communications settings—user manuals, news and a CEO blog were provided to allow employees to retrieve useful information from the platform. Furthermore, participation options (as a swarm) such as votes, comment sections, "like" and "share" options within the news stream and the CEO blog were introduced. Finally, tools for collaboration as a community and sharing were developed and tested such as groups, forums and consultations.

3.2 Building a Transformation Framework

Based on the results of field study, a framework was developed with the goal to describe the main factors affecting transformation of corporate communications in the age of digital media (Fig. 2).

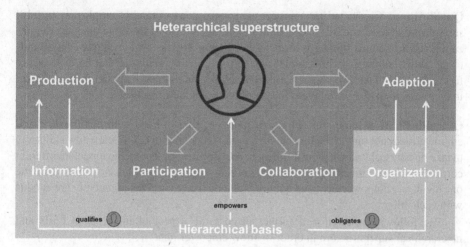

Fig. 2. Transformation framework for digitalized corporate communications

Consistent with the literature reviewed above, the model in Fig. 2 starts with the idea of employee empowerment (center), then it models transformation from a traditionally hierarchical organization towards a hybrid organization combining hierarchical and heterarchical structures. It is therefore not radical in its aim but builds on and maintains hierarchical structures. The hierarchical basis (grey area in Fig. 2) provides structure such as a digital platform and designs processes to qualify and obligate employees in their roles as corporate communicators. Furthermore, the hierarchical basis is accountable for information (left grey area) and organization (right grey area) regarding the transformation itself. As a result, the basically hierarchical organization aims at maintaining a heterarchical superstructure that empowers, qualifies and obligates employees to participate in corporate communications, to produce content for different channels and to collaborate through adoption of newly provided digital tools.

3.3 Main Driving Forces of Transformation in Digitalized Corporate Communications

In order to enhance a) production of communication content, b) adoption of a provided platform and c) participation in votes and comment sections, etc. and d) collaboration in groups and forums, the following three driving forces were defined within the transformation framework model: *empowerment*, *qualification* and *obligation*.

Empowerment. The company needs to empower employees to be content providers in the sense of allowing them not only to produce communication content, but also to edit and publish it. Too much control between writing and publishing acts as a showstopper. It slows down processes and counteracts the dynamics of social media. Furthermore, controlling communicates mistrust and the idea that there is right and wrong. Both effects prevent the flow of content to social media. Therefore, empowerment is crucial in the involvement of employees in corporate social media.

Qualification. Connected to empowerment is the need to qualify employees to fulfil semi-professional standards in corporate communications. At the same time, the organization needs to adjust standards to an adequate semi-professional level that corresponds to the skills employees either already have (e.g. writing skills) or can be evolved. In fact, companies face two choices: either to lower standards or heighten the investment in measures to qualify employees to contribute to digital media need.

Obligation. We assume that obligation must go hand in hand with qualification and empowerment not only to enable but also to motivate employees to learn new skills and to take on new tasks and responsibilities. In retrospect, after testing the model in different corporate cultures, this third driving force is called into question since obligation, on the one hand, and empowerment and qualification, on the other hand, apparently are at odds with each other.

The following section will further discuss the aspect of hierarchical basis and heterarchical superstructure in order to allow empowerment.

3.4 Hierarchical and Heterarchical Orientation in Corporate Communications or How to Empower Employees in Corporate Communications

The main lesson learnt from the above project and main reason to develop a new model (Fig. 2) was the fact that eliciting participation and collaboration pose more of a problem for organizations than distributing content or information. Information in corporate communications flows traditionally top-down: Leaders set the agenda for an information channel, content is produced and spread by corporate communications managers who have sole control over what is published on it. Therefore, hierarchical structures harmonize with a mainly top-down and "one-to-many" communication orientation regarding the information flow. Participation and collaboration, on the other hand, require heterarchic structures because collaboration, sharing and dialogue ("many-to-many") require dynamic agenda setting, freedom of writing and freedom of editing and publishing.

Social Media Require Organizational Transformation. Social media work in a very different way—not only regarding pace and style—but also in regard to the number of contributors. To exploit the potential of social media, a company has to ensure that it is used by more than only a few contributors. The more contributors and the more diverse these contributors are, the higher the likelihood that more valuable content is created. Furthermore, social media per definition serve as a way to exchange written and audio-visual messages and connect their contributors and users in a social network that resembles more a community held together by common interests and by individual expertise than by social structure.

Qualification and Obligation. Organizations that want to qualify a major part of the workforce (maybe even all employees) to be able to contribute to corporate communications are challenged in two ways. The first challenge is to provide writing skills including editing and publishing skills; the second challenge is the adaption of new roles with more responsibilities. This second challenge addresses psychological aspects of digital transformation.

If a company can rely on an academically advanced workforce, qualification efforts are more limited. Detailed guidelines (online and offline), adequate coaching as well as a reliable and patient support are needed so that academically educated employees can meet the journalistic and media-appropriate editorial expectations. Depending on the basic skills of the individual employee, a certain amount of training by the organization will be necessary. If, however, a major part of the employees lacks advanced or even basic writing skills, the challenge is huge. One way to deal with it would be to appeal to the workforce to seek higher qualification in the formal educational system in form of an additional tertiary degree. Another option would be to establish large training programs or implement other intensive measures to qualify employees. No matter which options a company chooses, there is one major restriction: To force employees to learn new skills and to take on more responsibilities is not a good option as it is neither effective nor efficient.

In addition to providing someone with the necessary technical and journalistic skills, it will also be necessary to sensitize the employee to the needs of online communication by discussing topics, such as:

- reacting to comments (both positive and negative).
- copyright law when, for example, using sources.
- working with pictures and video material with due respect to data protection laws.

The above items are only a few of the most important requirements of a semi-professional use of corporate social media. In the following, we present the learnings form a follow-up exploratory study.

4 Learnings from a Follow-Up Exploratory Study

4.1 Concept of the Exploratory Study

In order to learn more about how to set up digital corporate communications based on the transformation framework (Fig. 2), we designed a concept for a collaborative blog, a common corporate communications tool. In this blog, around thirty members of an institute at a university of applied sciences publish didactical solutions to overcome the so-called "post-meal coma", sometimes also referred to as "food coma" or "graveyard-slot" during conferences. The German term for it translates as "soup-coma". The soup-coma refers to the attention deficit after a lunch break; when students are digesting food, they often feel a bit tired and dazed. This, of course, is unfortunate for a study program that depends on students' attention. Therefore, lecturers tend to include short interludes in their programs to quickly restore their students' attention after such a break. The blog aims at collecting these interludes to share solutions for a commonplace problem and to attract public attention, to draw parallels to certain study programs and ultimately to attract new students. These motivations are also typical in corporate communications.

To do this in an adequate form and as a contribution to corporate communications, the concept includes specific requirements regarding the formal aspects of contributions [30]. These requirements mainly comprise three aspects: the contribution consists of a) structured text, b) audio-visual content and c) metadata (e.g. picture description) and links to other content on the institutional website or the internet.

Data is collected through observation and interviews with contributors in different roles. In an action-research-scenario, learnings are applied and settings are adapted to keep the blog and study up and running.

4.2 Learnings

Unsurprisingly, infrastructure is the easy part. We set up a WordPress blog, a YouTube channel and used Cognito forms to create a template for the blogpost. The form is a major balancing act between obligation (elements that are compulsory) and empowerment (permission to free expression). As a measure of qualification, we use explanatory remarks in the form to declare why certain information is required. The provided infrastructure includes supportive features such as guidelines, background information or contact information on how to reach first level support. Apart from support, costs are low after everything is set up.

The reviewing and publishing process and the corresponding roles undergo a major change in digitalized corporate communications. In a traditional corporate communications context, a professional in corporate communications (together with his or her supervisor) reviews a contribution and either accepts, re-works or rejects it. In larger firms with a professional corporate communications department, there might also be a copy-editing process to ensure correct spelling, adherence to corporate design and corporate language. In smaller firms, however, reviewing and copy-editing are often combined in one role. The major change in a dynamical digital setting is that no supervisor is involved. This means that contributions will not be rejected and that peers review and publish communication content. Reservations against this major change concern quality and responsibility issues. In a heterarchical setting, responsibility for content as well as its form are handed over to the contributors and their peers who act as reviewers and publishers. It is the collective that moves to the centre of content production rather than an individual and specialized employee or team.

Review criteria are not subject to arbitrariness, but a set of communicated guidelines. At the same time, there is no compulsory obligation to adhere to guidelines. Moreover, guidelines are subject to modifications if the collective objects to certain rules or establishes better procedures. In other words, during the starting phase there is a predefined set of loose rules to guide everyone involved that can—and in a best-case scenario will—evolve.

The role of the content manager encompasses setting up and handling the infrastructure including supportive features. In addition, the content manager organizes the contributions (when) and roles (who, what) and offers support if needed. She or he collects all data for the blog post: structured text, pictures, audio-visual content, metadata, links. The content manager then takes care of technical handling of the content in the blog. As videos are involved, this includes feeding a YouTube channel and linking the blog to this channel. First, the blogpost is set up as a draft. Then the content manager notifies the reviewer/publisher as soon as the post is ready to be reviewed and subsequently published. The content manager acts as first-level supporter, especially concerning the production of audio-visual content. As the role of the content manager is centralized in one person (during a certain period), while production, review and publishing are ideally performed by many, the content manager causes most costs.

Finally, all roles are interchangeable, meaning that every producer of a contribution can switch his or her role to reviewer/publisher and vice versa or even become a content manager. This has several consequences. For example, employees experience the roles and the related liabilities from different perspectives (producing, reviewing, publishing, managing). Another consequence can and should be that employees share responsibility while collaborating in the best sense of the word pursuing the company's overall goals. Yet another consequence can be that employees learn from each other and that they build new skills, trust and social cohesion.

5   Conclusion

As a preliminary result, we present a corporate communications content model for a contemporary approach to corporate communications in the age of digitalization (Fig. 3). It focuses on content in the age of digitalization that needs to be shaped in a multimodal and online-adapted way. Content consists of written parts combined with audio-visual parts optimized with metadata and links. Figure 3 also shows processing members of staff in alternating roles of content producer, content manager and content reviewer/publisher. The model claims that the main requirements—besides a collective with a shared goal, a working infrastructure and adaptable guidelines—are enough time and budget.

In this heterarchic approach, the organization empowers its employees by providing infrastructure, assigning tasks and roles to a collective and by qualifying them mainly through supportive infrastructure, learning by doing and learning from each other. In contrast to traditional organizations with hierarchical structures, the roles of content producer (writing and recording of audio-visual recordings), content manager as well as reviewers and publishers are not exercised by delegated communications specialists, but by everyone in the company. Finally, empowerment not only means to allow staff to produce, manage, review and publish communication content on corporate channels but also to value their work and effort. Therefore, budget to fund this empowerment is also crucial. If employees across an organization are empowered to communicate, the model may also help create more content. Thus, the increased demand for valuable and authentic content for larger audiences on multiple channels can be met.

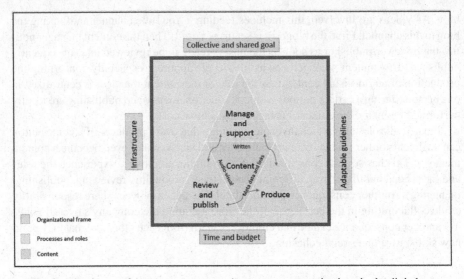

Fig. 3. Big picture of content management/corporate communications in the digital age

References

1. Hübner, H.: The Communicating Company. Towards an Alternative Theory of Corporate Communication. Physica-Verlag, Heidelberg (2007)
2. Göldi, S.: Grundlagen der Unternehmenskommunikation. Werbung, Public Relations und Marketing im Dienste der Corporate Identity. hep, Bern (2005)
3. Van Riel, C.B.M., Fombrun, C.: Essentials of Corporate Communications. Routledge, New York (2007)
4. Cornelissen, J.: Corporate Communication. A Guide to Theory and Practice, 3rd edn. Sage, Los Angeles (2011)
5. Argenti, P.: Corporate Communication, 7th edn. McGraw Hill, New York (2015)
6. Beger, R.: Present-Day Corporate Communication. A Practice-Oriented State-of-the-Art Guide. Springer, Singapore (2018). https://doi.org/10.1007/978-981-13-0402-6
7. Lerbinger, O.: Corporate Communication. An International and Management Perspective. Wiley Blackwell, Hoboken (2019)
8. Christensen, L.T., Cornelissen, J.: Bridging corporate and organizational communication. Review, development and a look to the future. Manag. Commun. Q. 25(3), 383–414 (2011)
9. Helm, S.: Employees' awareness of their impact on corporate reputation. J. Bus. Res. 64(7), 657–663 (2011)
10. Falkheimer, J., Heide, M.: Strategic communication in participatory culture. From one- and two-way communication to participatory communication through social media. In: Holtzhausen, D., Zerfass, A. (eds.) The Routledge Handbook of Strategic Communication, pp. 337–349. Routledge, New York (2015)
11. Hart, L.: Social media. In: Doorley, J., Garcia, H. (eds.) Reputation Management. Routledge, New York (2011)
12. Postman, J.: SocialCorp. Social Media Goes Corporate. New Riders, Berkeley (2009)
13. Loader, B.D.: Networking democracy? Social media innovations and participatory politics. Inf. Commun. Soc. 14, 747–769 (2011)

14. Kaak, E.-J.: Mention communication—think organisation: agile communication in the digital era. In: Klewes, J., Popp, D., Rost-Hein, M. (eds.) Out-Thinking Organizational Communications. MP, pp. 129–143. Springer, Cham (2017). https://doi.org/10.1007/978-3-319-41845-2_10

15. Kraft, C., Peter, M.K.: Die digitale transformation: eine Begriffserklärung. In: Peter, M.K. (ed.) KMU-Transformation. Als KMU die digitale Transformation erfolgreich umsetzen. Fachhochschule Nordwestschweiz, Olten (2017)

16. Klewes, J., Popp, D., Rost-Hein, M.: Digital transformation and communications: how key trends will transform the way companies communicate. In: Klewes, J., Popp, D., Rost-Hein, M. (eds.) Out-Thinking Organizational Communications. MP, pp. 7–31. Springer, Cham (2017). https://doi.org/10.1007/978-3-319-41845-2_2

17. Kirf, B., Eicke, K.N., Schömburg, S.: Unternehmenskommunikation im Zeitalter der digitalen Transformation. Wie Unternehmen interne und externe Stakeholder heute und in Zukunft erreichen. Springer, Wiesbaden (2018). https://doi.org/10.1007/978-3-658-15364-9

18. Göldi, S., Waldau, M.: Wie gelingt Kollaboration? Ein Transformationsrahmen für die Unternehmenskommunikation. Wissensmanagement 8, 36–39 (2015)

19. Klewes, J., Popp, D., Rost-Hein, M.: Managing the digital transformation: ten guidelines for communications professionals. In: Klewes, J., Popp, D., Rost-Hein, M. (eds.) Out-Thinking Organizational Communications. MP, pp. 187–195. Springer, Cham (2017). https://doi.org/10.1007/978-3-319-41845-2_14

20. Rumpold-Preining, M.: The changing role of the chief marketing officer: unlocking the power of data-driven communication. In: Klewes, J., Popp, D., Rost-Hein, M. (eds.) Out-Thinking Organizational Communications. MP, pp. 65–71. Springer, Cham (2017). https://doi.org/10.1007/978-3-319-41845-2_5

21. Shin, H., Picken, J., Dess, G.: Revisiting the learning organization: how to create it. Organ. Dyn. 46, 46–56 (2017)

22. Sprafke, N.: Kompetente Mitarbeiter und wandlungsfähige Organisationen. Zum Zusammenhang von Dynamic Capabilities, individueller Kompetenz und Empowerment. Springer, Wiesbaden (2016). https://doi.org/10.1007/978-3-658-13035-0

23. Huq, R.A.: The Psychology of Employee Empowerment. Concepts, Critical Themes and a Framework for Implementation. Gower, Fanham (2015)

24. Lee, M.Y., Edmondson, A.C.: Self-managing organizations: exploring the limits of less hierarchical organizing. Res. Organ. Behav. 37, 35–37 (2017)

25. Bernstein, E., Buch, J., Canner, N., Lee, M.: The big idea beyond the holacracy hype. The overwrought claims and actual promise of the next generation of self-managed teams. Harv. Bus. Rev. 94(7–8), 38–49 (2016)

26. Gino, F., Staats, B.R., Hall, B.J., Chang, T.Y.: The Morning Star Company. Self-Management at Work. Harvard Business School Case No. 9-914-013. Harvard Business School Publishing, Boston (2016)

27. Baldwin, C.Y.: In the shadow of the crowd. A comment of valve's way. J. Organ. Des. 4(2), 5–7 (2015)

28. Spreitzer, G.: Taking stock: a review of more than twenty years of research on empowerment at work. In: Cooper, C., Barling, J. (eds.) Handbook of Organizational Behavior, pp. 54–73. Sage, Thousand Oaks (2008)

29. Dolata, U., Schrape, J.F.: Zwischen Individuum und Organisation. Neue kollektive Akteure und Handlungskonstellationen im Internet. Stuttgarter Beiträge zur Organisations-und Innovationsforschung, SOI Discussion Paper 2013-02. Institut für Sozialwissenschaften, Stuttgart (2013)

30. Göldi, S., Zachlod, C.: Die Top 5 SEO-Massnahmen beim Online-Texten. In: Peter, M.K. (ed.) KMU-Transformation: Als KMU die Digitale Transformation erfolgreich umsetzen. Forschungsresultate und Praxisleitfaden, pp. 9–17. Fachhochschule Nordwestschweiz, Olten (2017)

Implementing Robotic Process Automation for Auditing and Fraud Control

Luke Griffiths and Hendrik Willem Pretorius(✉) ⓘ

University of Pretoria, Pretoria, South Africa
Henk.Pretorius@up.ac.za

Abstract. The cost of fraud continues to be a problem for many organizations in the global economy. This study explores how robotic process automation may offer a way forward for organizations to reduce fraud and advance organizational audit effectiveness for detecting potential fraud areas and cases.

The research was performed by conducting a literature review that considered 22 articles (through a selection process) on the relevant research themes of robotic process automation, fraud and auditing.

The findings suggest that organizations should consider robotic process automation as a means for reducing fraud opportunities in organizations. Robotic process automation may also assist organizations to advance their audit efficiency and effectiveness.

The paper conclude by proposing a theoretical framework for the implementation of robotic process automation in fraud control and auditing. A number of new theoretical questions arose during this analysis. This include, the potential use of robotic process automation by fraudsters in support of organizational fraud and secondly, the new skills required by auditors to be effective in an intelligent workplace.

Keywords: Robotic process automation · Fraud · Audit · Systematic literature review

1 Introduction

The challenges posed by fraud are significant. The annual, global losses caused by occupational fraud exceeds seven billion US Dollars [1]. One form of occupational fraud, namely asset misappropriation, caused the collapse of various banks in Iran [3]. In general, occupational fraud is widely recognized as a contributing factor to banking crises across the globe [4]. Except for asset misappropriation, other forms of occupational fraud exist namely corruption and financial statement fraud [2].

The significance of fraud as an organisational problem, necessitates the need for an organizational audit function, involved in fraud detecting and control [5]. Organizations should take the necessary precautions to reduce the risk associated with occupational fraud.

One precaution that organizations may consider is the use of robotic process automation. Robotic process automation refers to software tools which automate the execution

© Springer Nature Switzerland AG 2021
A. Gerber and K. Hinkelmann (Eds.): Society 5.0 2021, CCIS 1477, pp. 26–36, 2021.
https://doi.org/10.1007/978-3-030-86761-4_3

of tasks by using the same interface that a human actor would [6]. By reducing repetitive human interaction with computer systems, robotic process automation aims to improve return on investment through automation and streamlined organizational business processes [6]. This is against the backdrop that the most common methods for concealing occupational fraud include the creation of fake physical documents, the creation of fake transactions and the altering of transactions in an accounting system [1]. Minimising interaction with computer systems could potentially decrease the risk of fraud. Robotic process automation may also be beneficial for the audit function by automating many audit tasks [7].

This convergence of technology and people into the same workspace to solve a global problem aligns with the goal of society 5.0 to integrate Industry 4.0 technology with human ideals [28]. Robotic process automation maintains the industrial focus expected from such technology [28] with the goal of addressing illegal, fraudulent activity [7], contributing to the economic advancement envisioned by society 5.0 [29].

The purpose of this systematic literature review is to explore, how robotic process automation may offer ways for organizations to reduce the risk of fraud and advance their audit effectiveness. The study is a generic study, not bound to a specific industry or geographical location.

2   Research Method

The section will briefly discuss the process that was performed during the systematic literature review to answer the following research question:

How can robotic process automation be used in organizations to reduce potential fraud and advance audit effectiveness?

2.1   Search Terms

The following search terms were used in relevant academic journal databases: "robotic process automation" AND ("fraud" OR "audit").

2.2   Selection Criteria and Quality Assurance

Table 1 presents the selection criteria (what was included and excluded) for the literature review.

2.3   Source Selection and Data Extraction

The search terms were applied to the following database sources for the literature review: EBSCOhost, ScienceDirect and ProQuest.

The search results were filtered to only include academic works. The database search returned 135 articles. After duplicate articles were removed, 125 articles remained. Article title and abstracts were then screened for relevance and only 66 articles remained. The remaining full-text articles were assessed for appropriateness (using the inclusion and exclusion criteria) and 44 articles were excluded with reasons. Finally, a total of 22 articles were consulted during this literature review, which was carefully captured in Microsoft Excel.

Table 1. Selection criteria for the literature review.

Inclusion criteria	Exclusion criteria
1. Peer-reviewed articles	1. Non peer-reviewed articles
2. Articles that focus on robotic process automation, auditing and fraud control	2. Articles whose focus is not robotic process automation, auditing and fraud control
3. Articles published in the last 3 years for the most current research	3. Non English articles whose full-text is not available
4. Relevant articles in any industry and geographic location	4. Articles older than 3 years, for the most current research
5. Articles published in the last 3 years for the most current research	

3   Analysis and Discussion

During the systematic literature review, relevant literature themes emerged. These themes are: the automation of mundane tasks (19 relevant articles), process identification for robotic process automation (8 articles), data standardization (5articles), robotic process automation (RPA) vendors (5 articles), the changing role of the auditor (7 articles) and RPA threats (9 articles). A discussion of these literature themes follow.

3.1   Process Automation

The literature indicates that robotic process automation (RPA) is mostly used to automate and replace mundane audit tasks that allow employees and auditors to shift their focus to other organizational tasks [7–25].

Mundane audit tasks involve tasks such as audit evidence gathering [10, 25, 26], but RPA also saves employees time through automation that helps them to be highly efficient [26]. The time saved allowed employees to focus less on repetitive tasks and more on skill-intensive, value-adding activities such as the use of professional judgement to make decisions [10].

By automating tedious, manual processes, RPA allows auditors to expand the scope of organizational audits [25]. RPA software flag audit exceptions and errors which require expert intervention or further investigation [8, 12, 21, 23, 26]. The ability to quickly gather audit evidence across an entire population allows for continuous, real-time analyses of audit evidence [8, 23, 27].

The nature of RPA as a software solution which performs highly repetitive, predictable tasks also means that the process can be well documented and lead to increased audibility of automated tasks [21–23]. This means that RPA can be programmed to follow control requirements and therefore increase confidence in control tests [23] and compliance [9, 18, 20, 22, 24, 28].

The literature, therefore, indicates that the role of RPA in auditing and fraud control is primarily to improve the efficiency and effectiveness of audit engagements and automating evidence gathering and analysis to allow for wider audit scope and therefore an increase the ability to detect fraudulent activity. RPA can allow for standardizing, documenting and speeding up of audit engagements and high-risk activities and can aid auditors in performing their duties.

Furthermore, RPA can be used outside of the audit function to standardise organizational controls and ensure adequate documentation and compliance with control requirements to reduce he opportunities for fraud to take place [27, 28].

3.2 Process Identification for RPA

The literature analysed, indicates that there is no consensus on which activities should be automated by robotic process automation. However, there is a need to automate processes which are highly structured and repetitive in nature [7, 10, 13, 15, 17, 19, 22, 25], although the specific functional areas or tasks are not specified [13].

In other words, structured audit tasks which are well defined are best suited to RPA automation techniques [22, 25], such as substantive audit procedures [10]. Expert involvement is required to identify which processes can be automated and how to optimise the solution [15, 17]. Understanding how to automate the processes is equally as important as identifying the processes for robotic process automation [10, 19].

An example from the literature is the use of robotic process automation to automate substantive procedures testing loan valuation, recording and disclosure [10]. Data was collected from source reports, prepared for loading into Microsoft Access and automatically execute the desired audit tests [10], where it was able to detect the expected anomalies faster than an auditor could [10].

Processes are identified for automation based on task data structure and repetitive, predictable workflow. RPA is sometimes classed as part of the wider intelligent process automation (IPA) environment [7, 15, 21, 25]. This means that RPA could potentially be integrated with other intelligent automation tools such as tools that involves machine learning [22] to further enhance its effectiveness [25, 26].

Also note that RPA automate existing processes rather than replacing them and may therefore automate existing control weaknesses and inadequacies [18]. While RPA does not necessitate process reengineering [24], it could perhaps be a driver of audit engagement and fraud control improvement to enable its use [19].

3.3 Data Standardization

RPA requires quality data to perform adequately [13]. When a robotic process automation solution is being considered, the format, source and compatibility of related data must be considered [7, 15].

In the literature, there are two dimensions to data standardization. First, organizations that implement RPA need to consider cross-functional organizational data needs [20] and their related controls [13]. Furthermore, organizations which aim to reduce fraud using RPA should ensure that the data needed is of the correct level of detail, quality and security [13]. Just as RPA can cause incorrect decision making if implemented with poorly designed process, poor data and data standards can lead to similar problems.

The second dimension for data standardization is audit data standards. In order for RPA software, when used by the audit function, to give consistent and reliable results, the data dictionary, labels and preparation methods for auditing should be defined and followed by the audit function [10, 15].

To conclude, the successful use of RPA in organizations to address fraud and enhance audit interventions require strict data standardization and governance considerations.

3.4 RPA Vendors

In the literature, a number of articles refer to specific vendors for implementing RPA solutions [14, 15, 19, 22, 25]. Only one literature source mention the development of in-house RPA solutions [15].

In other words, in-house development for audit and fraud control RPA systems does not appear as widespread as vendor-provided solutions. It further appears that RPA solutions developed in-house may be used in conjunction with vendor purchased solutions to address fraud and audit control needs in an organization [15].

3.5 The Changing Role of the Auditor

As mentioned earlier, one of the roles of RPA in auditing and fraud control is the replacement of mundane tasks, allowing employees to focus on more challenging, value-adding tasks.

This implies that the role of auditors will change to better fit the new role demands that RPA offers. Data analytics is one area that is transformed when using RPA [25]. RPA allows for more data to be collected and processed than if similar processes had to be conducted manually [25]. Data can also be analyzed in conjunction with other artificial intelligence technologies [25]. Auditors will therefore need a good understanding of analytics and artificial intelligence techniques in order to achieve the best results from the use of RPA. This is aligned to the claim that accountants will be required to develop more technical skills for the RPA environment, such as data management [26]. The call for technical skills development in accounting students [23, 26] indicates the need for professionals in this environment to embrace changing technological needs in the audit and accounting space.

The fact that RPA tools can flag suspicious transactions or records [8, 12, 21, 23, 26] for examination by experts means that a greater emphasis will be placed on professional judgement [8, 10]. Auditors will need to be able to interpret flagged records adequately which may require fraud examination, analytical or forensic investigation perspective [8, 23]. This perspective and professional expertise cannot be automated like the more structured, well-defined tasks which RPA targets [10]. The need for auditors will, therefore, not be significantly impacted by the use of RPA, especially considering the increased scope of audit engagements which RPA enables [25].

There is further no consensus on what the more challenging tasks undertaken by employees and auditors will be. The literature only indicates that analysis and more challenging tasks (because of the automation of mundane tasks) will be a focus for auditors and that professional judgement and technical skills will be required. As more audit and accounting professionals develop their IT skills, in-house solutions could become more common. This points to a convergence of IT and audit principles and skills.

3.6 RPA Threats

RPA has implications with regards to governance, control and risk management in the organization.

Firstly, governance strategies of organizations will either need to incorporate RPA directly into existing governance frameworks, or create new separate decentralized RPA-specific governance structures to address the organizational changes brought about by RPA [13]. In either case, governance structures should be in place before any RPA implementation takes place [21].

Secondly, risk management strategies need to consider the effects of RPA [23]. Processes and process constraints may not be automated correctly in RPA software, which may lead to incorrect process results and unexpected process exceptions that carry risk [22]. Privacy and security concerns also affect the risk environment. Digital evidence gathering during auditing may potentially exposes sensitive data [15, 22]. In other words, there may be an increase in the risk of organizational cybersecurity breaches. These risk areas will require adjustments to the risk register of the organization and may lead to the modification of auditing standards [8].

Changes in governance and risk will further necessitate changes to the control environment. In order to address the security risks created by using RPA, controls will need to be implemented which aim to mitigate those risks. The organisation should implement controls which ensure the confidentiality, integrity, accessibility, accountability, authenticity and reliability of data used by the RPA software [24]. There should also be controls which address the possibility of faulty RPA workflow [12]. With these new controls in place, there will also be a need to audit the RPA system itself [12, 23] to determine their adequacy and effectiveness.

Another problem posed using RPA in audit and fraud control is the use of RPA by fraudsters. Robotic process automation may be abused by its users to more easily commit fraud [16]. The relationship between RPA and fraud still needs to be thoroughly investigated [16].

However, implementation of RPA in the process of disclosing information constituting a banking secret to authorities was found to mitigate the risk non-compliance in areas such as protection of information and meeting statutory obligations [24]. Robotic process automation may therefore also provide a means to address some compliance threats by reducing errors in critical processes.

Organizations need to consider various applications of RPA and the effects on the organizational governance, risk and control environment to ensure strategic goals are met.

4 An RPA Implementation Framework in Audit and Fraud Control

From the systematic literature review analysis and discussion, seven pre-conditions were identified (derived from Sect. 3) when implementing RPA for fraud control and auditing. A discussion of these pre-conditions follow, after which an implementation framework for RPA in auditing and fraud control is proposed.

4.1 Pre-conditions for RPA in Auditing and Fraud Control

Seven pre-conditions (in no particular order) were identified for the successful implementation of RPA in fraud control and auditing. These pre-conditions may serve as a checklist that organizations may use for implementing RPA in fraud control and auditing.

Definition of Expected Outcomes: An organization should have a clear vision of the goals, objectives and role of a RPA implementation project. If there are clear goals, objective and roles defined for RPA in the target environment, appropriate decision of the correct processes can follow, assisting in successful implementation [10, 19, 22, 25]. After implementation, the design can be evaluated against the defined goals, objectives and roles for RPA in the organization.

Structured Processes: A successful RPA implementation initiative requires that processes are already well structured and meet organizational goals [10, 18, 22, 25]. Furthermore, processes targeted for RPA projects or engagements should already be well optimized and fit for purpose.

Involvement of Experts: The RPA solution should be implemented through collaboration with experts. This includes process experts who understand the process being automated, audit and fraud experts who can guide the project regarding control best practice, as well as information technology experts who can provide insight into the data and technical environment [8, 10, 15, 17, 19].

Data Standardisation: RPA requires structured data to perform adequately, therefore it is necessary to standardize data [22, 25]. As consequence, if a RPA solution is implemented in a fraud control context, cross-functional data is available [20] which will be well understood and can be leveraged easily. If the RPA solution is being implemented in an audit context, then data standardization also refers to the audit data standards which should be in place to ensure consistent, easily interpreted results [10, 15].

Evaluation of Threats: An evaluation of the threats which may occur in the target environment should be conducted. The changes which may occur in the governance, risk and control environment of the organisation as a result of a RPA solution being implemented [12, 13, 15, 22, 24] should be taken into consideration so that they can be responded to appropriately [21].

Solution Procurement: Organizations should decide whether a vendor RPA solution will be purchased, or an in-house solution will be developed, or a combination of both [15]. The type of solution which will be used may affect the time, cost, skill requirement and quality of the RPA project [14, 15, 19, 22, 25].

Skill Requirements: An organization need to determine whether or not it has the necessary skills to successfully implement a RPA solution. There will be a need for process, audit and IT experts [8, 23, 25, 26], which may not be present in the organisation. If an in-house solution is required, there will be a need for RPA developer skills [15]. These skillsets are needed to successfully implement a RPA solution which meets the organisational goals.

4.2 An Implementation Framework

An implementation framework for RPA in auditing and fraud control is proposed that combine the identified literature themes of this study. The proposed framework involves the phases of *Process Identification* [7, 10, 13, 15, 17, 19, 22, 25], then *RPA Design and Construction* (and the technical skills involved) [23, 26] and finally the *Results Evaluation* (or analytics) [25] presented by the software (see Fig. 1).

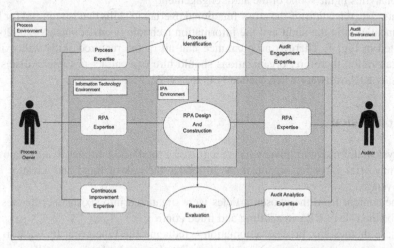

Fig. 1. An implementation framework for RPA in auditing and fraud control

The RPA pre-conditions for auditing and fraud control (Sect. 4.1) may assist to prevent and detect fraud. These pre-conditions apply to both the audit environment and the existing process environment. In the audit environment, it is at least the auditor who will need to consider these pre-conditions and on the process environment, it is at least the process owner, as illustrated in the proposed implementation framework.

Process identification involves the identification of processes which are best suited for automation to meet organizational or audit engagement objectives. These are typically simple and structured tasks whose output is needed for later tasks [7, 10, 13, 15, 17, 19, 22, 25].

The framework considers the design and construction of the RPA solution to be a part of the organization's intelligent process automation environment [7, 15, 21, 25]. The organization implementing the RPA solution, should consider RPA within the context of any existing IT and intelligent process automation strategy.

The framework considers results evaluation to be any usage of the output of the RPA system to determine the existence of fraud and how best to prevent it from occurring in future.

The three high-level phases described in the framework involve various skills which are needed for the implementation of RPA. The skills will also differ between the process and audit environments.

The first phase, *Process Identification*, requires identifying processes for automation that requires process and audit expertise in the context of that specific process environment.

The second phase, *The RPA Design and Construction*, requires RPA development expertise, regardless of the environment the automation takes place in.

Lastly, *Results Evaluation* of the automated process will either cause changes to the implemented process to further reduce fraud in the process environment, or be used in audit analytics in the scope of the audit engagement.

This research confirms the cross-functional overlap in skills that is required for RPA implementation in the audit and the information technology environments [23, 26], as indicated in Fig. 1. There is no guarantee that all of the required skills will exist in an organization therefore, organizations should hire or contract in these skillsets and necessary RPA software when needed [14, 15, 19, 22, 25].

5 Conclusion

This systematic literature review has recognized a total of 22 articles that explain how RPA may offer ways for organizations to reduce the risk of fraud and advance audit effectiveness.

The content from the chosen articles were organized into six distinct themes that describe the role of RPA in auditing and fraud control.

These themes are: process automation – reducing the time spent by auditors and employees on mundane, repetitive tasks that allow for greater focus on challenging and value-adding tasks; the changing role of the auditor – proposing an expansion of auditor skills to include more technical skills required to make best use of RPA in auditing and fraud control; RPA vendors – that indicate most organizations make use of RPA vendors with the necessary skills and expertise to implement RPA solutions rather than embarking on in-house development; RPA threats – RPA implementations have an impact the governance, risk and control environment of organisations; process identification for RPA – processes automated identified for RPA should be structured or semi-structured in nature; data standardization – the successful use of RPA in organizations to address fraud and enhance audit interventions require strict data standardisation and governance considerations.

Finally, this review contributes to the body of knowledge by presenting a list of pre-conditions for the successful use of RPA in auditing and fraud control. Furthermore, a RPA implementation framework was proposed, that organizations, practitioners and researchers may consider in audit and fraud control environments.

References

1. Association of Certified Fraud Examiners: Global Study on Occupational Fraud and Abuse Report to the Nations **10** (80) (2018)
2. Association of Certified Fraud Examiners (2019). https://www.acfe.com/rttn2016/images/fraud-tree.jpg

3. Nia, E.H., Said, J.: Assessing fraud risk factors of assets misappropriation: evidences from iranian banks. Procedia Econ. Finance **31**(15), 919–924 (2015)
4. Suh, J.B., Nicolaides, R., Trafford, R.: The effects of reducing opportunity and fraud risk factors on the occurrence of occupational fraud in financial institutions. Int. J. Law Crime Justice **56**, 79–88 (2019)
5. Petraşcu, D., Tieanu, A.: The role of internal audit in fraud prevention and detection. Procedia Econ. Financ. **16**(May), 489–497 (2014)
6. van der Aalst, W.M.P., Bichler, M., Heinzl, A.: Robotic process automation. Bus. Inf. Syst. Eng. **60**(4), 269–272 (2018). https://doi.org/10.1007/s12599-018-0542-4
7. Huang, F., Vasarhelyi, M.A.: Applying robotic process automation (RPA) in auditing: a framework. Int. J. Account. Inf. Syst. **35**, 100433 (2019)
8. Appelbaum, D., Nehmer, R.: The coming disruption of drones, robots, and bots: how will it affect CPAs and accounting practice. CPA J. **87**(6), 40–44 (2017)
9. Asquith, A., Horsman, G.: Let the robots do it!-Taking a look at Robotic Process Automation and its potential application in digital forensics. Forensic Science International: Reports (2019)
10. Cohen, M., Rozario, A., Zhang, C.: Exploring the use of robotic process automation (RPA) in substantive audit procedures. CPA J. **89**(7), 49–53 (2019)
11. Hale, A., VanVleet, E., Butt, J., Hollis, T.: The "Power of With": Combining humans and machines to transform tax. International Tax Review, N.PAG-N.PAG (2020)
12. Kaya, C.T., Turkyilmaz, M., Birol, B.: RPA Teknolojilerinin Muhasebe Sistemleri Üzerindeki Etkisi. Muhasebe ve Finansman Dergisi **82**, 235–250 (2019)
13. Kokina, J., Blanchette, S.: Early evidence of digital labor in accounting: Innovation with Robotic Process Automation. Int. J. Account. Inf. Syst. **35**, 100431 (2019)
14. Madakam, S., Holmukhe, R.M., Jaiswal, D.K.: The future digital work force: robotic process automation (RPA). J. Inf. Syst. Technol. Manage. **16**, 1–17 (2019)
15. Moffitt, K.C., Rozario, A.M., Vasarhelyi, M.A.: Robotic process automation for auditing. J. Emerg. Technol. Account. **15**(1), 1–10 (2018)
16. Nickerson, M.A.: Fraud in a world of advanced technologies: the possibilities are (unfortunately) endless: certified public accountant. CPA J. **89**(6), 28–34 (2019)
17. Osman, C.C.: Robotic process automation: lessons learned from case studies. Informatica Economica **23**(4), 66–75 (2019)
18. Raju, P., Koch, R.: Can RPA improve agility. Strategic Finance **100**(9), 68–69 (2019)
19. Rozario, A.M., Vasarhelyi, M.A.: How robotic process automation is transforming accounting and auditing. CPA J. **88**(6), 46–49 (2018)
20. Shroff, M.: How intelligent finance decodes data. Treasury Risk, 1–4 (2020)
21. Steinhoff, J., Lewis, A., Everson, K.: The march of the robots. J. Gov. Financ. Manage. **67**(1), 26–33 (2019)
22. Syed, R., et al.: Robotic Process Automation: contemporary themes and challenges. Comput. Ind. **115**, 103162 (2020)
23. Tucker, I.: Are you ready for your robots? Strategic Finance **99**(5), 48–53 (2017)
24. Wojciechowska-Filipek, S.: Automation of the process of handling enquiries concerning information constituting a bank secret. Banks Bank Syst. **14**(3), 175–186 (2019)
25. Zhang, C.: Intelligent process automation in audit. J. Emerg. Technol. Account. **16**(2), 69–88 (2019)
26. Lin, P., Hazelbaker, T.: Meeting the challenge of artificial intelligence: what CPAs need to know. CPA J. **89**(6), 48–52 (2019)
27. Hradecká, M.: Robotic internal audit-control methods in the selected company. AGRIS On-Line Papers Econ. Inform. **2**(2), 31–42 (2019)

28. Ferreria, C., Serpa, S.: Society 5.0 and social development: contributions to a discussion. Manage. Organ. Stud. **5**(4), 26–31 (2018)
29. Potocan, V., Matjaz, M., Nedelko, Z.: Society 5.0: balancing of Industry 4.0, economic advancement and social problems. Kybernetes **50**(3), 794–811 (2020)

Design Parameters of Multidimensional Reward Systems Based on Preference Analysis of Students of Business Information Systems (Bachelor and Master) at the University of Applied Sciences Northwestern Switzerland

Fabian Heimsch[✉] [iD] and Erhard Lüthi

University of Applied Sciences and Arts Northwestern Switzerland, 4600 Olten, Switzerland
fabian.heimsch@fhnw.ch

Abstract. In Switzerland, there is currently a major shortage of skilled workers in many companies and organisations. A particular bottleneck can be seen in the area of IT professions. The lack of qualified employees is a challenge for future education and training and intensifies the current competition for today's necessary and urgently sought talent in the IT sector. In this context, it will be crucial in the future how attractive and individualized compensation systems can be designed for potential employees. Needs-based compensation packages should help to attract and ultimately retain future IT professionals. The aim of this study is to measure the preferences of students of business informatics at the FHNW to analyse which elements of total rewards management are crucial for the choice of a future employer. The results will help companies optimise the total rewards system according to their needs or include those factors that can be expected to provide the best benefits for future employees. Thus, not only the total monetary value, but also the composition of financial and non-financial elements must be included in this overall consideration.

The aim is to provide decision-makers in organisations with targeted information that will allow them to design optimal incentive packages to be an attractive employer for students of business informatics or potential employees in the informatics field.

Keywords: Web-tool reward design · Discrete choice analysis · Data driven business analytics · Flexible wage systems · Employer attractiveness

1 Introduction

There is currently a significant shortage of skilled workers in many companies and organisations. This situation can be observed among others, mostly in the field of IT-professionals. The lack of qualified employees is a challenge for future education and training and intensifies the current competition for today's necessary, and urgently sought talent in the information sector. It will be crucial how attractive and individualised

© Springer Nature Switzerland AG 2021
A. Gerber and K. Hinkelmann (Eds.): Society 5.0 2021, CCIS 1477, pp. 37–45, 2021.
https://doi.org/10.1007/978-3-030-86761-4_4

remuneration systems can be designed for potential employees in this context. Needs-oriented customised remuneration packages should help to attract and ultimately retain IT professionals. Employer brand Randstad's latest study (2021) has also shown that companies should take a closer look at these questions because at-tractive salary and benefits remain the most important drivers overall. The discussion on the design of company-specific remuneration systems is broad and intensive to-day. However, this is often done from a purely corporate perspective. The question of how employees perceive and assess these remuneration systems is often ignored. The consideration of the remuneration from the employee side is essential from a scientific as well as a practical point of view. The perceived satisfaction with the remuneration system not only has a relevant influence on the attraction but also on the behaviour and the attitude of the employees to their work and their employer.

In the concepts of total rewards (Thompson 2002, p. 9), it is evident that nowadays a modern reward sys-tem will not only focus on the employee's payment but take more attractive non-financial benefits into account, like work-life balance, flexible working hours, the possibility to work at home, etc. The total rewards approach is an advanced human resources management model that supports enterprise development and increases the enterprise's attractiveness. This study aims to measure the preferences of students of computer sciences at the University of Applied Sciences and Arts (FHNW) to analyse which elements of total rewards are decisive for the choice of a future employer. In addition, the results provide decision-makers in organisations with specific information that allows them to design optimal incentive packages to be an attractive employer for students of computer sciences or potential employees in this industry. For the realisation of the project, a practice-oriented integration of partner companies is planned from the beginning. Therefore, the aim is to collect and analyse data and develop a web implementation that promises a successful transfer into practice and can also be evaluated in terms of its benefits.

For the analysis, we will use a discrete choice experiment (DCE). A discrete choice experiment is a choice or decision-based method for analysing consumer preferences. DCEs have become a common technique in economics, addressing a wide range of policy questions in the transport economy (Hensher et al. 2005, p. 693), environmental economics (Hanley et al. 2001, p. 436) and health economics (de Bekker-Grob et al. 2012, p. 153). In human resource economics, preference measurement has only found its way into the field in recent years. This study aims to expand the research aspect to include individualisation and flexibility in remuneration based on the total reward model.

The following practice-relevant questions are to be answered:

- Which design parameters of a multidimensional compensation package are essential for computer sciences students when choosing a future employer?
- How likely are respondents to accept a job with specific attributes?
- Are there different design parameters depending on the age, gender, or other relevant factors of the students included in the decisions and can thus lead to additional employer benefits?

Knowing these job preferences of computer sciences students can finally help better understand the significant attributes for them.

Discrete Choice Model Design

For the analysis of the design parameters of multidimensional reward systems, the different factors, being preferences that influence the acceptance decision for a job, are examined. This method goes beyond traditional qualitative assessments and provides quantifiable data that can better guide the selection of the most appropriate strategies for recruitment. It also goes beyond traditional ranking and rating exercises, which do not provide information on the strength of preference or trade-off. The method derives from Characteristics Theory of Value (Lancaster 1966, p. 133; Aus-purg and Liebe 2011, p. 305) and Random Utility Theory (McFadden 1974, p. 106). Based on the above, utility is presented as a function of an alternative's characteris-tics and the person-specific characteristics of the decision maker. In this way, student n will choose job i if the following condition is met:

$$U_{nj} > U_{ni} \; \forall i \neq j \in \tag{1}$$

The random utility model assumes that utility (U_{nj} = denotes the utility for alternative j at decision maker n) consists of two components:

- V_{nj} = explainable benefit, which can be observed and in an...
- ϵ_{nj} = unobservable variable (this latent variable consists in characteristics such as un-traceable properties of the service, or product such as unapparent differences or er-rors in the measurement itself).

The benefit for the students, taking into account the mentioned components for job i, can be defined as follows:

$$U_{ni} = V_{ni} + \varepsilon_{ni} = f(\alpha_1 + \beta_1 x_{1n} + \beta_2 x_{2n} + \dots + \beta_m x_{mni} + \varepsilon_n) \tag{2}$$

β in this case provides the preference variable for each specification of the job. Since the total utility cannot be determined directly, the probability (P) with which students n will prefer job i to job j is examined:

$$P_{ni} = P(U_{ni} > U_{nj}) \forall i \neq j \in \tag{3}$$

Before defining the characteristics and their attributes, the underlying preference structure model must be specified. Since in the present study not every characteristic can be objectively graded in terms of utility between the individual characteristics, a partial utility model is used as a basis and is consequently described by a deterministic and a probabilistic term.

It is planned to analyze the stated preferences of the respondents. Stated preferences mean that the preference of the students towards different alternatives is directly evident under experimental conditions since a limited number of choices (choice set) is presented. In contrast, revealed preferences mean the real situation where the set of alternative choices is not apparent. The disadvantages of the stated preference method are:

- respondents are faced with a hypothetical choice without having to experience the direct consequences of their choice (do respondents take the survey seriously enough?)

– difficulty of a real representation of the labour market situation
– large heterogeneity among the respondents

We want to minimise the first disadvantage by using a sensitivity analysis (some classes of the business informatics courses are thus surveyed repeatedly). We plan to address the second point with expert interviews and focus group discussions and thus be sure that we only map choice sets that also correspond to reality. Since we are conducting the survey among business informatics programs at the FHNW, we can conduct an initial survey with a relatively homogeneous group.

We plan to implement three discrete choice procedures to analyse stated prefer-ences and methodologically adhere to Greene (2005, 2010).

1. Mixed Multinomial Logit and Latent Class Modelling
2. Bayesian Hierarchical Modelling
3. Generalised Multinomial Logit

At present, the alternatives mentioned (Latent Class Models, Bayesian Hierarchical Modeling, Generalised Multinomial Logit) are no longer so computationally intensive and thus offer a valuable possibility to obtain additional information within the scope of a sensitivity analysis.

In addition, the extended models under points 2 and 3 are less constrained with re-spect to modelling assumptions. For example, the most commonly used mixed multi-nomial logit procedure is based on the so-called Independence of Irrelevant Alterna-tives (IIA) assumption. A consequence of this assumption is that a standard logit model is not always appropriate since it assumes that there is no correlation between unobserved factors and choice alternatives. The fulfillment of the IIA assumption can be checked with a Hausman test. If the assumption is not fulfilled, further mod-eling approaches can be used (points 2 and 3 from the previous list). This extended modeling ensures that the model finally used allows a concrete and scientifically sound transfer to practice, and verifies the best research methods are used for evalua-tion.

Preference Measurement and Implementation of the Analysis – Stated Choice Experiment
The design parameters defined using expert discussions and focus group interviews are transferred into so-called "choice sets". In this process, hypothetical job offers are gen-erated based on the possible characteristics of the performance parameters' levels and presented to the participants for selection.

For illustration purposes, a selection from a possible choice set is shown below in the simplified form. For this example, we can hypothetically specify the following attributes:

- Place of work with 4 levels: 4600 Olten, 8152 Glattbrugg, 4001 Basel and 6110 Wolhusen (LU)
- Annual salary (100%) with 5 levels: 72'000, 78'000, 84'000, 90'000, 96'000 CHF
- Weekly working hours 100% with 4 levels: 36 h, 38 h, 40 h, 42 h
- Number of holiday weeks 100% per year with 3 levels: 4 weeks, 5 weeks, 6 weeks

- Expected workload (workload flexibility) with 5 levels: 60%, 80%, 100%, 60–80%, 80–100%
- Home office with 3 levels: no home office, 1 weekday home office, 2 weekdays home office (Fig. 1)

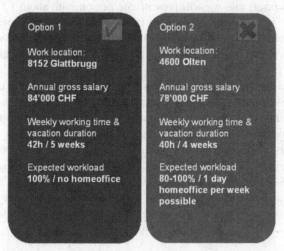

Fig. 1. Illustrative example of a choice set for measuring the monetary valuation of multidimensional reward systems

Even this relatively simple (hypothetical) configuration allows the design of $4·5·4·3·5·3 = 3600$ different choice cards. However, the participants cannot judge 3600 choice cards (with 3600 choice cards; there are $\frac{3600·3599}{2} = 6.5$ millions binary choice tasks).

This problem can be solved in different ways:

Restriction of the choice cards: In the above example, it is not plausible that, for example, an expected workload of 60% or 60–80% would appear together with the option of 2 weekdays home office. Moreover, salary and workplace will correlate: In Zurich and Basel (metropolitan areas), the wage tends to be higher than in peripheral areas (e.g. Olten or Wolhusen). We will find out more about these restrictions in indi-vidual interviews with recruiting experts from ICT companies in the region to ensure that only practice-relevant choice-sets are represented in the survey.

Experimental design: In addition to the complete design just presented (3600 choice cards) and a possible reduced design, there is the possibility of orthogonal, fractional or optimal (efficient) design. These algorithms allow a further considerable (!) reduction of the choice set that a respondent has to answer (typically 5–15). However, the disadvantage of reduced designs to full designs is that only main ef-fects and no interactions can be estimated. In addition, participant-specific covari-ates are asked, such as mode of study (full-time vs. part-time), gender, age, migration background, work experience and family situation.

Using suitable software packages (Stata and R), the study design is formed according to criteria commonly used in practice. These criteria include, for example, the optimal D-efficiency of the study design, which is influenced by the number of choic-es presented in the choice experiment and the number of participants. Also, the choices' values must have a minimum overlap (within a choice set, the values should be used as often as possible and in a balanced way).

We assume a priori that we will present one person with about 12 choices (target group of business information technology students. Currently, there are 6 classesin the Bachelor's programme and 2 class courses in the Master's programme with 30–40 participants per class so that the necessary sample size of n = 300 can be achieved (Louviere et al. 2000).

Survey: Once the experimental design is fixed, the choice cards for the partici-pants will be formed. We plan to use the Questback survey tool (browser-based) to conduct the choice experiment. During the experiment, the database with the answers will be automatically expanded. The advantage is that the survey becomes easily scalable. After completing the first phase with students from FHNW, we plan to in-volve other technical courses at universities of applied sciences and universities (in-cluding Kalaidos FH, ZHAW, BFH, HSR, FHGR and the business engineering courses at ETH Zurich).

The illustration below shows the above choice set on a smartphone or laptop/iPad. If a user selects option 1 (green tick on the left), the database is displayed as follows (Fig. 2):

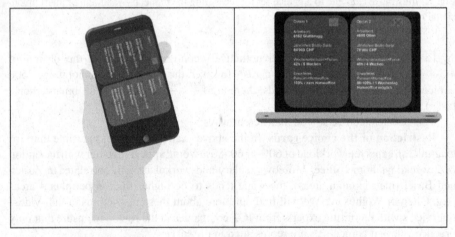

Fig. 2. Choice sets displayed in an illustrative web tool

The "third" option in the last data line is a dropout option, i.e. the non-selection of both proposed alternatives.

Emission of Results to ICT Companies and Future Developments, Transfer to Research and Teaching

The aim of the first data collection among business informatics students at the FHNW

Table 1. Illustrative data set collected after completing a choice card by individual 131

ID	Year	Mode	Gender	Nationality	Age	...	Location	Salary	Weekly work-time (hours)	Holidays (weeks)	Workload (%)	Home-office (days p. week)	Choice
131	2021	ft	m	CH	26	...	8152	84 K	42	5	100	0	1
131	2021	ft	m	CH	26	...	4600	78 K	40	4	80	1	0
131	2021	ft	m	CH	26	...	DROPOUT-OPTION						0

is to calibrate a multivariate discrete choice model. The purpose is, among other things, the monetary evaluation of design parameters x_j of employment contracts. This can be expressed via the marginal rate of substitution with non-monetary covariates x_j:

The unit of measurement of the marginal rate is $\frac{\Delta S}{\Delta x_j}$. It indicates how much salary can be foregone on average (ΔS), if an attribute of the employment contract changes (Δx_j), for example, one day more home office per week is granted. This information allows ICT companies to optimally design employment contracts via non-monetary components such as working time flexibilisation, etc.

For this purpose, the data set (anonymised) is stored in a specially programmed web tool as a prototype with the calibration algorithm. In follow-up projects, this web tool will be made available to companies so that the continuously updated monetary evaluations of the design parameters of employment contracts by students can be visualised on the basis of the surveys collected and the preferences derived from them.

Planned functionalities: A user of the web tool can stratify the data set according to his or her wishes, for ex-ample, by only evaluating the attributes of female students. For example, women may value a working day in a home office higher than men, but men may value a lower working time per week monetarily higher. Thus, users can create hypothetical employment contracts with design parameters via a drop-down menu and estimate individual performance parameters' monetary effects (including estimation uncer-tainties) utilizing graphical visualizations.

Planned further developments and transfer of the results: This study's result can be a database for corporate and organisational decision-makers who want to understand better the relative importance of different attributes for choosing a job in information systems. Companies and organisations can create adequate total compensation packages based on the quantitative information from the DCE. Such information as the stated pref-erences of business informatics students will also be important for designing appropriate recruitment and retention strategies.

After successfully completing this initialisation project, the project steps and the results will also be presented in the textbook "Statistik im Klartext" (author Fabian Heimsch). Concerning research, much has been published in the context of DCE appli-cations. However, the project provides new and innovative insights, especially for human resource management, to promote employer attractiveness and employee loyalty in the context of total rewards management. The use with regard to sensitivity analyses, e.g. Bayesian Hierarchical Modelling, can also be published in peer-reviewed scientific and practice-oriented journals.

In addition, an expansion of the basis via other universities of applied sciences and universities is planned (e.g. ETH Zurich, University of Applied Sciences Rap-perswil, University of Applied Sciences Chur, etc.). This will further increase the use-fulness of the web tool for companies (e.g. ICT companies in the canton of Grau-bünden are more likely to want to align themselves with the responses of the students of Graubünden). Furthermore, the data and answers can be used to identify any changes in ICT students' preferences over time and publish these through the appro-priate channels.

References

1. Auspurg, K., Liebe, U.: Choice-Experimente und die Messung von Handlungsentscheidungen in der Soziologie. Köln Z Soziol **63**, 301–314 (2011)
2. Bekker-Grob, D., Esther, W., Ryan, M., Gerard, K.: Discrete choice experiments in health economics: a review of the literature. Health Econ. **21**, 145–172 (2012)
3. Hanley, N., Wright, R., Mourato, S.: Choice modelling approaches: a superior alternative for environmental valuation? J Econ. Surv. **15**, 435–462 (2001)
4. Hensher, D., Rose, J., Greene, W.: Applied Choice Analysis, Cambridge University Press, Cambridge (2005)
5. Greene, W.: Modelling Ordered Choices, Cambridge University Press, Cambridge (2010)
6. Lancaster, K.J.: A new approach to consumer theory. J. Polit. Econ. **74**, 132–157 (1966)
7. Louviere, J., Hensher, D., Swait, J.: Stated Choice Methods: Analysis and Application, 1st edn. Cambridge University Press, Cambridge (2000)
8. McFadden, D.: Conditional logit analysis of qualitative choice behavior. In: Zarembka, P. (ed.) Frontiers in Econometrics, Academic Press, New York, pp. 105–142 (1974)
9. Randstat: Employer Brand Research 2021 (2021). https://f.hub-spotusercon-tent00.net/hubfs/2249108/REBR/Randstad%20Employer%20%20Research_Switzerland.pdf
10. Thompson, P.: Total Reward, CIPD House, London (2002)

Role of Innovation Competitive Advantage on Strategic Orientation Dimensions and Sustainable Growth of SMEs in Nigeria

Danjuma Tali Nimfa[✉], Ariful Islam, Ahmad Shaharudin Abdul Latiff, and Sazali Abdul Wahab

Putra Business School, Universiti Putra Malaysia, 43400 Serdang, Selangor, Malaysia
nimfad@unijos.edu.ng

Abstract. The purpose of this study was to examine the role of innovation competitive advantage on strategic orientation dimensions of (entrepreneurial orientation, market orientation, and resource orientation) on the sustainable growth of SMEs. This study used a total of 217 responses adopting the cross-sectional survey research design from manufacturing SMEs owners/founders. The results were analysed using PLS-SEM via SmartPLS version 3.3.3. The major findings established that entrepreneurial orientation did not directly link with the sustainable growth of SMEs. The study confirmed that market orientation and resource orientation revealed a direct and significant positive link with the sustainable growth of SMEs. Similarly, innovation competitive advantage has a direct significant positive association with the sustainable growth of SMEs. Likewise, entrepreneurial orientation and market orientation have a direct and significant positive relationship with innovation competitive advantage. However, resource orientation did not significantly relate to innovation competitive advantage. The findings validated that innovation competitive advantage mediated the relationship between entrepreneurial orientation, market orientation, and the sustainable growth of SMEs. Finally, innovation competitive advantage did not mediate between resource orientation and sustainable growth of SMEs, which have not previously been proven in empirical studies. This study was designed to address the existing gaps and provide reasons to prove them. This study is indeed one of the remarkable studies in the context of SMEs, which integrates these selected variables into a single model. The originality focused on the role of innovation competitive advantage on strategic orientation dimensions and sustainable growth of SMEs that are relevant to Society 5.0.

Keywords: Entrepreneurial orientation · Market orientation · Resource orientation · Innovation competitive advantage · Sustainable growth of SMEs

1 Introduction

Integrating sustainability into enterprise strategic planning is necessary for modern changing landscape. A value-driven approach may be crucial to sustaining long-term growth in the development of business strategies. Therefore, the sustainable growth of

© Springer Nature Switzerland AG 2021
A. Gerber and K. Hinkelmann (Eds.): Society 5.0 2021, CCIS 1477, pp. 46–62, 2021.
https://doi.org/10.1007/978-3-030-86761-4_5

SMEs reflects the product of the founders' strategic choices and the external environment dynamic attributes (Wawira 2013; Sony 2019; Srisathan et al. 2020). The SMEs are uprising at various rates in any climate or business context. Such success inconsistencies indicate that entrepreneurs' strategic choices can influence the enterprise growth; SMEs make up 99% of all companies (Sustainability Knowledge Group 2019). In addition, they contribute 70% of global jobs and the major contributors to value manufacturing SMEs, contributing between 50% and 60% of the estimated value-added. The SMEs total employment is up to 45% and 33% GDP in developing economies (Sustainability Knowledge Group 2019). These data clearly show that the position of SMEs in sustainable growth is crucial to realise the sustainability goal, which confirms the bond between SMEs and sustainability (Silvestre and Țîrcă 2019). The achievement of small and medium enterprises (SMEs) in a country is a key area of study. The incredible success or lack of progress of small and medium enterprises in every economy is important to the success of such an economy (Schmitt 2018). In view of this, past research has shown that absolutely far-reaching empirical model still remain to be found to illustrate the sustainable growth of SMEs and the ways they should grow to succeed (Diaz et al. 2021) Therefore, not much has been detailed in respect of sustainable growth of small and medium enterprises. Baker (2014) found that innovation simply refers to total creativity, improvement, invention and the involvement of everyone in the enterprise in new ideas for the advancement of the organisation. Since growth across borders and global competitiveness has strengthened, the importance of innovation has grown and has become a core necessity central to an enterprise's sustainable growth performance in the indigenous or local and foreign marketplace (Saqib and Satar 2021). In other sittings Sheng et al. (2013) maintained that knowledge stickiness had shown a significant effect on innovation competitive advantage, and knowledge transfer also had a significant impact on innovation competitive advantage. Therefore, the role of innovation competitive advantage on strategic orientation dimensions of entrepreneurial orientation, market orientation and resource orientation with sustainable growth of SMEs has not been addressed in the prior work of scholars. Similarly, Society 5.0 has emerged as a result of rapid innovation of interconnected devices, which are now extremely sophisticated and widely used around the world, and it has managed to cause a massive culture shift (Salgues 2018), which has an influence on sustainable growth of SMEs especially in the context of Nigeria. Thus, these motivational Knowledge gaps would be ascertained in addition to lack of empirical research on the effects of entrepreneurial orientation, market orientation, resource orientation and sustainable growth of SMEs in Nigeria. This study is needed because it attempt to investigate the role of innovation competitive advantage in the bond between strategic orientation dimensions such as entrepreneurial orientation, market orientation and resource orientation on the sustainable growth of small and medium enterprises (SMEs) in Nigeria.

2 Literature Review and Hypotheses Development

2.1 Theory

The dynamic capabilities theory was employed in this study. Dynamic capabilities theory (DCT) maintains that competitive gain of enterprises can be centred on unique processes, ways of coordinating and combining, shaped by the precise level of investment about the organisation, (Teece et al. 1997), such as the hard-to-trade knowledge business plan, additional value of the enterprise and the paths of transformation that it has engaged. Entrepreneurial orientation (Sharma and Kumar 2021), market orientation (Fitriany et al. 2020), resource orientation (Paladino 2007) and innovation competitive advantage (Sheng et al. 2013) are currently viewed as dynamic capabilities and robust strategies that can foster sustainable growth of SMEs (Teece 2007; Nimfa et al. 2019). Academics such as Teece (1997); Newey and Zahra (2009) had advanced dynamic capability theory and their claims and models. While these scholars have placed great importance on the development of business strategies aimed at entrepreneurship, technology, knowledge management, innovation and sustainable profitability, they have not sufficiently incorporated viable practices such as the sustainable growth of SMEs into their models. From the context of SMEs, previous studies have identified the entrepreneurial orientation (Nofiani et al. 2021) market orientation (Randhawa et al. 2020); resource orientation (Sahi et al. 2020), and innovation competitive advantage (Sheng et al. 2013, Whalen and Han 2017) as basic capabilities, smart enough to foster sustainable growth of SMEs. From the viewpoint of dynamic capabilities theory, numerous intensities of entrepreneurial orientation, market orientation, resource orientation and innovation competitive advantage provide available capabilities and resources that can promote sustainable growth of SMEs (Teece 2007; Hussain et al. 2020; Gutierrez Rodriguez et al. 2020). This study has contributes to improving the effectiveness of dynamic capabilities theory that SME owners/founders who embrace an entrepreneurial orientation, market orientation and resource orientation; and innovation competitive advantage, can witness the continued delivery of sustainable growth of SMEs and improved business efficiency. Accordingly, this research adopted the dynamic capabilities theory as the basis for explaining the relationship between the variables chosen in the framework to underpin the theoretical lenses, as shown in Fig. 1.

2.2 Entrepreneurial Orientation and Sustainable Growth of SMEs

Entrepreneurial orientation makes a firm quite willing to take advantage of opportunities (Stephens and Kim 2015). Previous literature on entrepreneurial orientation (EO) Ali et al. (2020) indicated that entrepreneurial orientation, market orientation, and total quality management are positively and significantly related to the organisational sustainable growth of SMEs. Accordingly; Beliaeva et al. (2020) found that there was a positive influence of entrepreneurial orientation and relatively insignificant effect of market orientation as component of strategic orientation. Kumar and Das (2020) reported that entrepreneurial orientation was mast related with the selection of new added value or in the face of growing competition. Covin and Wales (2019) noted that entrepreneurial orientation is part of a new business that has a strategic orientation based on the extent to which the company has a sustained risk-taking structure of appropriate strategic behaviour. In addition, entrepreneurial orientation in new enterprises could indeed grow while acquiring essential low-cost economic resources and converting them into high-value imitative products where competitive environments are not balanced (Yin et al. 2020; Nimfa and Gajere 2017). This occurred due to difficulties in obtaining resources to sustain business operations, economic expansion and technological innovation (Cui et al. 2018; Ying et al. 2019). Hence, this study hypothesised that:

H1: Entrepreneurial orientation (EO) has a direct positive effect on sustainable growth of SMEs.

2.3   Market Orientation and Sustainable Growth of SMEs

Narver and Slater (1990) claimed that a firm that enhances its own market orientation would also strengthen market growth through business segments made up of primary commodities and non-commodity products. In other words, it must build a sustainable and remarkable value for the customer (Silbergh 2019). Recent studies has revealed that higher-level market orientation dimensions have a significant effect on the performance of women-owned small and medium enterprises (Porter and Kramer 2019). Dogbe et al. (2020) found that market orientation is dedicated to the recognition of market dynamics and the exchange of knowledge with organisational members in order to deliver the best strategic orientation initiatives to the customer. Sahi et al. (2020) confirmed that the level of market orientation for operating activities as part of the strategic direction was significant. However, market orientation and entrepreneurial orientation do not have a positive and significant impact on strategic orientation and business performance (Novita et al. 2020). Conversely, this link continue to be stronger under strategic decision responsiveness and higher-level dimensions of entrepreneurial orientation (Yu et al. 2019). Thus, this study stated that:

H2: Market orientation (MO) has a direct positive effect on sustainable growth of SMEs.

2.4   Resource Orientation and Sustainable Growth of SMEs

The resource orientation also showed significant and positive interactions with all four performance measures evaluated, and most of these relationships were strengthened by the conditions of the industry (Chmielewski and Paladino 2007). Likewise, survey on resource orientation revealed a positive and significant relationship with performance indicators that were assessed in an industrial conditions that support resource capabilities (Cheng et al. 2020). Resources and capacities must have unique characteristics before making a significant contribution to the strategic advantage of the firm (Teece et al. 1997). The decision on resource orientation for innovation should be at a strategic level as the organisational strategy is largely restricted and dependent on the firm's resource profile' (Zhang and Walton 2017). Literature review on resource orientation showed that resources and capabilities are sources of sustained value when they are valuable. In addition, valuable resources allow the enterprise to develop and implement strategies to improve its operational efficiency (D'Amato et al., 2020; Alnawas and Farha 2020). Therefore, the hypothesis of this study suggested that:

H3: Resource orientation (RO) has a direct positive effect on sustainable growth of SMEs.

2.5 Relationship Between the Role of Innovation Competitive Advantage and Entrepreneurial Orientation, Market Orientation and Resource Orientation on Sustainable Growth of SMEs

Previous studies have attempted to acknowledge the direct and significant link between innovation competitive advantage and sustainable growth of SMEs (Whalen and Han 2017). Sheng et al. (2013) indicated that transfer of knowledge had a strong association with innovation competitive advantage. In a similar vein, current research has confirmed that innovation competitive advantage has a direct affiliation with organisational culture; and innovation competitive advantage partially mediates the connection between organisational culture and sustainable growth of SMEs (Nimfa et al. 2021a). Studies have also shown that entrepreneurial orientation has an important connection with innovation-oriented enterprises (Al Mamun et al. 2018; Kiyabo and Isaga 2020). On the other hand, Ledwith and O'Dwyer (2008) outlined some clear differences between the influence of product release, market orientation and product advantage on product capabilities and business quality in small and large enterprises. Research findings have shown that resource orientation is positively linked to progress and innovation of new products, while the sustainable use of resources promotes the business's technology capabilities (Paladino 2007; Kumar et al. 2012). Woschke et al. (2017) stated that resource imbalance would have a progressive impact on accelerated growth, but not technological innovation in SMEs. Based on the above discussion, there is a limited empirical survey on the mediating role of innovation competitive advantage between entrepreneurial orientation, market orientation and resource orientation, and sustainable growth of SMEs. Accordingly, the following hypotheses were suggested:

H4: Innovation competitive advantage has a direct positive effect on sustainable growth of SMEs.

H5: There is a significant relationship between entrepreneurial orientation and innovation competitive advantage.

H6. There is a significant relationship between market orientation and innovation competitive advantage.

H7. There is a significant relationship between resource orientation and innovation competitive advantage.

H8: Innovation competitive advantage mediates between entrepreneurial orientation and sustainable growth of SMEs.

H9: Innovation competitive advantage mediates between market orientation and sustainable growth of SMEs.

H10: Innovation competitive advantage mediates between resource orientation and sustainable growth of SMEs.

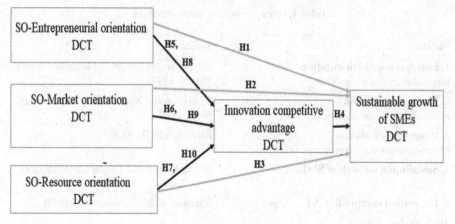

Fig. 1. Theoretical framework

3 Methodology

The current research is empirical (based on primary data), descriptive (analysis of the relationship between variables). Deductive (testing of hypotheses), and quantitative (involves analysis of quantitative data collection using a structured questionnaire). The population of the study includes manufacturing SMEs, enterprise year of incorporation, employees, enterprise assets based, highest qualification and owner responsibilities. Based on the most recent data provided by Manufacturers Association of Nigeria (MAN 2017), the Nigerian manufacturing sector consists of 3,012 manufacturing firms, presently registered in official directory records. These firms are part of a broad spectrum of business sizes.

3.1 Measurement

The analysis of the suggested theoretical framework was carried out using the accepted and validated questionnaire from previous empirical studies with a few adjustments to fit the current study outlined in Table 1. Five points Likert scale used for measuring all variables 1 = strongly disagree and 5 = strongly agree. In order to assess whether the theoretical and practical eligibility criteria have been met, copies of the research instrument (questionnaire) were sent to 3 practitioners and 3 scholars. Five research variables, items used as measurement and sources are outline in Table 1. The structured questionnaire covers a total of 27 questions used to measure 5 study variables. All variables were used as Mono-dimensional variables.

3.2 Data Collection

A list including the contact details of most of the initial population of 3012 manufacturing firms was obtained from the official Manufacturers Association of Nigeria (MAN) website. Initial contact via telephone call was placed to roughly 1124 of these firms

Table 1. Measurement of study variables

Variable	Items	Source
1. Entrepreneurial orientation Mono-dimensional construct	5	(Cheng and Huizingh 2014; Gatignon and Xuereb 1997)
2. Market orientation Mono-dimensional construct	6	(Gatignon and Xuereb 1997; Narver and Slater 1999)
3. Resource orientation Mono-dimensional construct	6	Paladino (2007, 2008)
4. Sustainable Growth of SMEs	6	Arora, Kumar and Thapar (2018); Eggers et al. 2013)
5. Innovation competitive Advantage	6	Sheng et al. 2013; Nimfa et al. 2020
Total number of items	27	

using a simple random sampling method. The unit of analysis used was organisational (the owners/founders) who has the strategic knowledge of the SMEs. The structured questionnaire was administered to 540 manufacturing firms that decided to participate in the research, together with a cover letter consisting of all required clarifications. The mail survey, which was sent to the respondents via a Google form, was the data collection technique used in this study.

Only 217 usable copies of the questionnaire were returned from these firms, response rate was 40.19% and population-wide representation was 7.20%. Owing to their pragmatic knowledge of strategic management of manufacturing companies, owners were selected as the primary respondents. A number of respondents, 20% of organisational research work is considered acceptable (Saleh and Ndubisi 2006; Rogelberg and Stanton 2007). The SMEs survey rate of response in developing countries (for example, Nor-Aishah et al. (2020) received 146 (14.6%), Basah (2018) received 203 (20.83%), Ghobakhloo and Ching (2019) received 177 (32.82%), and Ebrahim et al. (2012) received 256 (20.8%) these were considered acceptable. Therefore, the response rate of 217 (40.19%) for this study was considered acceptable in research. The methods of data analysis used for this study was Partial Least Square Structural Equation Modelling (PLS-SEM) with the aid of SmartPLS statistical software analysis (Hair et al. 2019a, 2020).

4   Discussion and Conclusion

The descriptive analysis shows that more than half of the respondents 139 (64.1%) owners/founders and only 78 (35.9%) were senior management employees had participated in this analysis. The highest qualification possessed by 116 (53.5%) respondents had no degree but were skilled, whereas 101 (46.5%) respondents were bachelor degree and above. Followed by the assets (excluding land and buildings) for 138 (63.6%) SMEs are between 5 million Naira and less than 50 million Naira, while 79 (36.4%) SMEs documented assets worth between 50 and below 500 million Naira. Amongst the SMEs, 113

(52.1%) and 104 (47.9%) hired 10–49 and 50–199 full-time employees, accordingly. The majority of the respondents 163 (71.5%) SMEs had been recognised for 5 years or more incorporation, while 54 (24.9%) SMEs had been incorporated in less than 5 years. Table 2 provides a demographic information summary of the results as follows:

Table 2. Demographic Information

Items		Frequency	Percentage (%)
1. Your responsibility in the enterprise	Owner/Founder	139	64.1
	Senior management employee	78	35.9
	Total	**217**	**100**
2. Your highest qualification	Bachelor degree and above	101	46.5
	No degree/skilled	116	53.5
	Total	**217**	**100**
3. What is your enterprise assets based (excluding land and building)	5 million Naira to <50 million Naira	138	63.6
	50 million Naira to <500 million Naira	79	36.4
	Total	**217**	**100**
4. How many full-time employees are hired in your enterprise?	10–49	113	52.1
	50–199	104	47.9
	Total	**217**	**100**
5. How long has your enterprise incorporated?	Less than 5 years	54	24.9
	5 years or more	163	71.5
	Total	**217**	**100**

4.1 Measurement Model Assessment

In order to assess the model, this study used the Partial Least Squares method to the structural equation model (Hair et al. 2019a). The statistical software used was the SmartPLS version 3.3.3, which generates an incremental combination of the main method of analysis that relates to construct measurements and path analysis that captures the structural model of all constructs. The Partial least squares (PLS) approach was considered most appropriate, mainly based on small sample size (Hair et al. 2019b). This study used 217 sample size, and a bootstrapping process with 500 samples of data was used. A study by (Hair et al. 2017a) recommended a two-step process when evaluating PLS-SEM. This approaches include determining measurement model and assessing structural model. Henseler (2017) stated that it may be irrelevant to assess the structural model without first evaluating the measurement model. Therefore, this study considered the evaluation of measurement model prior to the assessment of the structural model (Hair et al. 2017b). The findings revealed that the composite reliability (CR) value for sustainable of SMEs was 0.903. Meanwhile, the composite reliability (CR) value for innovation competitive advantage was 0.859, followed by entrepreneur orientation (0.914), market orientation with 0.893 and resource orientation with 0. 901 as illustrated in Table 3. The Cronbach Alpha value for sustainable growth of SMEs was 0.866 which indicates excellent internal consistency. Meanwhile, the Cronbach Alpha value for innovation competitive advantage was 0.782, which indicates good internal consistency. The Cronbach Alpha value for entrepreneurial orientation was 0.874, market orientation with 0.840 and resource orientation was 0.863 which all indicated excellent internal consistency (Hair et al. 2019a), shown in Table 3:

Table 3. Construct reliability and validity

	CA	CR	AVE
EO	0.874	0.914	0.726
ICA	0.782	0.859	0.604
MO	0.840	0.893	0.676
RO	0.863	0.901	0.647
SGSMEs	0.866	0.903	0.652

Note: EO = Entrepreneurial orientation, ICA = Innovation Competitive advantage, MO = Market Orientation, RO = Resource Orientation, and SGSMEs = Sustainable Growth of SMEs

Convergent-validity assessed by AVE for sustainable growth of SMEs was 0.652, followed by innovation competitive advantage with 0.604, entrepreneur orientation with 0.726, market orientation was 0.676 and resource orientation with 0.647 as illustrated in the Table 3 above. Discriminant validity was measured using the Fornell-Larcker Criterion for this model (Hair et al. 2019a) as shown in Table 4. The findings indicate that for all reflective constructs, the square root of average variance extracted [AVE] (diagonal) was higher than the causal relationships (off-diagonal).

4.2 Structural Model Assessment

When the reliability and validity of the measurement model was achieved, the structural model was examined. The path coefficient (hypothesis test) as well as the coefficient of determination (R2 value) were tested in the structural model. In this study, the coefficient of determination (R2 value) was 0.894 (89.4%) and 0.745 (74.5%) for sustainable growth of SMEs and innovation competitive advantage. In order to evaluate the path

Table 4. Fornell-Larcker

	EO	ICA	MO	RO	SGSMEs
EO	0.852				
ICA	0.809	0.777			
MO	0.855	0.841	0.822		
RO	0.843	0.794	0.848	0.804	
SGSMEs	0.865	0.844	0.904	0.903	0.807

Note: EO = Entrepreneurial orientation, ICA = Innovation Competitive advantage, MO = Market Orientation, RO = Resource Orientation, and SGSMEs = Sustainable Growth of SMEs

coefficient (hypothesis tested), a single-tailed SmartPLS test with a 5% significance level was performed to evaluate the P value and T statistics to test the significance or insignificance of the hypotheses. Baron and Kenny (1986); MacKinnon (2011) has been used to test the relationship between entrepreneurial orientation, market orientation, resource orientation, and sustainable growth of SMEs with any mediation effect of innovation competitive advantage. The findings of the structural model, referred to as the inner model, are shown in Table 5.

The first hypothesis of this study, H1 has predicted that entrepreneurial orientation did not have a direct significant positive link with sustainable growth of SMEs, therefore it was not supported at a 0.01 level of significance ($\beta = 0.118$, t = 1.676, p > 0.05) as illustrated in Table 5. Hypothesis 2 (H2) of this study confirmed that market orientation has a direct and significant positive link with sustainable growth of SMEs ($\beta = 0.334$, t = 3.100, p < 0.01), therefore, H2 was strongly supported. Also, H3 revealed that resource orientation has a direct significant positive connection with sustainable growth of SMEs, the results was strongly supported with ($\beta = 0.391$, t = 4.128, p < 0.01). The fourth hypothesis of this study, indicated that innovation competitive advantage has a significant positive association with sustainable growth of SMEs, which was supported at a value 0.01 level of significance ($\beta = 0.163$, t = 2.890, p < 0.01). Furthermore, in hypothesis 5 (H5), show a significant relationship between the entrepreneurial orientation and innovation competitive advantage. Based on the findings, entrepreneurial orientation has a direct significant and positive relationship with innovation competitive advantage ($\beta = 0.235$, t = 3.093, p < 0.01). Based on hypothesis (H6), the result shows that market orientation has a direct and significant positive relationship with innovation competitive advantage, that was supported at a value 0.01 level of significance ($\beta = 0.495$, t = 4.333, p < 0.01). On the other hand, hypothesis 7 (H7), results show that resource orientation did not significantly relate to innovation competitive advantage ($\beta = 0.182$, t = 1.829, p > 0.05), hence H7 was not supported. Furthermore, hypothesis (H8), indicated that innovation competitive advantage mediates the between entrepreneurial orientation and sustainable growth of SMEs, therefore, the result was supported by a 0.05 level of significance ($\beta = 0.038$, t = 2.010, p < 0.05). Hypothesis nine (H9), revealed that innovation competitive advantage mediates the relationship between market orientation and sustainable growth of SMEs, the result was supported by a 0.01 level of significance ($\beta = 0.081$, $t = 2.665$, $p < 0.01$). Finally, hypothesis ten (H10), confirmed that innovation competitive advantage did not mediates between resource orientation and sustainable growth of SMEs, therefore, the result was not supported at 0.01 level of significance ($\beta = 0.030$, $t = 1.556$, $p > 0.01$).

Table 5. Path coefficient

	Original sample	Sample mean	(STDEV)	T statistics	P value
1. EO -> SGSMEs	0.118	0.105	0.070	1.676	ns 0.094
2. MO -> SGSMEs	0.334	0.347	0.108	3.100	**0.002
3. RO -> SGSMEs	0.391	0.400	0.095	4.128	***0.000
4. ICA -> SGSMEs	0.163	0.150	0.056	2.890	**0.004
5. EO -> ICA	0.235	0.225	0.076	3.093	**0.002
6. MO -> ICA	0.495	0.511	0.114	4.333	***0.000
7. RO -> ICA	0.182	0.177	0.099	1.829	ns 0.068
8. EO -> ICA -> SGSMEs	0.038	0.034	0.020	2.010	*0.045
9. MO -> ICA -> SGSMEs	0.081	0.075	0.030	2.665	**0.008
10. RO -> ICA -> SGSMEs	0.030	0.027	0.019	1.556	ns 0.120

Note: Entrepreneurial orientation, ICA = Innovation Competitive advantage, MO = Market Orientation, RO = Resource Orientation, and SGSMEs = Sustainable Growth of SMEs
P values asterisks: ns = P > 0.05; * = P ≤ 0.05; ** = P ≤ 0.01; *** = P ≤ 0.001

5   Conclusion

This study examined the role of innovation competitive advantage on strategic orientation dimensions of entrepreneurial orientation, market orientation and resource orientation on sustainable growth of SMEs. The initial assessment was to demonstrate the variable links between entrepreneurial orientation, market orientation, resource orientation and sustainable growth of SMEs. In addition, this study investigates the role of innovation competitive advantage between entrepreneurial orientation, market orientation and resource orientation on sustainable growth of SMEs a path not previously established by scholars (Tajeddini et al. 2020; Diabate et al. 2019). The empirical findings have shown that entrepreneurial orientation did not have a direct significant link with sustainable growth of SMEs. The study confirmed that market orientation and resource orientation revealed a direct and significant positive link with sustainable growth of SMEs. Similarly, it was also found that innovation competitive advantage has a direct significant positive association with sustainable growth of SMEs. Relatedly, the results proved that entrepreneurial orientation and market orientation have a direct and significant positive relationship with innovation competitive advantage. Nevertheless, resource orientation did not significantly relate to innovation competitive advantage. Accordingly, the findings demonstrated that innovation competitive advantage mediated the relationship between entrepreneurial orientation, market orientation and the sustainable growth of SMEs. Finally, it was reported that innovation competitive advantage did not mediates between resource orientation and sustainable growth of SMEs, which have not previously been proven empirical studies. Also, the findings revealed that innovation competitive advantage has a significant positive association with sustainable growth of small and medium enterprises. This finding is consistent with the views of previous studies (like Sheng et al. 2013; Nimfa et al. 2021a). These results indicate that when entrepreneurial-oriented SME managers are involved in promoting innovation competitive advantage pathways that are particularly beneficial to SMEs, and dynamic capabilities in nature, sustainable growth of small and medium enterprises would certainly succeed (Whalen and Han 2017). In addition, entrepreneurial orientation and market orientation did not have a direct significant connection to sustainable growth of SMEs, which could be the result of tougher regulations and global pandemics where SMEs are strategizing for success in business before thinking about sustaining SMEs (Islam and Wahab 2021b).

In this study, results of the mediation analysis, found that innovation competitive advantage mediates the relationship between entrepreneurial orientation, market orientation and sustainable growth of SMEs. This outcome was in tandem with the views of existing studies, such as (Nofiani et al. 2021; Dickel 2018) who disclosed that innovation and ambidexterity of social networks mediates the link between entrepreneurial orientation and performance of small and medium enterprises. Finally, the results confirmed that innovation competitive advantage did not mediate between resource orientation and sustainable growth of SMEs. This study contributes to the growing literature on innovation competitive advantage, sustainable growth of SMEs and dynamic capabilities theory, while showcasing the role of innovation competitive advantage for sustainable growth of SMEs. These results show that the strategic orientation dimensions (of entrepreneurial orientation, market orientation and resource orientation) can be influenced by innovation competitive advantage for sustainable growth of SMEs. Hence, the data collected support the finding of this study, and uncover the importance of innovation, competitive advantage as a driver of strategic orientation dimensions (entrepreneurial orientation, market orientation and resource orientation) to improve sustainable growth of SMEs.

5.1 Practical Implications

This study offers valuable insights for managerial practice in the SMEs sector. The strategic orientation dimensions of entrepreneurial orientation and market orientation and resource orientation are teamsters of innovation competitive advantage, resulting in higher sustainable growth of SMEs. Understanding the backgrounds of sustainable growth of SMEs will benefit SME managers that engage in a superior level of entrepreneurial orientation, market orientation, and resource orientation processes nurtured through innovation competitive advantage which can improve sustainable growth of SMEs. Therefore, SME managers that promote innovation competitive advantage strategy may gain the benefits that come from building a strong association between entrepreneurial orientation, market orientation, resource orientation and sustainable growth of SMEs. The combination of entrepreneurial orientation and market orientation has a robust influence through innovation competitive advantage on sustainable growth of SMEs. Also, these outcomes show that resource orientation has a strong link with sustainable growth of SMEs. Thus, market orientation is an important impetus for sustainable growth of SMEs. Furthermore, these findings show that innovation competitive advantage positively influence sustainable growth of SMEs. Finally, the findings of this study highlighted the important role of innovation competitive advantage in the setting of the prevailing market competitiveness, where innovation competitive advantage is a key strategic capability and resource that pilot the leading spot in sustainable growth of SMEs. SME Owner and managers need to understand that efficient managing of innovation competitive advantage as the dynamic capabilities is a dominant tool for upholding sustainable growth in SMEs. Furthermore, Society 5.0 encompasses social structure as well as all the Sustainable Development Goals (SDGs), such as sustainable policy, economic growth, the development of new successful models, increased and efficient manufacturing, secure and sophisticated environmental services, reasonable and smart infrastructure use for SMEs' sustainable growth. In Nigeria, where SMEs innovation activities are rated low, these can be fostered through the role of innovation competitive advantage.

5.2 Limitations and Future Research Direction

This study examined the relationship between entrepreneurial orientation, market orientation, resource orientation, innovation competitive advantage and sustainable growth of SMEs. This study only focus on the economic perspective of sustainable growth of SMEs. Future research could provide additional insights by exploring the potentially mediating role of innovation competitive advantage, and explore sustainable growth of SMEs in term of social, economic and environmental factors. Future research should explore the insignificant direct effects of entrepreneurial orientation, market orientation to sustainable growth of SMEs, and as well resource orientation and innovation competitive advantage for large enterprises, multinational look into the insignificant direct effect between resource orientation and innovation competitive advantage to underscore the cause factors prevented the relationships to be significant. Also investigate into the insignificant affiliation between innovation competitive advantage on resource orientation and sustainable growth of SMEs. Another limiting factor is that the data for this study was obtained in a single manufacturing SMEs in Nigeria, floating the query in generalising of results to enterprises in other sectors and developing countries.

References

Al Mamun, A., Mohiuddin, M., Fazal, S.A., Ahmad, G.B.: Effect of entrepreneurial and market orientation on consumer engagement and performance of manufacturing SMEs. Manage. Res. Rev. 41(1), 133–147 (2018)

Ali, G.A., Hilman, H., Gorondutse, A.H.: Effect of entrepreneurial orientation, market orientation and total quality management on performance: evidence from Saudi SMEs. Benchmarking. Int. J. 27(4), 1503–1531 (2020)

Alnawas, I., Farha, A.A.: Strategic orientations and capabilities' effect on SMEs' performance. Market. Intell. Plan. **38**(7), 829–845 (2020)

Arora, L., Kumar, S., Thapar, M.L.: The anatomy of sustainable growth rate of Indian manufacturing firms. Global Bus. Rev. **19**(4), 1050–1071 (2018)

Baker, D.R.: Innovation and value creation: a cross-industry effects study of patent generation. A published Ph.D. dissertation, School of Business and Technology, Capella University, pp. 1–99 (2014)

Baron, R.M., Kenny, D.A.: The moderator-mediator variable distinction in social psychological research: conceptual, strategic, and statistical considerations. J. Pers. Soc. Psychol. **51**(6), 1173 (1986)

Basah, N.H.: Effect of export and intermediary cultural similarity on relationship between quality and export performance of SMEs. A published Ph.D. thesis, Graduate School of Management, University Putra Malaysia, pp. 1–286 (2018)

Beliaeva, T., Shirokova, G., Wales, W., Gafforova, E.: Benefiting from economic crisis? Strategic orientation effects, trade-offs, and configurations with resource availability on SME performance. Int. Entrep. Manage. J. **16**(1), 165–194 (2018). https://doi.org/10.1007/s11365-018-0499-2

Cheng, C.C., Huizingh, E.K.: When is open innovation beneficial? The role of strategic orientation. J. Prod. Innov. Manag. **31**(6), 1235–1253 (2014)

Cheng, Z., Wang, H., Xiong, W., Zhu, D., Cheng, L.: Public-private partnership as a driver of sustainable development: toward a conceptual framework of sustainability-oriented PPP. Environ. Dev. Sustain., 1–21 (2020)

Chmielewski, D.A., Paladino, A.: Driving a resource orientation: reviewing the role of resource and capability characteristics. Manag. Decis. **45**(3), 462–483 (2007)

Covin, J.G., Wales, W.: Crafting high-impact entrepreneurial orientation research: some suggested guidelines. Entrep. Theory Pract. **43**(1), 3–18 (2019)

Cui, L., Fan, D., Guo, F., Fan, Y.: Explicating the relationship of entrepreneurial orientation and firm performance: underlying mechanisms in the context of an emerging market. Ind. Market. Manage. 71, 27–40

D'Amato, D., Veijonaho, S., Toppinen, A.: Towards sustainability? Forest-based circular bioeconomy business models in Finnish SMEs. Forest Policy Econ. **110**, 101848 (2020)

Diabate, A., Sibiri, H., Wang L., Yu, L.: Assessing SMEs' sustainable growth through entrepreneurs' ability and entrepreneurial orientation: an insight into SMEs in Côte d'Ivoire. Sustainability **9**, 11, 7149 (2019)

Diaz, A., Schöggl, J.P., Reyes, T., Baumgartner, R.J.: Sustainable product development in a circular economy: implications for products, actors, decision-making support and lifecycle information management. Sustain. Prod. Consump. **26**, 1031–1045 (2021)

Dickel, P.: Exploring the role of entrepreneurial orientation in clean technology ventures. Int. J. Entrep. Ventur. **10**(1), 56–82 (2018)

Ebrahim, N.A., Ahmed, S., Rashid, S.H.A., Wazed, M.A., Taha, Z.: Virtual collaborative R&D teams in Malaysia manufacturing SMEs. In: Advanced Materials Research, vol. 433, pp. 1653–1659. Trans Tech Publications Ltd. (2012)

Eggers, F., Kraus, S., Hughes, M., Laraway, S., Snycerski, S.: Implications of customer and entrepreneurial orientations for SME growth. Manag. Decis. **51**(3), 524–546 (2013)

Fitriany, F., Brasit, N., Nursyamsi, I., Kadir, N.: The influence of entrepreneur insight, market orientation, knowledge-sharing capabilities, on the performance and competitiveness of SMEs in Makassar Indonesia. Int. J. Multicult. Multirelig. Underst. **7**(7), 392–411 (2020)

Gatignon, H., Xuereb, J.M.: Strategic orientation of the firm and new product performance. J. Mark. Res. **34**(1), 77–90 (1997)

Ghobakhloo, M., Ching, N.T.: Adoption of digital technologies of smart manufacturing in SMEs. J. Ind. Inf. Integr. **16**, 100107 (2019)

Hair, J.F. Jr., Sarstedt, M., Ringle, C.M., Gudergan, S.P.: Advanced Issues in Partial Least Squares Structural Equation Modeling, pp. 1–27. Sage Publications, Thousand Oaks (2017a)

Hair, J.F., Jr.: Next-generation prediction metrics for composite-based PLS-SEM. Ind. Manage. Data Syst. 121(1), 5–11 (2020)

Hair, J.F., Hult, G.T.M., Ringle, C.M., Sarstedt, M.A.: Primer on Partial Least Squares Structural Equation Modeling (PLS-SEM), 2nd edn. Sage, Thousand Oaks (2017b)

Hair, J.F., Ringle, C.M., Gudergan, S.P., Fischer, A., Nitzl, C., Menictas, C.: Partial least squares structural equation modeling-based discrete choice modeling: an illustration in modeling retailer choice. Bus. Res. 12(1), 115–142 (2018). https://doi.org/10.1007/s40685-018-0072-4

Hair, J.F., Risher, J.J., Sarstedt, M., Ringle, C.M.: When to use and how to report the results of PLS SEM. Eur. Bus. Rev. 31(1), 2–24 (2019)

Henseler, J.: Partial least squares path modeling. In: Leeflang, P., Wieringa, J.E., Bijmolt, T.H.A., Pauwels, K.H. (eds.) Advanced Methods for Modeling Markets, pp. 361–381. Springer, Cham (2017). https://doi.org/10.1007/978-3-319-53469-5

Hilman, H., Kaliappen, N.: Market orientation practices and effects on organizational performance: empirical insight from Malaysian hotel industry. Sage Open 4(4), 2158244014553590 (2014)

Islam, A., Jerin, I., Hafiz, N., Nimfa, D.T., Wahab, S.A.: Configuring a blueprint for Malaysian SMEs to survive through the COVID-19 crisis: the reinforcement of quadruple helix innovation model. J. Entrep. Bus. Econ. 9(1), 32–81 (2021)

Islam, A., Wahab, A.S.: The intervention of strategic innovation practices in between regulations and sustainable business growth: a holistic perspective for Malaysian SMEs. World J. Entrep. Manage. Sustain. Dev. Vol. ahead-of-print No. ahead-of print (2021). https://doi.org/10.1108/WJEMSD-04-2020-0035

Kiyabo, K., Isaga, N.: Entrepreneurial orientation, competitive advantage, and SMEs' performance: application of firm growth and personal wealth measures. J. Innov. Entrep. 9(1), 1–15 (2020). https://doi.org/10.1186/s13731-020-00123-7

Kumar, K., Boesso, G., Favotto, F., Menini, A.: Strategic orientation, innovation patterns and performances of SMEs and large companies. J. Small Bus. Enterp. Dev. 19(1), 132–145 (2012)

Kumar, S., Das, S.: Integrated framework of strategic orientation, value offerings and new venture performance. DECISION 47(1), 3–17 (2020). https://doi.org/10.1007/s40622-020-00232-y

Ledwith, A., O'Dwyer, M.: Product launch, product advantage and market orientation in SMEs. J. Small Bus. Enterprise Dev. 5(1), 96–110 (2008)

MacKinnon, D.P.: Integrating mediators and moderators in research design. Res. Soc. Work Pract. 21(6), 675–681 (2011)

Manufacturers Association of Nigeria: Annual report review of Year 2016 (MAN, 2017). https://www.manufacturersnigeria.org/ReviewAndResearch. Accessed 20 Jan 2021

Narver, J.C., Slater, S.F.: The effect of a market orientation on business profitability. J. Market. 54(4), 20–35 (1990)

Narver, J.C., Slater, S.F.: The effect of market orientation on business profitability. In: Deshpandé, R. (ed.) Developing a Market Orientation, pp. 45–78. SAGE Publications, Thousand Oaks (1999)

Nimfa, D.T., Gajere M.C.: Small scale enterprises innovation and youths empowerment for local economic growth in Kanam L.G.A of Plateau State-Nigeria. IOSR J. Bus. Manage. (IOSR-JBM) 19(10–3), 1–12 (2017)

Nimfa, D.T., Latiff, A.S.A., Wahab, A.S.: Upper echelon theory versus dynamic capabilities theory relativeness for current sustainability of entrepreneurs. Paper presented at Putra Business School Research and Innovation (PURE) Colloquium Series 1, UPM Serdang, Selangor, Malaysia, 26th June 2019 (2019)

Nimfa, D.T., Latiff, A.S.A., Wahab, A.S., Etheraj, P.: Effect of organisational culture on sustainable growth of SMEs: mediating role of innovation competitive advantage. J. Int. Bus. Manage. 4(2), 01–19 (2021)

Nimfa, D.T., Latiff, A.S.A., Wahab, S.A.: Theories underlying sustainable growth of small and medium enterprise. Afr. J. Emerg. Issues 3(1), 43–66 (2021). https://ajoeijournals.org/sys/index.php/ajoei/article/view/15. Accessed 15 Feb 2021

Nimfa, D.T., Latiff, A.S., Wahab, S.A.: Instrument for testing innovation on the sustainable growth of manufacturing SMEs in Nigeria. J. Econ. Manage. Sci. 3(2), 57 (2020)

Nofiani, D., Indarti, N., Lukito-Budi, A.S., Manik, H. F.G.G.: The dynamics between balanced and combined ambidextrous strategies: a paradoxical affair about the effect of entrepreneurial orientation on SMEs' performance. J. Entrep. Emerg. Econ. Vol. ahead-of-print No. ahead-of print (2021). https://doi.org/10.1108/JEEE-09-2020-0331

Novita, L., Parawansa, D.A., Maming, J.: The effect of market orientation and entrepreneurial orientation on business performance with marketing capabilities as a mediation variable (case in public Bank of Makassar City). Hasanuddin J. Appl. Bus. Entrepr. 3(1), 101–113 (2020)

Paladino, A.: Analyzing the effects of market and resource orientations on innovative outcomes in times of turbulence. J. Prod. Innov. Manag. 25(6), 577–592 (2008)

Paladino, A.: Investigating the drivers of innovation and new product success: a comparison of strategic orientations. J. Prod. Innov. Manag. 24(6), 534–553 (2007)

Porter, M.E., Kramer, M.R.: Creating shared value. In: Lenssen, G.G., Smith, N.C. (eds.) Managing Sustainable Business. An Executive Education Case and Textbook, pp. 327–350. Springer, Dordrecht (2019). https://doi.org/10.1007/978-94-024-1144-7_16

Rogelberg, SG., Stanton, M.J.: Introduction: understanding and dealing with organizational survey nonresponse, pp. 195–209 (2007)

Sahi, G.K., Gupta, M.C., Cheng, T.C.E.: The effects of strategic orientation on operational ambidexterity: a study of indian SMEs in the industry 4.0 era. Int. J. Prod. Econ. 220, 107395 (2020)

Saleh, A.S., Ndubisi, N.O.: An evaluation of SME development in Malaysia. Int. Rev. Bus. Res. Papers 2(1), 1–4 (2006)

Salgues, B.:. Society 5.0: industry of the future, technologies, methods and tools. Wisley-ISTE, 1–302 (SKG, 2019) (2018). ISBN 978-1-119-52763-3

Saqib, N., Satar, M.S.: Exploring business model innovation for competitive advantage: a lesson from an emerging market. Int. J. Innov. Sci. Vol. ahead-of-print No. ahead-of-print (2021). https://doi.org/10.1108/IJIS-05-2020-0072

Schmitt, U.: Supporting the sustainable growth of SMEs with content-and collaboration-based personal knowledge management systems. J. Entrepr. Innov. Emerg. Econ. 4(1), 1–21 (2018)

Sheng, M.L., Chang, S.Y., Teo, T., Lin, Y.F.: Knowledge barriers, knowledge transfer, and innovation competitive advantage in healthcare settings. Manage. Decis. 513, 461–478 (2013)

Silbergh, D.: Sustainability and sustainable development. In: Environment Scotland, pp. 16–41. Routledge (2019)

Silvestre, B.S., Țîrcă, D.M.: Innovations for sustainable development: moving toward a sustainable future. J. Cleaner Prod. 208, 325–332 (2019)

Sony, M.: Implementing sustainable operational excellence in organizations: an integrative viewpoint. Prod. Manuf. Res. 7(1), 67–87 (2019)

Srisathan, W.A., Ketkaew, C., Naruetharadhol, P.: The intervention of organizational sustainability in the effect of organizational culture on open innovation performance: a case of Thai and Chinese SMEs. Cogent Bus. Manage. 7(1), 1717408 (2020)

Stephens, R.A., Kim, S.S.: A Study on the effects of strategic orientations on dynamic capabilities and international performance: evidence from Korean firms. Int. Manage. Rev. 19(4), 243–275 (2015)

Sustainability Knowledge Group: The importance of SMEs role in achieving sustainable development. https://sustainabilityknowledgegroup.com/the-importance-of-smes-role-in-sustainability/. Accessed 21 July 2019

Tajeddini, K., Martin, E., Ali, A.: Enhancing hospitality business performance: the role of entrepreneurial orientation and networking ties in a dynamic environment. Int. J. Hosp. Manage. **90**, 102605 (2020)

Teece, D.J.: Explicating dynamic capabilities: the nature and microfoundations of (sustainable) enterprise performance. Strateg. Manag. J. **28**(13), 1319–1350 (2007)

Teece, D.J., Pisano, G., Shuen, A.: Dynamic capabilities and strategic management. Strateg. Manag. J. **18**(8), 509–533 (1997)

Wawira, N.P.: Factors influencing sustainable growth in small and medium enterprises: a case of Avery East Africa limited. A published Master degree thesis in Arts, project planning and management, University of Nairobi, Kenya, pp. 1–55 (2013)

Whalen, E.A., Han, J.: The innovative competitive advantage: a case study of two pioneering companies. International CHRIE (2017)

Woschke, T., Haase, H., Kratzer, J.: Resource scarcity in SMEs: effects on incremental and radical innovations. Manage. Res. Rev. **40**(2), 195–217 (2017)

Yin, M., Hughes, M., Hu, Q.: Entrepreneurial orientation and new venture resource acquisition: why context matters. Asia Pac. J. Manage. (2020). https://doi.org/10.1007/s10490-020-097 18-w

Ying, Q., Hassan, H., Ahmad, H.: The role of a manager's intangible capabilities in resource acquisition and sustainable competitive performance. Sustainability **11**(2), 527 (2019)

Yu, J., Kang, S., Moon, T.: Influence of market orientation and e-marketing capability on marketing performance in Chinese SMEs. Internet e-commerce Res. **19**(5), 59–76 (2019)

Zhang, J.A., Walton, S.: Eco-innovation and business performance: the moderating effects of environmental orientation and resource commitment in green-oriented SMEs. R&D Manage. **47**(5), E26–E39 (2017)

A Knowledge Base About Non-pharmaceutical Interventions to Support Hospitals in Responding to Pandemic Situations

Franck Polin[✉] and Emanuele Laurenzi

FHNW University of Applied Sciences and Arts Northwestern Switzerland,
Von-Roll Strasse, 10, 4600 Olten, Switzerland
franck.polin@alumni.fhnw.ch, emanuele.laurenzi@fhnw.ch

Abstract. The ability to properly respond to a biological disaster such as the Covid-19 pandemic is fostered by making knowledge available quickly and consistently. In absence of a vaccine, knowledge about appropriate actions that prevent the spread of the virus (i.e., non-pharmaceutical interventions - NPIs) becomes essential to save lives. This is especially the case in hospitals, as everyone, including healthcare personnel, is exposed to a high risk of infection. Within this context, decision makers about NPIs in hospitals are constantly under pressure. They have to quickly interpret numerous, lengthy and ever-changing regulatory documents, coming from multiple public authorities for the creation of internal security protocols against the spread of the virus. This is a knowledge intensive task calling for support to ensure an efficient response to a pandemic situation. In this paper, a knowledge base is presented, which consists of an ontology, semantic rules and queries about NPIs. The knowledge base was systematically engineered by considering both (a) official regulatory documents of multiple public authorities and (b) expert knowledge from a Swiss hospital. The ultimate goal of this work is to support decision makers in the creation of consistent security protocols about NPIs. The approach is evaluated via the implemented knowledge base which proves that questions relevant for a decision maker are automatically answered.

Keywords: Emergency management · Response · Knowledge base · Decision making · Non-pharmaceutical interventions · Biological disaster · Covid-19 pandemic

1 Introduction

Similar to the influenza pandemic [1] and the SARS-cov-1 epidemic of 2003 [2, 3], the COVID-19 pandemic [4] was yet another biological disaster that brought health organizations, especially hospitals, into exceptional emergency situations. Knowledge in such situations is the main determining factor that counts to help reducing losses.

The year 2019 and 2020 have been characterized by a series of cumulative learnings with respect to how to cope with a pandemic situation by governments and organizations. Eventually, these learnings have been crafted into disaster response measures [5],

© Springer Nature Switzerland AG 2021
A. Gerber and K. Hinkelmann (Eds.): Society 5.0 2021, CCIS 1477, pp. 63–76, 2021.
https://doi.org/10.1007/978-3-030-86761-4_6

which can be grouped into two main categories: pharmaceutical and non-pharmaceutical interventions [6]. Non-pharmaceutical interventions (NPIs) include any kind of intervention that is not directly related to the use of medical drugs and vaccines. Among other things, they include preventing and controlling infections from a disease but also contact management such as social distancing and quarantines. NPIs are highly relevant to fight infectious diseases, especially when no effective treatment like a vaccine is available. Hence, public health authorities and the health care systems around the world needed to take quick and consistent decisions on the management of such measures. For example, during the first weeks of the Covid-19 pandemic, managers in hospitals were required to make decisions on personal protective equipment (PPE) policy. However, the initial lack of knowledge in the subject matter, has led to inappropriate advises across countries [7], e.g. using homemade masks, or using mask types like FFP3 that are equipped with an exhalation valve, that don't prevent the spread of pathogens by the wearer, and are there-fore not recommended in the context of the Covid-19 pandemic [8].

The knowledge acquired over time led to new and increasingly appropriate regulation and advice from public health authorities, then adopted by health organizations. However, these instructions come in the form of long official documents also known as regulatory documents. These shall be interpreted by specialized hospital personnel (e.g. COVID-19 taskforce) with the purpose to create internal security protocols.

Hence, a high cognitive effort is required to interpret such regulatory documents, which is time-consuming. The issue becomes even more problematic and error prone when regulatory documents come from different sources. In federal countries like Switzerland, local governmental entities issue more specific and sometimes contradicting regulations. For example, the canton of Basel-City authorized extraordinary exemptions of quarantine only under specific circumstances and for a limited timeframe whereas the Swiss Federal Office of Public Health did not specify such exemptions.

To tackle the proposed problem, this paper presents a knowledge base consisting of machine-interpretable NPIs, aiming to support hospital personnel who need to make decisions on how to apply those as well as to create consistent security protocols.

Section 2 describes the related work around knowledge bases that support decision-making for disaster response. Next, Sect. 3 presents the adopted methodology. Sections from 4 to 6 explain the scope, design and implementation of the knowledge base, respectively. Section 7 shows the evaluation of the approach through the implemented artifact and finally we discuss the conclusion and outlook in Sect. 8.

2   Related Work

The dissemination of knowledge during pandemics to inform decision-making was identified as a critical issue that greatly impacts a response to a biological disaster [4, 9–11]. For instance, following the Ebola disease outbreak in 2013, Moon et al. [10] insisted on the critical need to produce and disseminate knowledge and denounce the fact that "reliable systems" for the sharing of knowledge were not established.

Hristidis et al. [12] point to the relevance for businesses to make use of knowledge bases to set in place decision support systems in emergency situations such as disasters. They also conclude that further improvements "upon the functionalities and/or methodologies of the existing disaster management systems" are required. Their contribution aims at the "facilitation of collaboration between "emergency management officials and private businesses" to reduce the losses caused by crises. Moreover, another key issue identified by Hristidis et al. [12] is making existing knowledge ma-chine-interpretable with the use of semantics (i.e., RDF) to increase the overall quality of query results.

Xu and Zlatanova [13] and Babitski et al. [14] solve the semantic interoperability issues within a disaster response by using knowledge bases with regards to geo-information and resource management, respectively.

The authors in [5, 15, 16] exploited knowledge bases to improve the availability of knowledge and support decision-making within disaster responses. Specifically, for biological disasters, the identified critical knowledge covers various domains such as disease surveillance [17–19], personnel management [20, 21], use and management of equipment [22], contaminated waste management [23].

In like manner, Farias et al. [24] present an approach for designing a "tool that could integrate multiple information sources" in a healthcare facility, within the con-text of a biological disaster, and that could support decision-making about the management of limited resources. Regarding NPIs, Desvars-Larrive et al. [25] developed a "specific hierarchical coding scheme" for those so as to better monitor the decisions implemented by states and support future emergency management. Differently from them, our work is not limited to a data set, but the knowledge base contains also rules and queries tailored to the need of the decision makers.

This paper builds upon those related works to tackle the domain of the multiple regulatory documents dictating non-pharmaceutical interventions within the Covid-19 pandemic and investigates how a knowledge base covering this domain could support healthcare personnel in their decision-making within a biological disaster response.

3   Research Methodology

The methodology applied for this research work follows the design science research (DSR) [26]. As explained by Van Der Merwe et al. [27], the dual value of applying DSR methodology is that it brings in relevance with the identification of business needs from the research environment (people, organizations and technology) and rigor from the application of "foundations" and "methodologies" from the "knowledge base" available in scientific literature. To add more rigor in the creation of the knowledge base, the DSR phases were supplemented with Noy and McGuinness's ontology engineering approach [28].

As a result, each DSR phase was instantiated as follows:

In the Awareness of Problem phase, the scope of the knowledge base was defined with a list of competency questions and rules which were written in natural language. The list of the questions and rules were created by expert interviews and documentation analysis. Specifically, three expert interviews were conducted with a manager of the Covid-19 taskforce of Spitex Basel. The first interview followed a semi-structured approach. The second interview served to create a use case (see Sect. 7) and to gather related documents. The last interview had the purpose to confirm the acquired knowledge and avoiding misunderstanding.

In the Suggestion phase, the knowledge base was conceptualized. Hence, concepts and relations were derived from the competency questions and rules. It is good engineering practice to identify ontologies of which the concepts can be extended to address the requirements of a new application domain [29, 30]. This approach has the convenience of making use of already established semantics, thus of not starting from scratch. Hence, based on the domain requirements framed by the set of competency questions and rules, an existing ontology was identified, and the related concepts were extended accordingly.

In the Development phase, the concepts, relations queries and rules were formalized with W3C standard languages.

In the Evaluation phase, the approach was evaluated by implementing a use case though the formalized knowledge base. For this, functionalities of TopBraid Composer™ were used to show the expected results upon execution of semantic rules and queries against the ontology.

4   Scope of the Knowledge Base

The scope of the knowledge base concerns the support of decision-making in the creation of security protocols. Acting in accordance with current NPIs requires from a hospital to analyze the regulatory documents issued by public health authorities and then to retrieve the knowledge necessary to create its own guidelines, which are transcribed into internal security protocols.

Following the guide of Noy and McGuinness [28], the scope of the knowledge base was captured by defining a list of competency questions and rules written in natural language. While the questions set the scope by framing the specific concepts and relations that shall be retrieved, the rules capture the decision logic and are relevant to keep the knowledge base updated. In fact, rules allow the inferencing of new concepts based on the existing ones.

As mentioned in Sect. 3, both questions and rules were derived from findings identified with expert interviews and by analyzing regulatory documents and security protocols. What came out was the identification of important issues that should be addressed by the knowledge base. For space reasons, only a small set of competency questions and rules are reported.

First, it should be possible to trace back a given element within the security protocols to the relevant regulatory documents and issuing public health authority. From this, competency questions were defined such as:

1. What regulatory documents does the Federal Office for Public Health dictate? What document regulates the reasons for a close contact quarantine?
2. What quarantine measures are regulated by the document "Instruction on Quarantine for persons arriving in Switzerland"?

Second, an additional finding was that a hospital needed to determine what entity would finance any loss of earnings resulting from the NPIs. For example, while the cantonal office compensates the quarantine of a health employee due to a close contact with a positively tested person, it does not if the quarantine follows a travel to a country with an increased risk of infection. This kind of decision logic was captured in the form of competency rules, e.g.:

1. **If** A health employee is in quarantine **AND** If this health employee's quarantine is a quarantine due to a close contact with a positively tested person **AND** A cantonal office has ordered this health employee's quarantine, **Then** This health employee's quarantine is financed by this cantonal office.
2. **If** A health employee is in quarantine **AND** If this health employee's quarantine is a quarantine because of travelling in a country with an increased risk of infection, **Then** This health employee's quarantine is financed by him/herself.

Another example is about quarantine exemptions:

3. **If** A health employee is in quarantine **AND** If this health employee is tested negative **AND** If this health employee is not symptomatic **AND** A cantonal office has authorized special quarantine exemptions, **Then** This health employee is exempted from following a quarantine to work.

Rules allows the inference of new "explainable" information. Explainability of conclusions was found to be a very important factor for some NPIs. Following on the first example, reasons about who finances a quarantine can be identified by tracing back to the reasons for a quarantine. Regarding the second example, reasons relevant for quarantine exemptions for a health employee can be identified, i.e. negative to the Covid-19 test, no symptoms, and cantonal office authorization. Hence, the questions were framed as follows:

1. Why is the health employee following a quarantine?
2. Why is a health employee exempted from a quarantine?

5 Conceptualization of SPECO

An ontology is a "[...] formal, explicit specification of a shared conceptualization [29]. In our case, an ontology was first conceptualized and then formalized (see Sect. 6 for the ontology formalism).

As mentioned in Sect. 3, the list of competency questions and rules was used to select an existing ontology. The main driving criteria for selection were the following: the ontology contains relevant concepts and relations for an enterprise, in particular documentation and organizational aspects. Additional nice-to-have selection criteria were: (a) the ontology is freely available, and (b) extending the ontology has already been proven to be successful in other research works.

The enterprise ontology ArchiMEO [31] was selected as a basis for the design of the new ontology as it matched with all the criteria. ArchiMEO contains relevant concepts and relations of an enterprise and was successfully extended to address various application domains such as supply risk management, experience management, workplace learning and business process as a service. Additionally, ArchiMEO includes, among other ontologies, the Document and Knowledge Meta Ontology and the Organizational Meta Ontology, which contain document and organizational aspects, respectively. Figure 1 depicts the relations among the considered ontologies and introduces the new ontology as an extension of ArchiMEO.

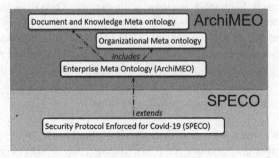

Fig. 1. The new ontology SPECO as an extension of ArchiMEO

The considered classes from ArchiMEO are shown in Sect. 6. The new classes, related taxonomy, class instances and relations were derived entirely from the competency questions and rules. The new ontology takes the name of SPECO, which stands for "Security Protocol Enforced for Covid-19 Ontology".

A visual representation of an excerpt of SPECO is shown in Fig. 2. Specifically, classes were defined and refer to the main concepts of SPECO's application domain, including regulatory documents about NPIs for the Covid-19 pandemic (e.g. laws, instructions sheets), involved organizations who interpret these documents, then create and enforce security protocols and the people who follow those. Additionally, the reasons that justify the application of NPIs were also categorized as separate classes.

Properties were assigned to these classes such as the "URL" property indicating where a given regulation document can be found. Similarly, the data-type properties "date of start", "date of end" and "minimum period" were attributed to the classes of "quarantine" and "isolation".

An important aspect modelled into SPECO are the relationships between classes, properties and individual instances. Those take the form of object-type properties. For example, the object type property "finances" relates an instance of the class "Cantonal Office" to an instance of the class "Quarantine". Class instances of every class were created, and the corresponding property values filled. Individual instances of the class "Instruction Sheet" correspond to regulatory documents for Covid-19 like "Instructions on Quarantine" dictated by the Federal Office for Public Health, itself an instance of the class "Federal Office". Similarly, the instance "Law on epidemics" of the class "Law", is a regulatory document dictated by the instance "Federal Council" of the class "Federal Office". It is important to note that not all property values are filled, as some of those are inferred based on the competency rules defined within SPECO (see Sect. 7).

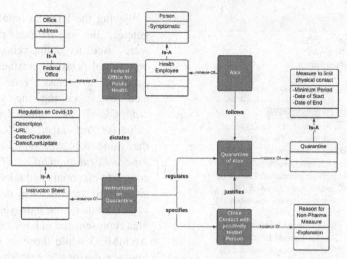

Fig. 2. Object-type and datatype properties, instances and their classes in SPECO

6 Formalization of SPECO

The conceptualized ontology is formalized through the ontology language RDF(S), which extends the Resource Description Framework Schema (RDF). The competency questions and rules are formalized with the SPARQL Protocol and RDF Query Language (SPARQL). Both standards RDF(S) and SPARQL are maintained by the W3C. For space reasons, this section elaborates only on the formalism of the ontology. Examples for the formalized queries and rules are reported directly in the evaluation section (Sect. 7) along with the use case.

The decision for the ontology language is in line with the design principle of ArchiMEO [31] where the language expressiveness is chosen according to the purpose of the ontology, i.e. types of facts that are important to deduce, represent and retrieve. Similarly, in our case the purpose is to retrieve facts or to infer new facts about NPIs and not to classify instances automatically. Therefore, the body of knowledge does not need to be constrained with axioms, which would unnecessarily increase the complexity of the ontology. A lightweight ontology language expressed in RDF(S), in contrast to OWL and its sub-languages (e.g. OWL-DL) also has the benefit of a better maintainability. First, it favors a higher simplicity, as it is constraint-free. If constraints are required, they can be added using the Shape Constraints Language (SHACL). Second, it offers a higher degree of agility, as changes can be implement-ed quickly. Namely, if the decision logic changes, only the semantic rules are affected and not the ontology. In our work this is an important aspect to consider as regulations about NPIs change frequently. Last, it holds the Unique Names Assumption (UNA), meaning that different names refer to different things. This is valuable in our approach as each instance in SPECO (e.g. for persons, institutions or regulations) has a unique identifier.

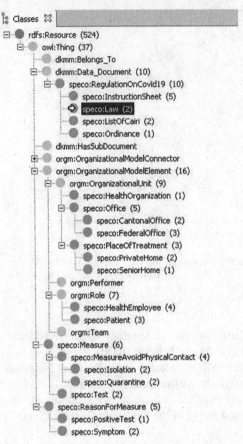

Fig. 3. Overview of the classes in speco.ttl (Color figure online)

Following the RDF(S) ontology languages, the pre-defined properties were used to define classes, taxonomy of classes, instances. For example, the class "*Law*" is created by specifying the value for "*rdfs:Class*" as "*speco:Law*", the value for "*rdfs:label*" as "*Law*", and the value for "*rdfs:subClassOf*" as "*speco:RegulationOnCovid19*". The complete taxonomy and related extension from ArchiMEO is depicted in Fig. 3. Namely, the light-yellow bubbles represent the classes taken from ArchiMEO while those in dark yellow are the newly extended classes for SPECO. Concepts from the Document Knowledge Meta Ontology have the prefix *dkmm* while those from the Organizational Meta Ontology have the prefix *orgm*. Intuitively, concepts from SPECO have the prefix *speco* (see the rightmost tier of concepts in Fig. 3).

For the specification of attributes and relations, we borrowed the OWL properties: data-type property and object-type property so as to have a better human interpretability between the two. The expressiveness of the language was not compromised as the reasoning capabilities remain the same.

The name specification used to specify both the data-type and object-type properties follow the convention *subjetcPredicateObject*. This convention favors the good understandability about what relationship type is represented by a given property and the two classes it binds. This is notably effective in allowing a better readability by the end user of the knowledge base and also to differentiate between the names of properties and their sub-properties.

For example, the datatype property "*speco:quarantineHasMiminum_Period*", of a class "*speco:Quarantine*" with data type "*Integer*", is formally represented as follows:

```
speco:quarantineHasMinimum_Period
    rdf:type  owl:DatatypeProperty;
    rdfs:domain  speco:Quarantine;
    rdfs:range  xsd:integer;
    rdfs:label  "Minimum Period".
```

Similarly, the object-type "*speco:federalOffice_Dictates_RegulationOnCovid19*" has as domain the class "*FederalOffice*", represents the relationship "dictates" and has as range the class "*RegulationOnCovid19*". Sub-object-type properties were created to specify the range of existing properties. For example, the aforementioned property was further specified with *speco: federalOffice_Dictates_Law*, where the class "*Law*" is a subclass of "*RegulationOnCovid-19*". Figure 4 shows the remaining sub-properties of *speco:federalOffice_Dictates_RegulationOnCovid19* that were implemented in the ontology editor.

Fig. 4. Object-type property and its sub properties in TopBraid Composer™

Finally, the class instances were formalized too. In Fig. 3, the numbers in parentheses next to each class name indicate the number of instances. Let's consider the example of "*speco:Federal_Office_Public_Health*", which is an instance of the class "*speco:FederalOffice*". In the domain of SPECO, the federal office for public health dictates four essential documents that are "*Instruction on Quarantine*", "*Instruction on Isolation*", "*Instruction for Testing Ambulatory Sector*" and "*Instruction Quarantine for persons arriving in Switzerland*". Hence, all those documents are instances of the class "*speco:InstructionSheet*" and are resources assigned to the same object-type property: "*federal_Office_Dictates_Instruction_Sheet*". The complete version of SPECO is freely available in a GitHub repository[1].

7 Evaluation of SPECO

This work is evaluated by executing a use case in the created knowledge base. The use case comprises the competency questions and rules that were initially derived. Hence, in line with Noy and McGuinness's suggestion [28], the approach is validated when proving that the knowledge base is able to answer the expected answers.

The use case applied in this research work explores a situation in which the activities of the above-mentioned Swiss hospital Spitex, in the canton of Basel-City, were heavily impacted by the Covid-19 pandemic. This organization dispatches health employees to care for patients at their private homes or in senior homes. Like hospitals, it was of great importance that its employees abide to the non-pharmaceutical interventions set in place by public health authorities, especially considering that a large part of the patients that they care for are over 65 years old, thus having a higher risk of an aggravated Covid-19 infection. Failing to do so could have seriously hurt the organization due to multiple reasons. On the one hand, the reputation of the health organization could have been

---

[1] https://github.com/BPaaSModelling/ArchiMEO

jeopardized as soon as the care provided by its employees was considered unsafe in the eyes of the patients. On the other hand, the temporary inability to work of employees caused by quarantine and isolation measures lead to financial losses.

Hence, decision-making about the security protocols to enforce quickly became a complex and sensitive issue. The health organization was compelled to gather and interpret the regulatory documents made available by Swiss public health authorities, such as the Federal Office for Public Health. Unfortunately, handling the available information proved challenging. As explained above, because of the dynamic nature of the epidemiological situation, and as the state of knowledge about the Sars-Cov-2 virus evolved regularly, the public health authorities of Switzerland often adapted and tweaked their regulatory documents. Furthermore, relevant information did not come from a single source.

In this context, selected hospital personnel are put in charge of the decision-making about security protocols for this health organization, named Covid-19 task-force. Additionally, a health employee named Alex is working in the same health organization. When Alex is required to go into quarantine, the Covid-19 taskforce should be able to provide clear information about this specific quarantine measure to various stakeholders.

As the Covid-19 taskforce informs and guides all these decisions, it could theoretically make use of the available but long regulatory documents and come up with all the necessary information by itself. However, given the variety of questions asked by the several stakeholders, and the previously mentioned fast-paced evolution of the regulation about NPIs, its task would quickly become overwhelming and therefore prone to errors. The knowledge base SPECO is therefore implemented into the decision-making process to significantly facilitate the job of the Covid-19 taskforce as it enables such reasoning to be done automatically.

For example, SPECO indicates the reason that justifies Alex's quarantine, what regulatory document provides detailed explanations for it, as well as who is responsible for compensating the loss of earnings caused by Alex's temporary inability to work.

Following the example of Alex's quarantine, a demonstration is provided of how such reasoning can be made by SPECO. Let's imagine that the contact tracing ser-vices of the canton of Basel-City have just notified Alex that he has been in close contact with a person that was tested positive for Covid-19 and that he should go into quarantine. The Covid-19 taskforce is going to ask the following questions to SPECO:

1. What document is there that provides detailed explanations about close contact quarantines?
2. Who is going to compensate the loss of earnings caused by Alex's quarantine?

To answer the first question, the following query is executed:

```
SELECT ?subject
WHERE {?subject speco:regulationOnCovid19_Specifies_ReasonForMeasure
       speco:Close_Contact_With_Positively_Tested_Person . }
```

The query consists in asking SPECO with the function "SELECT" to find any instance for which a given statement in the knowledge base can be made. The function "WHERE" specifies that statement.

As shown in Fig. 5, when executed, the query provides the result "*speco: Instruction_Quarantine*" (on the right side). In fact, this instance of the class "*InstructionSheet*" is defined within SPECO to be specifying the reason for quarantine "*speco:Close_Contact_With_Positively_Tested_Person*". This test exemplifies how SPECO is able to answer the defined competency question.

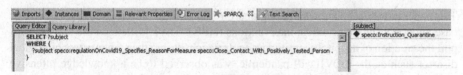

Fig. 5. SPARQL query for the described competency question and result upon execution

Next, the competency rule nr.1 (detailed above) is used to infer automatically the answer to the second question. It is formalized in SPECO as follows:

By using the function "CONSTRUCT", the semantic rule adds the value "*speco: Quarantine_Of_Alex*" to the property "*speco:cantonalOffice_Finances_Measure*". The function "BIND" associates this value to an instance of the class "*speco:CantonalOffice*", if the three conditions (specified also with the function "WHERE") are met (Fig. 6).

```
CONSTRUCT {?this speco:cantonalOffice_Finances_Measure speco:Quarantine_Of_Alex }
WHERE {
speco:Alex speco:healthEmployee_Follows_Quarantine speco:Quarantine_Of_Alex .
speco:Close_Contact_With_Positively_Tested_Person speco:reasonForMeasure_Justifies_Measure speco:Quarantine_Of_Alex .
?this speco:cantonalOffice_Orders_Measure speco:Quarantine_Of_Alex .
BIND (speco:CantonalOffice(speco:Quarantine_Of_Alex) as ?s).
}
```

Fig. 6. SPARQL rule for the competency rule nr.1

As shown in Fig. 7, once executed, the semantic rule was able to infer that the instance "*speco:Basel_City*" is in charge of financing Alex's quarantine. This test exemplifies how SPECO is able to provide the expected answer to the defined competency rule.

[Subject]	Predicate	Object
◆ speco:Basel_City	▥ speco:cantonalOffice_Finances_Measure	◆ speco:Quarantine_Of_Alex

Fig. 7. Answer provided upon execution of the described competency rule

Additionally, another utility linked to the semantic rule is that the inferred knowledge provided upon execution can be stored into SPECO, thereby keeping the knowledge base updated. This new knowledge can then be utilized for other queries and rules and is linked to the rest of SPECO's elements. Following the example of Alex's quarantine, the newly inferred information about its financing is asserted into the knowledge base. Technically, the instance "*speco:Quarantine_Of_Alex*" is associated to the instance "*speco: Basel_City*" via the object-type property "*speco:cantonalOffice_Finances_Measure*".

Overall, SPECO has been able to answer the questions asked by the Covid-19 taskforce. This excerpt shows that a proof of concept for the design approach was obtained.

8   Conclusion and Outlook

This paper introduces a knowledge engineering approach for the creation of a knowledge base about non-pharmaceutical interventions (NPIs). The knowledge base aims to support the creation of hospital security protocols which, during the response to a biological disaster such as the COVID-19 pandemic, was observed to be a knowledge intensive task. For this, the new ontology called SPECO was developed rigorously, along with semantic rules and queries. SPECO extends the enterprise ontology ArchiMEO, which provided a wide range of relevant concepts and relations of an enterprise to start from. As of today, the knowledge base counts 942 triples.

The evaluation was conducted by executing a real-world use case on the knowledge base. The use case was conceived from two sources both from Spitex Basel: the hospital's security protocols (documentation) and semi-structured expert interviews. The execution results validated the presented approach. Namely, the knowledge base was able to correctly answer to the competency questions and rules derived from the identification of issues relevant for the hospital's Covid-19 taskforce.

This research is yet a concrete example of how Machine Reasoning approaches are a well-established practice of Artificial Intelligence that shall be taken advantage of for the resolution of problems afflicting Society 5.0 such as pandemic situations.

As a future work, the knowledge base can be extended to answer time- and geographic-related questions, e.g. "Is Canada listed as a country with an increased risk of infection on the 25th of June?". Moreover, to facilitate the maintainability of SPECO also by a non-ontology expert (e.g., adapt or enter new concepts from the regulatory documents) the AI-based modelling environment AOAME [32] can be adopted as it allows the automatic transformation of graphical models into ontologies.

References

1. Burton, D.C., Confield, E., Gasner, M.R., Weisfuse, I.: A qualitative study of pandemic influenza preparedness among small and medium-sized businesses in New York City. J. Bus. Contin. Emerg. Plan. **5**(3), 267–279 (2011)
2. Krumkamp, R., et al.: Evaluation of national pandemic management policies-a hazard analysis of critical control points approach. Health Policy **92**(1), 21–26 (2009). https://doi.org/10.1016/j.healthpol.2009.01.006
3. McDonald, L.C., et al.: SARS in healthcare facilities, Toronto and Taiwan. Emerg. Infect. Dis. **10**(5), 777–781 (2004). https://doi.org/10.3201/eid1005.030791
4. Djalante, R., Shaw, R., DeWit, A.: Building resilience against biological hazards and pandemics: COVID-19 and its implications for the Sendai Framework. Prog. Disaster Sci. **6**, 100080 (2020). https://doi.org/10.1016/j.pdisas.2020.100080
5. Beyer, M., Hare, J., Sallam, R.: COVID-19 Demands Urgent Use of Graph Data Management and Analytics. Gartner Research, April 2020

6. Aledort, J.E., Lurie, N., Wasserman, J., Bozzette, S.A.: Non-pharmaceutical public health interventions for pandemic influenza: an evaluation of the evidence base. BMC Public Health **7** (2007). https://doi.org/10.1186/1471-2458-7-208

7. AFP: Coronavirus and face masks: how countries have shifted their advice to the public. The Local (2020). https://www.thelocal.com/20200405/coronavirus-and-face-masks-how-countries-have-changed-their-advice/

8. Swiss National Covid-19 Taskforce: Clarification on face mask types, architecture, quality, handling, test and certification procedures (2020). https://sciencetaskforce.ch/en/policy-brief/clarification-on-face-mask-types-architecture-quality-handling-test-and-certification-procedures/

9. Bentz, J.A., Blumenthal, D.J., Potter, A.B.: It's all about the data: responding to international chemical, biological, radiological, and nuclear incidents. Bull. Atomic Sci. **70**(4), 57–68 (2014). https://doi.org/10.1177/0096340214539117

10. Moon, S., et al.: Will Ebola change the game? Ten essential reforms before the next pandemic. The report of the Harvard-LSHTM Independent Panel on the Global Response to Ebola. The Lancet **386**(10009), 2204–2221 (2015). https://doi.org/10.1016/S0140-6736(15)00946-0

11. Shearer, F.M., Moss, R., McVernon, J., Ross, J.V., McCaw, J.M.: Infectious disease pandemic planning and response: incorporating decision analysis. PLoS Med. **17**(1), e1003018 (2020). https://doi.org/10.1371/journal.pmed.1003018

12. Hristidis, V., Chen, S.C., Li, T., Luis, S., Deng, Y.: Survey of data management and analysis in disaster situations. J. Syst. Softw. **83**(10), 1701–1714 (2010). https://doi.org/10.1016/j.jss.2010.04.065

13. Xu, W., Zlatanova, S.: Ontologies for disaster management response. In: Li, J., Zlatanova, S., Fabbri, A.G. (eds.) Geomatics Solutions for Disaster Management. LNGC, pp. 185–200. Springer, Heidelberg (2007). https://doi.org/10.1007/978-3-540-72108-6_13

14. Babitski, G., Probst, F., Hoffmann, J., Oberle, D.: Ontology design for information integration in disaster management. In: Informatik 2009–Im Focus das Leben, pp. 3105–3119 (2009)

15. Purohit, H., Kanagasabai, R., Deshpande, N.: Towards next generation knowledge graphs for disaster management. In: Proceedings of the 13th IEEE International Conference on Semantic Computing, ICSC 2019, pp. 474–477 (2019). https://doi.org/10.1109/ICOSC.2019.8665638

16. Tan, Y., Liu, W., Yang, Z., Du, X., Liu, Z.: Pattern-based ontology modeling and reasoning for emergency system. IEICE Trans. Inf. Syst. **E101D**(9), 2323–2333 (2018). https://doi.org/10.1587/transinf.2017EDP7383

17. Collier, N., et al.: A multilingual ontology for infectious disease surveillance: rationale, design and challenges. Lang. Resour. Eval. **40**(3–4), 405–413 (2007). https://doi.org/10.1007/s10579-007-9019-7

18. Hripcsak, G., et al.: Syndromic surveillance using ambulatory electronic health records. J. Am. Med. Inform. Assoc. **16**(3), 354–361 (2009). https://doi.org/10.1197/jamia.M2922

19. Samoff, E., et al.: Integration of syndromic surveillance data into public health practice at state and local levels in North Carolina. Public Health Rep. **127**(3), 310–317 (2012). https://doi.org/10.1177/003335491212700311

20. Sasangohar, F., Moats, J., Mehta, R., Peres, S.C.: Disaster ergonomics: human factors in COVID-19 pandemic emergency management. Hum. Factors **62**(7), 1061–1068 (2020). https://doi.org/10.1177/0018720820939428

21. Witty, R., Analyst, V.P., Liu, V.: Overcoming COVID-19 Through Pandemic Preparedness, Gartner Research, February 2020

22. Jinia, A.J., et al.: Review of sterilization techniques for medical and personal protective equipment contaminated with SARS-CoV-2. IEEE Access **8**, 111347–111354 (2020). https://doi.org/10.1109/ACCESS.2020.3002886

23. Yu, H., Sun, X., Solvang, W.D., Zhao, X.: Reverse logistics network design for effective management of medical waste in epidemic outbreaks: insights from the coronavirus disease 2019 (COVID-19) outbreak in Wuhan (China). Int. J. Environ. Res. Public Health **17**(5) (2020). https://doi.org/10.3390/ijerph17051770

24. Farias, D.R., et al.: Data for decision making: Strategic information tools for hospital management during a pandemic. Disaster Med. Public Health Prep. **4**(3), 207–212 (2010). https://doi.org/10.1001/dmp.2010.29

25. Desvars-Larrive, A., et al.: A structured open dataset of government interventions in response to COVID-19. Sci. Data **7**(1) (2020). https://doi.org/10.1038/s41597-020-00609-9

26. Vaishnavi, V., Kuechler, B.: Design science research in information systems overview of design science research. Ais **45** (2004). https://doi.org/10.1007/978-1-4419-5653-8

27. Van Der Merwe, A., Gerber, A., Smuts, H.: ICT Education. In: Guidelines for Conducting Design Science Research in Information Systems Alta (2012). https://doi.org/10.1007/978-1-4419-1428-6_4268

28. Noy, N.F., McGuinness, D.L.: Ontology development 101: a guide to creating your first ontology. Stanford Knowledge Systems Laboratory (2001). https://doi.org/10.1016/j.artmed.2004.01.014

29. Studer, R., Benjamins, V.R., Fensel, D.: Knowledge engineering: principles and methods. Data Knowl. Eng. **25**(1–2), 161–197 (1998). https://doi.org/10.1016/S0169-023X(97)00056-6

30. Laurenzi, E., Hinkelmann, K., Reimer, U., Van Der Merwe, A., Sibold, P., Endl, R.: DSML4PTM: a domain-specific modelling language for patient transferal management. In: ICEIS 2017 - Proceedings of the 19th International Conference on Enterprise Information Systems, vol. 3, pp. 520–531. SciTePress (2017). https://doi.org/10.5220/0006388505200531

31. Hinkelmann, K., Laurenzi, E., Martin, A., Montecchiari, D., Spahic, M., Thönssen, B.: ArchiMEO: a standardized enterprise ontology based on the archimate conceptual model. In: MODELSWARD 2020 - Proceedings of the 8th International Conference on Model-Driven Engineering and Software Development, Modelsward, pp. 417–424 (2020). https://doi.org/10.5220/0009000204170424

32. Laurenzi, E., Hinkelmann, K., van der Merwe, A.: An agile and ontology-aided modeling environment. In: Buchmann, R.A., Karagiannis, D., Kirikova, M. (eds.) PoEM 2018. LNBIP, vol. 335, pp. 221–237. Springer, Cham (2018). https://doi.org/10.1007/978-3-030-02302-7_14

COVID-19 Contact Tracing Apps

Dennis Senn$^{(\boxtimes)}$ (iD) and Christina Loosli (iD)

FHNW, Olten, Switzerland
dennis.senn@students.fhnw.ch, christina.loosli@fhnw.ch

Abstract. As a response to the COVID-19 pandemic, many countries, including Switzerland, have put enormous efforts to break chains of infections using automated contact tracing apps for smartphones. As a result, different approaches such as centralized and decentralized apps with a wide range of frameworks have been deployed, including DP-3T and PEPP-PT. It immediately raised privacy concerns and intensified the importance of ensuring interoperability between the various apps, especially in border regions. Those frameworks were examined regarding its privacy architecture and interoperability, including usage of the tracing apps of Switzerland, France, and Germany. Applicable regulations such as the GDPR must be complied with, and user concerns and the general effectiveness of automated tracing applications respected. Finally, the conclusion answers the main objectives and provides an outlook with potential solutions.

Keywords: COVID-19 · Tracing apps · Interoperability · Regulations · Switzerland

1 Introduction

1.1 Problem Statement and Research Questions

The World Health Organization (WHO) has declared COVID-19 a global pandemic in March 2020. They suggested that contact tracing to be a key component in fighting the global spread of the virus [1]. However, using a manual backtracing approach as a measure is "time consuming, resource demanding, and prone to errors, since people might not remember all their contacts" [2]. Further, it is stated that digital contact tracing could help detect and interrupt the chain of infections as early as possible.

Regarding following the WHO's suggestion, Singapore was among the first countries to release its tracing app *TraceTogether* in March 2020 using a centralized approach. Compared to the countries analyzed in this work, Switzerland followed by publishing an official contact tracing app called *SwissCovid* by the end of May 2020. The Swiss app is open-sourced and using a decentralized approach based on DP-3T [3, 4]. The German *Corona-Warn-App* follows a decentralized approach, while the French *TousAntiCovid* chooses a centralized architecture [5, 6]. Besides preserving users' privacy and tracing apps to be an effective countermeasure against the spread of the COVID pandemic, interoperability between health authorities must be established. The necessity for

© Springer Nature Switzerland AG 2021
A. Gerber and K. Hinkelmann (Eds.): Society 5.0 2021, CCIS 1477, pp. 77–92, 2021.
https://doi.org/10.1007/978-3-030-86761-4_7

interoperability has been widely acknowledged and worked on with members from 10 different countries [7].

The main research questions are:

1. Which tracing apps and frameworks are used in Switzerland, France and Germany?
2. To what extend do those tracing apps provide interoperability?
3. Why is the population in these regions reluctant to use tracing apps?

1.2 Limitations

Due to the topic's actuality, most of the literature used throughout this paper could not be peer-reviewed. The authors has put great emphasis on carefully reviewing the integrity and correctness of the sources.

The main focus was analyzing frameworks directly correlating to the COVID-19 app of Switzerland, Germany, and France to describe the centralized and decentralized app tracing approach. There are numerous other frameworks used in different regions, but not described in detail. Regarding restrictions and limitations, this paper focuses predominantly on technical limitations because the author could not find substantial evidence of political reasons for separating contact tracing app development across countries.

2 Methodology

To establish the basis to answer the paper's objectives, existing frameworks had to be researched using databases such as Google Scholar and arXiv. For this purpose, the following keywords were used in different combinations: "covid", "tracing apps", "centralized", "decentralized", "DP-3T", "PEPP-PT", "Switzerland", "Europe", "Germany", "France". Additionally, along with examining the qualitative findings of various authors, the respective white papers of the frameworks were studied in depth. They were published publicly accessible at GitHub and GitLab.

To describe the tracing apps of Switzerland, France, and Germany, their correlating official websites published by the public health authorities were taken as a basis to analyze additional information being referenced. Moreover, public press releases from the countries, including the European Union, were collected and reviewed.

Regarding investigations of the frameworks' and apps' interoperability towards each other, Google searches and reviewing newspaper articles were used to accumulate hints of evidence. Each source assessed to be potentially valuable was traced back to its origin to verify its validity. The quality of information enormously varied across Switzerland, Germany, France, and the European Commission. Hence, the information found was only used when all doubts could be excluded.

Common user concerns towards tracing apps were extensively described in the papers found but were merely proven by conducted surveys. Therefore, appropriate surveys were assessed to underline the concern's meaningfulness where possible. Unfortunately, only a few surveys have been conducted to date.

3 Technical Aspect of Tracing Apps

To analyze Switzerland's potential for interoperability with its border regions, this section describes proximity tracing frameworks. Section 3.1 gives an overview of available frameworks and describes the centralized resp. the decentralized approach with the examples of PEPP-PT, DP-3T, and Apple-Google's Exposure Notifications. Section 3.2. deals with the effective implementation of tracing apps in Switzerland and its border countries France and Germany.

3.1 Proximity Tracing Frameworks

On the question of technology-based proximity tracing, various initiatives appeared. Their common goal is to detect chains of infections by tracking proximity while preserving user privacy, mainly classified into three types: decentralized, centralized, and hybrid. [2] listed the currently used frameworks in Table 1, differentiating them by type of approach, whether the source code is open-sourced, health authorities involved, and location data collected.

Table 1. Main characteristics of contact tracing frameworks [2]

Framework	Approach	Source code	Health authority	Location data collected
DP-3T	Decentralized	Open	Yes	No
Google/Apple	Decentralized	Proprietary	Yes	No
PEPP-PT NTK	Centralized	Open	Yes	No
ROBERT	Centralized	Open	Yes	No
BlueTrace	Centralized	Open	Yes	No
TraceSecure	Centralized	Not available	Yes	No
DESIRE	Hybrid	Not available	Yes	No
PACT (UW)	Decentralized	Open	Yes	No
PACT (MIT)	Decentralized	Not available	Yes	Optional
TCN	Decentralized	Open	Optional	No
OpenCovidTrace	Decentralized	Open	Yes	Yes
Whisper Tracing	Decentralized	Not available	No	Optional

Centralized. Both decentralized and centralized approaches have multiple implementations. To explain the mechanisms of centralized frameworks, PEPP-PT was elected as a reference because it finds use in the French tracing app *TousAntiCovid,* which will be explained in more detail in Sect. 3.2.

According to [2], key components of PEPP-PT are the users' smartphone having the app installed, a centralized backend server generating temporal IDs and receiving encounter messages, as well as a Push Notification Service that informs the user's locally installed apps to pull new information from the backend server. Similar to the decentralized approach, it requires Bluetooth and Push Notifications to be enabled for this approach to work. The interactions are divided into four steps: User registration, proximity tracing, infection notifications, and federation across other backends in Europe.

User Registration. To prevent the mass creation of user accounts, the user must register his app instance to the backend server. The registration involves a combination of proof-of-work (PoW) and a Captcha, which prevents denial-of-service (DoS) and mass registrations. When the user requests to register with the backend, those two challenges are sent to the app. The app will solve the PoW challenge itself, while the Captcha must be solved by the user. Both results will be returned to the backend server, which – provided that it is valid – answers with OAuth2 client credentials, consisting of a random *client_id* and a random *client_secret* over a TLS-secured network. Those short-lived credentials are used for every subsequent request to the backend server and allow inference to a "128-bit unique random pseudonym of the user" called PUID. This PUID is generated and stored on the backend server, along with the user's push notification ID [8].

Proximity Tracing. The backend server regularly generates global secret keys BK_t (whereas t refers to the short timeframe validity of, e.g., one hour) along with *Ephemeral Bluetooth IDs* (EBID) for each user AES-encrypted using the BK and their PUID separately. Because the EBID depends on the short-lived BK, the app can request multiple EBIDs from the backend server for a more extended period (e.g., two days). Starting from this point, the app begins to broadcast its contemporarily valid EBID via *Bluetooth Low Energy* (BLE) advertisements using BLE privacy feature, which enables the exchange of temporary addresses – *Resolvable Private Addresses* (RPK) – instead of fixed hardware addresses (MAC). This prevents backtracing the user's physical device. Consequently, only the backend server can determine the user's identity [8].

The users' app constantly scans other PEPP-PT apps and records all EBIDs received, the current time, and the connection's metadata. Metadata include the received signal strength (RSSI) and the signal power (TX/RX), which is used to estimate the duration and distance of contact between two users. The PEPP-PT architecture refers to this data as Contact/Time data (CTD) and will be deleted from the users' phone after the epidemiological relevant time (e.g., defined as 21 days) after receiving and thus, occurred contact [8].

Infection Notifications. When a user is diagnosed as COVID-19 positive, the collected CTD is uploaded to the backend (which is held up to three weeks) to evaluate which users are called "at-risk" contacts and shall be notified. To secure the data upload and ensure integrity, the user is provided with a *Transaction Authentication Number* (TAN) from the health authority, which needs to be uploaded along with the data. The CTD contains all recorded EBIDs and timestamps (t) that the server decrypts using the BK_t of the given time recorded. Affected PUIDs will receive a push notification, along with many randomly selected other PUIDs to avoid inference (called noise messages). The receiving apps use this notification to trigger a synchronization request to the backend server asking for the users' risk. In case of being at risk, the user receives instructions on how to proceed [8].

Federation Across Europe. Subject to the functional requirements of the PEPP-PT system, the federation across different countries and backend systems in Europe must be supported. Each country has the possibility to run its own backend and retain sovereignty over the data. This includes the decision on how EBIDs are constructed and how risk analysis is done [8].

For this purpose, the backend system must be able to determine the origin of the encountered EBIDs. An encrypted country code (ECC) as the first byte of an issued EBID guarantees that only the issuing backend can translate it back to the respective PUID. Consequently, EBIDs containing a foreign ECC must be forwarded to its "home backend" for risk analysis and user notification [8].

Decentralized. Decentralized proximity tracing frameworks differ from centralized approaches in that the core functionalities remain within the client app installed by the user. [9] emphasized that its main idea is to leave the backend server with minimal involvement and strengthen the user's privacy.

According to [2], the decentralized approach only requires a backend server and the mobile app installed on the users' smartphone. He defines the two main processes as generating and storing ephemeral IDs (EphIDs) and proximity tracing. However, the DP-3T whitepaper divides the process into setup, creating ephemeral IDs, local storage of observed EphIDs and secret day seed (SK), and decentralized proximity tracing [10].

Generation and Storing. Unlike centralized approaches, the user must not register his device. The app generates an initial secret day seed SK_t (where t represents the current day) and encrypts it using a cryptographic hash function. This SK is rotated each day depending on the previous secret seed by computing $SK_t = H(SK_{t-1})$, which, in case of a key being compromised, does not reveal every SK prior to it. Each day, the smartphone generates a list of EphIDs depending on the current SK. The app stores these EphIDs along with exposure measurement data (e.g., signal attenuation) and the timestamp and randomly broadcasts it using Bluetooth Low Energy (BLE) advertisements. Furthermore, the SKs are locally stored for a period of 14 days [10].

Proximity Tracing. When a user is diagnosed as COVID-19 positive, the health authority provides a code to the user which will be used to instruct the app to upload his seed SK_t, whereas t is the day the user is considered contagious. After the seed SK_t has been reported, the app deletes it and generates an entirely new one, therefore broadcasting newly derived EphIDs going onward. Registered users pull the collected positive pairs (SK_t and t) regularly from the backend server and check their locally stored EphIDs for existing entries. If there is a matching entry, the coherent exposure measurement data is passed for local exposure risk computation. In case of the calculated exposure score being above the threshold defined by the health authority, a local notification is shown to the user with the information of being potentially exposed to the virus along with additional information about how to proceed [10].

This process describes the "low-cost decentralized proximity tracing" design. However, the DP-3T white paper proposes two additional approaches: unlinkable decentralized proximity tracing and hybrid decentralized proximity tracing. The latter works similarly to Apple's and Google's Exposure Notification.

Exposure Notifications. On April 11, 2020, Apple and Google announced a joint effort to develop a Bluetooth-based contact tracing system. They intended to provide a solution for interoperability of tracing apps across mobile operating systems and countries if they actively choose to opt-in [11].

As described in the section above, the Exposure Notifications API (ENA) works similarly to the "hybrid decentralized proximity tracing" approach proposed by the DP-3T white paper [10]. However, unlike DP-3T and PEPP-PT, ENA is implemented at the operating system's level, providing a framework API to enable health authorities to implement it in their contact tracing apps.

When the user grants permissions to enable ENA, a temporary exposure key is generated to derive the encrypted Rolling Proximity Identifier (RPI). To prevent linkability, the RPI is rotated when the BLE advertiser address changes (random interval between 10 and 20 min). The RPI is broadcasted along with associated encrypted metadata (AEM), which contains protocol versioning and transmit power for risk analysis [2, 12].

Because the Exposure Notification System is built into the smartphone's operating system, vendor requirements need to be considered. For apple smartphones, ENA support was added to iOS at version 13.5 [13]. Starting with version 13.7, the Exposure Notification System can be enabled without the need to download a specific app. Since this excludes older iPhones (e.g., iPhone 6) to make use of ENA-based tracing apps, Apple has announced an update to iOS 12.5 [14]. For Android smartphones, Google has added support for Exposure Notifications for Android version 6 and above. However, version 10 and earlier needs the phone's location setting to be turned on, even though it does not use location data [15].

On May 25, 2020, Switzerland implemented ENA on a *SwissCovid* pilot app [16].

3.2   Tracing Apps of Switzerland and Its Border Regions

Switzerland. *SwissCovid* is the official contact tracing app of Switzerland. It was developed by FOITT, ETH, and EPFL and is operated by the Federal Office of Public Health (FOPH). *SwissCovid* uses a decentralized approach based on DP-3T and Exposure Notifications API. Its base source code is open-sourced at GitHub [3, 4].

Statistics published by the Federal Statistical Office [17], known as FSO, recorded 2.84 million app downloads while considering only 1.82 million installations being active (64.2%). The FSO [18] declares this survey to be based on automated configuration requests (every 6 h after activation of the app), counting the number of requests for 24 h and then dividing by 4.

A *SwissCovid* analysis of Vaudenay & Vuagnoux [19] observed that the app's core functionality is not open-sourced (referring to ENA) and, thus, outside of the control of the Swiss health authority. Additionally, SwissCovid requires users to consent to send personal information to Apple and Google, whereas the app itself is not allowed to collect such information [19, 20]. The FOPH does not mention ENA to be a component of the *SwissCovid* app. The DP-3T repository confirms the use of ENA but does not contain the actual source code of the app [3, 19].

France. *StopCovid* was the first COVID-19 contact tracing app in France, released on June 2, 2020 [21]. On October 22, 2020, the second app *TousAntiCovid* was released and served as an update, according to an article of The Connexion France [22]. The article further implies that relaunching the app was due to the missing traction of the former app. Many other newspapers, including Le Monde [23, 24], claimed that a new application was necessary as the former could not stand a significant number of concurrent requests. However, the official website of *TousAntiCovid* [5] does not justify the renewal of the app beyond doubt, e.g., added, updated, or removed core functionality. Instead, it announces *TousAntiCovid* as a mainly visually "enriched" version of the first *StopCovid* app.

TousAntiCovid, like its predecessor, uses a centralized contact tracing approach using the ROBERT[1] protocol – a candidate proposal for the PEPP-PT initiative [8, 25]. This protocol differs from PEPP-PT only in that it uses a pure polling-based approach to avoid the necessity of push notification services. Therefore, the app needs to ask (poll) for updates instead of retrieving them asynchronously (push). The ROBERT schema refers to it as *Exposure Status Requests* and occurs at least once per 15 min. This is a possible explanation as to why the central server could not handle the request load.

In contrast to the Swiss and German apps, *TousAntiCovid* is not using Exposure Notification. The health department argues that it does not comply with their choices made in terms of architecture [5]. An analysis of Cunche et al. [26] concludes that a drawback of using ENA is an increased "feasibility of a number of privacy attacks, exposing users declared infected to serious privacy threats".

According to metrics published by Etalab [27], the new *TousAntiCovid* app has been downloaded 5.86 million times, which cumulates to 8.56 million across both app versions. However, those numbers describe the downloads and activations (minus deregistrations) but do not include the number of effectively active users.

Germany. *Corona-Warn-App*, Germany's COVID-19 tracing app, was released on June 16, 2020 [28]. The official website [29] states that it was developed by Deutsche Telekom and SAP and was published by the Robert Koch Institute (RKI).

It is open-sourced at GitHub and based on Exposure Notification, inspired by the TCN[2] and DP-3T protocols [30]. According to [31], Germany decided to switch from a centralized PEPP-PT to a decentralized approach using Exposure Notification following the DP-3T protocol. This decision was made to meet data protection standards and to enable interoperability with other apps based on ENA.

According to statistics published by RKI [32], the app has been downloaded 23.8 million times across Android and iOS smartphones and has reported 115,426 positive test results as of December 9, 2020. However, this report does not include information about the number of active installations.

4 Interoperability of Tracing Apps

Because the spread of the virus does not stop at borders, the deployed apps from different countries should be able to interoperate with each other – especially for people

---

[1] ROBERT stands for "ROBust and privacy-presERving proximity Tracing protocol".
[2] TCN stands for "Temporary Contact Numbers".

living in border areas. However, according to [7], seamless interoperability is challenging because of different frameworks being used and regionally varying administrative boundaries. Users should not be required to install multiple apps for each region. Therefore, a wide range of deployment types must be supported, which Rosa et al. distinguished between: Single official deployment, concurrent deployment and aggregation-oriented deployment.

This section examines the interoperability of the Swiss, the German, and the French tracing apps. Section 4.1 focuses on technical requirements, and Sect. 4.2 describes the European Federation Gateway.

4.1 Technical Requirements

Rosa [7] as well as the European Commission agreed on technical specifications for interoperability with the primary requirement of using a decentralized approach. The Commission additionally assumes participating operators to rely on ENA [33]. Therefore interoperability requires the apps to:

- detect and collect Bluetooth beacons of users with different apps and decentralized tracing protocols,
- compute exposure risk analysis on encounter data regardless of the region it has been collected or health authorities being responsible,
- share data of positively diagnosed patients to the relevant users being at risk regardless of their active regions.

The proposal focused on the decentralized protocols DP-3T, PACT, TCN, and those relying on Exposure Notification. It describes a mechanism to handle the home region (active region) and the roaming regions (when traveling). It requires the operator of the app to provide the user with a list of compatible regions, which the user must maintain manually[3]. However, risk analysis in roaming regions will only be computed during the visit.

Enabling interoperability for centralized approaches such as PEPP-PT or ROBERT would be technically possible but severely weakens the users' privacy of decentralized systems [7]. Therefore, the European Commission [33] unambiguously requires operating tracing apps using a decentralized approach and relying on Exposure Notification. Thus, countries not using EAN are considered incompatible.

As examined in Sect. 3.2, Switzerland and Germany are principally compatible to interoperate, which is also confirmed on the official website of the *SwissCovid* app [4]. However, France is considered incompatible according to a list of apps from the European Commission because of its centralized approach [34]. This list (see Table 2) confirms 9 apps to be interoperable already. Most notably, the only countries being declared not even "potentially interoperable" includes France and Hungary solely.

---

[3] Technically, automated roaming regions management would be possible but requires sensitive location information.

Table 2. Mobile contact tracing apps in EU member states [34]

Country	Tracing app	Already interoperable	Potentially interoperable
Croatia	Stop COVID-19	Yes	Yes
Denmark	Smittestop	Yes	Yes
Germany	Corona-Warn-App	Yes	Yes
Ireland	COVID Tracker	Yes	Yes
Italy	Immuni	Yes	Yes
Latvia	Apturi Covid	Yes	Yes
Netherlands	CoronaMelder	Yes	Yes
Poland	ProteGO Safe	Yes	Yes
Spain	Radar Covid	Yes	Yes
France	TousAntiCovid	No	No
Hungary	VirusRadar	No	No

4.2 European Federation Gateway

On June 16, 2020, the European Commission announced in a press release that member states had agreed on technical specifications to provide "safe exchange of information between national contact tracing apps based on a decentralized architecture" [35]. This enables European countries to safely exchange the encounter information presumed they follow a decentralized approach and making use of Exposure Notification API.

To enable apps to share proximity and encounter information, the Commission had set up a single European Federation Gateway Service, known as EFGS, which went live on September 28, 2020 [33, 35, 36]. The EFGS enables backend-to-backend communication across all participating nations. On October 19, 2020, the European Commission [37] confirmed in a press release that the apps of Germany, Ireland, and Italy had been linked to this gateway service. Furthermore, the Commission stated that 20 apps in total could be interoperable.

To date, in addition to the countries joined previously mentioned, the following countries are registered with the EFGS: The Republic of Latvia, Spain, Denmark, Croatia, Poland, The Netherlands, and Cyprus [37, 38].

5 The Use of Tracing Apps

5.1 Regulations

Applications operated in Europe are subject to the regulations of the General Data Protection Regulation (GDPR). The GDPR dictates rules that also apply to the storing, processing, and sharing of personal data in the context of such apps. To not hinder taking measures to mitigate the COVID-19 pandemic, the European Data Protection Board [39] has released a statement that confirms to allow competent health authorities the processing of personal data in the context of the pandemic. However, applicable rules of the GDPR regarding data processing must be complied with (GDPR Art. 5).

Integration of Switzerland to the EFGS. The integration of Switzerland to the European Federation Gateway Service (EFGS) fails due to the lack of a bilateral health agreement, according to [40]. The finalization of a health agreement is a prerequisite for participation but continues to depend on the institutional framework agreement, Hess says. Instead, von der Leyen suggests that the tracing apps' interoperability could be provided in the short term through bilateral agreements between individual EU member states and Switzerland. However, this would require Switzerland to negotiate agreements with 27 member states [40].

5.2 User Concerns

According to [9], users' primary concern towards using automated app-based contact tracing includes battery usage, compatibility across operating systems and apps, consent withdrawal, and transparency. Each of those concerns will be examined in conjunction with a survey of [41] among 8088 respondents of the Republic of Ireland (where possible).

Battery Usage: Most of the tracing apps make use of Bluetooth technology. In fact, the apps of Switzerland, Germany, and France use BLE to broadcast encounter messages. According to Ahmet et al., battery usage depends on the implementation of the app and the communication with the backend server. [41] observed that 55% of respondents believe that using Bluetooth adversely affects their device's battery life. However, 63% use Bluetooth for other applications "every day" or "most days" (Table 3).

Table 3. Comparison of factors affecting device battery usage [9]

Arch	Encounter exchange	Downloads	Data upload	Processing at device
Centralized	BLE periodic exchange of short messages (TempIDs)	Periodic download of TempIDs (once in 15 min)	Upload all encounter messages for the past 21 days	Minimal
Decentralized	BLE periodic exchange of short messages (Chirps)	Download of seeds for positive cases (once in 24 h)	Upload seeds used for the past 21 days	High. Device periodically generates seeds/chirps

Comparing the information exchange and Bluetooth usage of centralized and decentralized approaches, Ahmet [9] show that both exchanges encounter messages and similarly upload data to the backend server. However, decentralized apps only download seeds for positive cases once every 24 h, whereas centralized apps download TempIDs once every 15 min. In contrast to this, the centralized architecture requires only minimal local processing because risk analysis is computed server-side.

Compatibility Across Operating Systems and Apps. In the survey of [41], the participants responded to the reason for installing tracing apps including, but not limited to: Protection of family and friends (79%), responsibility to the wider community (78%), and self-protection (65%). Because many smartphone operating systems are in use and many different devices, providing compatibility and interoperability must be considered a critical requirement.

Consent Withdrawal. Consent withdrawal refers to the ability of the users to stop sharing their data. Article 7 of the GDPR requires the right to withdraw the users' consent at any time. This includes the deletion of collected and processed data, such as collected within the data collection phase and the data uploaded to the server. Among the Irish survey participants, 41% are worried about possible technology company surveillance after the pandemic, and 33% of respondents fear the government would use these apps as an instrument for greater surveillance after the pandemic [41].

Regarding user privacy and security, Apple's Exposure Notification FAQ [42] states that each user must explicitly opt-in to enable it. Moreover, Google and Apple stated to disable ENA when it is no longer needed automatically.

Transparency. According to [9], there is public concern regarding the methods of the information being collected. Referring to the previous paragraph examining the fear of surveillance, Ahmet et al. further state that trust is another critical factor in user adoption.

[41] reported that 58% of respondents are definitely willing to install tracing apps, while only 6% denied it. Similarly, a multi-country study conducted by [43] with 5995 participants revealed the willingness to download such apps at 75%. Furthermore, 68% said they would probably or definitely keep the app installed, presumed they are able to opt-out (consent withdrawal).

On May 25, 2020, the FOPH [44] published a survey conducted with 2819 participants in Switzerland. 59% of respondents had agreed to install the SwissCovid app either definitely or "more likely". Additionally, reasons given against the installation included the following: insufficient data security (47%), fear of surveillance (29%), and extensive battery usage (19%).

5.3 Effectiveness

A study from Oxford University assessed it would take 80% of all smartphone users to use contact tracing apps to end the Covid-19 pandemic, or 56% of the world's population [45]. However, even lower adoption rates would still result in positive effects when combined with manual tracing, testing, and quarantine measures [46].

According to [47], the population's adoption of the contact tracing app remains the bottleneck. Predicting the apps' impact is difficult because it depends on factors such as the general penetration rate of digital solutions in society, compatibility across operating systems and concerns regarding privacy and security. [47] agree that tracing apps on a voluntary basis appears preferable, although a study shows that 68% of respondents would keep automatically installed apps [43].

[47] identifies "public trust" as a key dependency for the uptake of automated contact tracing but concludes with a list of extending factors to consider including establishing public health measures and infrastructure, limiting the number of apps available, and considering risk for privacy.

6 Discussion

Since the pandemic outbreak, a vast number of approaches, frameworks, and tracing apps have appeared. Undoubtedly, it became difficult to keep an overview of the tracing apps being in use. However, it could be determined that Switzerland and Germany both use Apple/Google Exposure Notification following the DP-3T suggested decentralized approach. France was identified to keep relying on a centralized approach even on their second attempt releasing a tracing app.

Nevertheless, with the introduction of the European Federal Gateway Service, the European Commission enabled countries participating using a decentralized approach along with ENA to communicate across country borders. Although this gateway would generally be compatible with centralized backends, it remains unclear if France is able or even willing to join. Given that Switzerland and Germany use an approach that is collecting encounter information on an operating system's level, they have ensured interoperability, especially for their inhabitants at border regions. Thus, users would only be required to enable ENA on their smartphones operating system settings.

Prevalent user concerns towards consenting to the use of tracing apps remain existent. In fact, the genuine reason for reluctance was proven to be the lack of trust in their governments, health authorities, and technology providers. The vast majority of respondents fear mass surveillance while the pandemic prevails, resp. thereafter. Indeed, centralized apps as France's *TousAntiCovid* holds huge potential regarding abuse by operating authorities.

Assuming most of the users do not have the required technical knowledge to either fully understand or evaluate the technology used, governments will not be able to increase public trust. Measures, as taken from the European Commission, such as aligning technical specifications as well as establishing a public gateway, should be taken globally. Exemplary, the World Health Organization's official website does not contain clearly visible information about tracing apps' deployment. Fortunately, the Swiss, German as well as the French health ministries provide sufficient information to their respective apps. However, putting this information together to a coherent overview is not even trivial for academic researchers.

7 Conclusion

The authors focused on examining the proximity tracing frameworks used in Switzerland, Germany, and France. The decentralized DP-3T and the centralized PEPP-PT approach were analyzed. Additionally, Google and Apple's joined effort building a cross-platform tracing framework Exposure Notification was identified as a potential solution to provide interoperability while preserving privacy across operating systems, devices, and apps. Consequently, the European Commission has enabled EU member states, which are making use of ENA, to communicate across country borders. However, sharing personally identifiable data falls within the legislation of the GDPR. Unfortunately, missing bilateral agreements with the European Union excludes Switzerland to participate with the EFGS. Apart from this, user concerns regarding battery impacts, compatibility, and data security continue to play a crucial role in the population's aversive attitude toward tracing apps. Moreover, pandemic containment's effectiveness is not based exclusively on an automated app but a combination of different measures.

To answer the research questions defined in Sect. 1.1. we examined that Switzerland and Germany both use a combination of DP-3T and Exposure Notification. France, however, uses a centralized approach based on ROBERT. Therefore, the Swiss and the German app are technically interoperable, but because Switzerland is not able to join the EFGS due to the lack of appropriate bilateral agreements, the user is required to switch his region manually when crossing borders. However, the French app is incompatible with both. The users' main reasons against the use of tracing apps include battery usage concerns, incompatibility, intransparency, and the fear of surveillance during and after the pandemic. Furthermore, the app's effectiveness depends on additionally taken actions.

While this research revealed the interoperability of the Swiss, German, and French apps, as well as the reasons for user's reluctance, the need for further surveys and investigations remains. Conducting them would help improve the understanding of why the tracing app's adoption stays below the level to support the pandemic's containment effectively.

One year after the pandemic outbreak, politicians now urge to a unified solution. According to an NZZ article [48], Switzerland should be able to join the EFGS before Easter 2021. It remains uncertain if France will be able to join the EFGS.

References

1. WHO: WHO Director-General's opening remarks at the media briefing on COVID-19 - 11 March 2020. https://www.who.int/director-general/speeches/detail/who-director-general-s-opening-remarks-at-the-media-briefing-on-covid-19---11-march-2020
2. Martin, T., Karopoulos, G., Hernández-Ramos, J.L., Kambourakis, G., Fovino, I.N.: Demystifying COVID-19 digital contact tracing: a survey on frameworks and mobile apps. Wirel. Commun. Mob. Comput. **2020**, 1–29 (2020). https://doi.org/10.1155/2020/8851429
3. DP3T: DP^3T Github. https://github.com/DP-3T/
4. Federal Office of Public Health, FOPH: SwissCovid app and contact tracing. https://www.bag.admin.ch/bag/en/home/krankheiten/ausbrueche-epidemien-pandemien/aktuelle-ausbru eche-epidemien/novel-cov/swisscovid-app-und-contact-tracing.html
5. Ministère des Solidarités et de la Santé, MSS: TousAntiCovid: réponses à vos questions. https://solidarites-sante.gouv.fr/soins-et-maladies/maladies/maladies-infectieuses/cor onavirus/tousanticovid
6. SAP Deutschland SE & Co. KG, SAP: Open-Source Project Corona-Warn-App. https://www.coronawarn.app/en/

7. de Rosa, P., et al.: Interoperability of decentralized proximity tracing systems across regions. https://drive.google.com/file/d/1mGfE7rMKNmc51TG4ceE9PHEggN8rHOXk/edit
8. PEPP-PT: PEPP-PT Data Protection Information Security Architecture Germany. https://github.com/pepp-pt/pepp-pt-documentation/blob/master/10-data-protection/PEPP-PT-data-protection-information-security-architecture-Germany.pdf
9. Ahmed, N., et al.: A survey of COVID-19 contact tracing apps. IEEE Access **8**, 134577–134601 (2020). https://doi.org/10.1109/access.2020.3010226
10. Troncoso, C., et al.: Decentralized Privacy-Preserving Proximity Tracing. Arxiv (2020)
11. Botham, L., Waldron, A.: Apple and Google partner on COVID-19 contact tracing technology. https://www.apple.com/au/newsroom/2020/04/apple-and-google-partner-on-covid-19-contact-tracing-technology/
12. Apple: Exposure Notification - Bluetooth Specification. https://covid19-static.cdn-apple.com/applications/covid19/current/static/contact-tracing/pdf/ExposureNotification-BluetoothSpecificationv1.2.pdf
13. Apple: About iOS 13 Updates. https://support.apple.com/en-om/HT210393
14. Apple: About iOS 12 Updates. https://support.apple.com/en-us/HT209084
15. Google: About the Exposure Notifications System and Android location settings. https://support.google.com/android/answer/9930236
16. EPFL: First pilot for the Google and Apple-based decentralised tracing app – EPFL. https://actu.epfl.ch/news/first-pilot-for-the-google-and-apple-based-decentr/
17. Federal Statistical Office, FSO: Swiss Covid Proximity Tracing App Monitoring. https://www.experimental.bfs.admin.ch/expstat/en/home/innovative-methods/swisscovid-app-monitoring.html
18. Federal Statistical Office, FSO: Calculation methods for estimating the number of active SwissCovid apps (2020)
19. Vaudenay, S., Vuagnoux, M.: Analysis of SwissCovid (2020)
20. Federal Office of Public Health, FOPH: SwissCovid App: Data Protection Statement & Conditions of Use. https://www.bag.admin.ch/bag/en/home/krankheiten/ausbrueche-epidemien-pandemien/aktuelle-ausbrueche-epidemien/novel-cov/swisscovid-app-und-contact-tracing/datenschutzerklaerung-nutzungsbedingungen.html
21. Inria: Le projet StopCovid, une solution numérique pour contribuer à la lutte citoyenne contre l'épidémie de Covid-19 I Inria. https://www.inria.fr/fr/le-projet-stopcovid
22. Connexion: How is France's new Covid app different from old one? https://www.connexionfrance.com/Practical/Your-Questions/How-is-France-s-new-Covid-app-different-from-old-one
23. Le Monde: Emmanuel Macron acte l'échec de l'application StopCovid et annonce une nouvelle version: «Tous anti-Covid». https://www.lemonde.fr/pixels/article/2020/10/14/emmanuel-macron-acte-l-echec-de-l-application-stopcovid-qui-sera-renommee-tous-anti-covid_6056049_4408996.html
24. Le Monde: TousAntiCovid: le lancement de l'application perturbé par des bugs. https://www.lemonde.fr/pixels/article/2020/10/23/tousanticovid-le-lancement-de-l-application-perturbe-par-des-bugs_6057158_4408996.html
25. Inria, AISEC, F.: ROBERT: ROBust and privacy-presERving proximity Tracing. https://github.com/ROBERT-proximity-tracing/documents/blob/master/ROBERT-specification-EN-v1_1.pdf
26. Cunche, M., Kessibi, G., Boutet, A., Castelluccia, C., Lauradoux, C., Roca, V.: Analysis of Diagnosis Key distribution mechanism in contact tracing applications based on Google-Apple Exposure Notification (GAEN) framework (2020)
27. Etalab: Métriques d'utilisation de l'application TousAntiCovid. https://www.data.gouv.fr/fr/datasets/metriques-dutilisation-de-lapplication-tousanticovid/

28. Dix, A.: Die deutsche Corona Warn-App – ein gelungenes Beispiel für Privacy by Design? Datenschutz und Datensicherheit - DuD **44**(12), 779–785 (2020). https://doi.org/10.1007/s11 623-020-1366-1

29. SAP Deutschland SE & Co. KG, SAP: Open-Source Project Corona-Warn-App – FAQ. https://www.coronawarn.app/en/faq/

30. CWA: Corona-Warn-App Github. https://github.com/corona-warn-app/cwa-documentation

31. Reuters: Germany flips to Apple-Google approach on smartphone contact tracing. https://www.reuters.com/article/us-health-coronavirus-europe-tech-idUSKCN22807J

32. Robert Koch Institut: Kennzahlen zur Corona-Warn-App. https://www.rki.de/DE/Content/InfAZ/N/Neuartiges_Coronavirus/WarnApp/Archiv_Kennzahlen/Kennzahlen_11122020.pdf?__blob=publicationFile

33. European Commission: European Proximity Tracing – An Interoperability Architecture for contact tracing and warning apps, 55 (2020)

34. European Commission: Mobile contact tracing apps in EU Member States | European Commission. https://ec.europa.eu/info/live-work-travel-eu/coronavirus-response/travel-during-coronavirus-pandemic/mobile-contact-tracing-apps-eu-member-states_en

35. European Commission: Coronavirus: Member States agree on an interoperability solution for mobile tracing and warning apps. https://ec.europa.eu/commission/presscorner/detail/en/ip_20_1043

36. Baldacci, E.: Contact tracing and warning apps and the European Federation Gateway Service (EFGS). IPEN Webinar on Contact Tracing apps (2020)

37. European Commission: Coronavirus: EU interoperability gateway. https://ec.europa.eu/commission/presscorner/detail/en/IP_20_1904

38. European Commission: National Joint Controllers and privacy policies. https://ec.europa.eu/health/sites/health/files/ehealth/docs/gateway_jointcontrollers_en.pdf

39. European Data Protection Board, EDPB: Statement on the processing of personal data in the context of the COVID-19 outbreak (2020). https://edpb.europa.eu/sites/edpb/files/files/news/edpb_statement_2020_processingpersonaldataandcovid-19_en.pdf

40. Hess, R.: Wegen Rahmenabkommen kein Anschluss an Corona-App: Schweiz soll mit allen 27 EU-Staaten einzeln verhandeln – Schweiz. https://www.bzbasel.ch/schweiz/wegen-rahmenabkommen-kein-anschluss-an-corona-app-schweiz-soll-mit-allen-27-eu-staaten-einzeln-verhandeln-139479249

41. O'Callaghan, M.E., et al.: A national survey of attitudes to COVID-19 digital contact tracing in the Republic of Ireland. Irish J. Med. Sci. (1971) **190**(3), 863–887 (2020). https://doi.org/10.1007/s11845-020-02389-y

42. Apple: Exposure Notifications - FAQ v1.2. https://covid19-static.cdn-apple.com/applications/covid19/current/static/contact-tracing/pdf/ExposureNotification-FAQv1.2.pdf

43. Altmann, S., et al.: Acceptability of app-based contact tracing for COVID-19: Cross-country survey evidence (Preprint). JMIR Mhealth Uhealth **8**, e19857 (2020). https://doi.org/10.2196/19857

44. Federal Office of Public Health, FOPH: SwissCovid-App: Studienbericht zur Bevölkerungsbefragung. https://www.bag.admin.ch/dam/bag/de/dokumente/cc/Kampagnen/covid-19/swisscovid-app-umfrage-mai2020.pdf.download.pdf/BAG_SwissCovidApp_Befragung_Mai_2020.pdf

45. Hinch, R., et al.: Effective Configurations of a Digital Contact Tracing App: A report to NHSX, 29 (2020)

46. O'Neill, P.H.: No, coronavirus apps don't need 60% adoption to be effective (2020). https://www.technologyreview.com/2020/06/05/1002775/covid-apps-effective-at-less-than-60-percent-download/

47. Ranisch, R., et al.: Digital contact tracing and exposure notification: ethical guidance for trustworthy pandemic management. Ethics Inf. Technol. 1–10 (2020). https://doi.org/10.1007/s10676-020-09566-8
48. NZZ: Corona: SwissCovid-App und Corona-Warn-App bald interoperable. https://www.nzz.ch/technologie/schweizer-und-deutsche-contact-tracing-apps-sollen-noch-vor-ostern-interoperabel-werden-ld.1604501

Moving Towards Society 5.0: A Bibliometric and Visualization Analysis

Noor Hidayah Shahidan(✉), Ahmad Shaharudin Abdul Latiff ⓘ,
and Sazali Abdul Wahab ⓘ

Putra Business School, Universiti Putra Malaysia, 43400 Serdang, Selangor, Malaysia

Abstract. This paper aims to provide a holistic approach for a brief understanding of the current state of literature of Society 5.0 by deciphering its characteristics, subjects, the geographical distribution of publications, keywords and general concepts by using bibliometric data retrieved from the Scopus database. We used descriptive analysis to examine publication characteristics, subjects and geographical distribution of published documents, Harzing's Publish or Perish to calculate citation metric and VOSviewer version 1.6.16 for data and network visualization. Through the network analyses of author and index keyword co-occurrences, research clusters were revealed from different perspectives. The bibliometric analysis indicates that Society 5.0 is heavily influenced by the advancement of the Industrial Revolution (IR) 4.0. The intellectual structure of the Society 5.0 literature is being dominated by engineering-related fields, artificial intelligence (AI), and the Internet of Things (IoT). Our analysis revealed the existence of a strong link in the temporal co-map between Sustainable Development Goals (SDGs) and Society 5.0. This paper also emphasizes on university's role as an important stakeholder in Society 5.0 ecosystem.

Keywords: Bibliometric study · SCOPUS · Society 5.0 · Emerging research topics

1 Introduction

The concept of Society 5.0 or also known as "super-smart society" was first introduced by the government of Japan in April 2016. The analysis outcome of the joint research report "The Evolution of ESG Investment, Realization of Society 5.0, and Achievement of SDGs" by Keidanren, the University of Tokyo, and the GPIF (Government Pension Investment Fund) (2020) quoted *"Society 5.0 is a sustainable, human-centered society in which the physical and cyber worlds are highly integrated by digital transformation, no one is left behind, and everyone works together to create safe and comfortable lives and new growth opportunities"* [1]. The IR 4.0 promotes digitalization and autonomous systems by using technologies such as the Internet of Things (IoT) and Artificial Intelligence (AI). These technologies operate the decision-making mechanisms that link human command to machines and electronic systems. However, the concept of IR 4.0 lacks human factors. A Japanese originated philosophy of Society 5.0 integrates the

A. Gerber and K. Hinkelmann (Eds.): Society 5.0 2021, CCIS 1477, pp. 93–104, 2021.
https://doi.org/10.1007/978-3-030-86761-4_8

Industry 4.0 technologies to create systems that harmoniously served the interest of society [2]. By combining cyberspace and physical space, Society 5.0 aims to leverage the digital transformation of IR 4.0 to create balance economic advancement to alleviate social problems through the provision of products and services.

This paper highlights the current state of the art of Society 5.0 literature corpus. The bibliometric review offers various advantages in term of examining the research domain from the perspective of a bird's eye view. Bibliographic analysis assists a researcher to understand the state of the art in the research area and means to justify the position of the research work concerning the existing studies. Besides, a researcher is also able to extract the emerging trends in the research area and determine the evolution of research topics [3]. Due to a vast number of academic publications, the bibliometric analysis offers a quantitative approach to analysing a vast number of published peer-reviewed documents effectively. The emergence of the Society 5.0 concept emphasizes the importance of multidisciplinary research and requires researchers with different expertise to collaborate harmoniously under one research team. Even though this research domain is still practically very new, it is crucial to examine how far it has been developed. Therefore, this bibliometric review addressed the following research questions.

1. What are the volume, research subject area, and geographic distribution of scholarship on Society 5.0?
2. What is the Intellectual Structure of the Society 5.0 Knowledge Base?

2 Methodology

In this study, we used the Scopus index database to search and extract documents. The reason for choosing Scopus as it covers comprehensive publications of reputable sources. The PRISMA (Preferred Reporting Items for Systematic Reviews and Meta-Analyses) guideline was adopted for this review (Fig. 1).

As of 6th March 2021, we managed to retrieve 142 documents published by entering the search query string of TITLE-ABS-KEY ("Society 5.0") into the Scopus search engine. These 142 documents were subjected to analysis. For the Scopus search, we did not specify any start date. Based on retrieved literature from the Scopus database, the earliest documents were published in 2017. To answer the first research question, we used descriptive statistics to analyse publication characteristics and geography of the Society 5.0 literature. The citation metric and frequencies were calculated by using Harzing's Publish or Perish. We answered the second research question by using Visualization of Similarities (VOS) viewer version 1.6.16 software (https://www.vosviewer.com/) for visualization of bibliometric maps and cluster determination in the Society 5.0 literature [4].

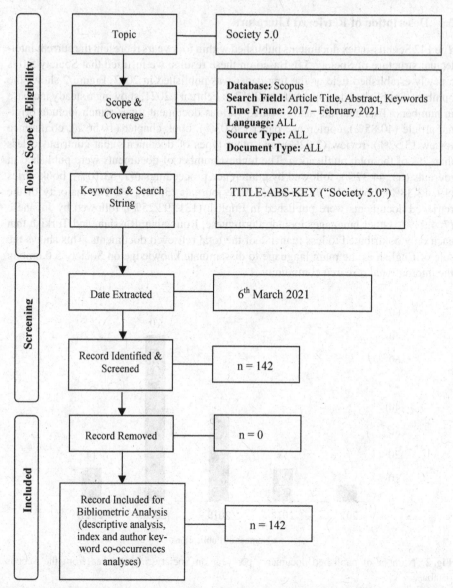

Fig. 1. PRISMA flow charts of procedures used in the identification of sources for the Society 5.0 bibliometric review

3 Findings

In this section, we present the results for the various bibliometric indicators such as the description of the retrieved literature, research subject areas, geographical distribution of publications and leading institutions, as well as key authors and intellectual structure of Society 5.0 knowledge base.

3.1 Description of Retrieved Literature

The 142 Scopus-index documents published within four years represent the current intellectual structure of Society 5.0. Based on these results, we justified that Society 5.0 is a newly established field as the first paper was published in 2017. Figure 2 shows the number of published documents from 2017 to February 2021, showing a steady increase in numbers. This analysis also revealed various document types which include original article (40.85%), conference paper (38.03%), book chapter (10.56%), conference review (3.52%), review (2.82%), and other types of documents that contributed less than 2% of the total publication. The highest number of documents were published in journals (63, 44.37%), followed by conference proceedings (47, 33.10%), book series (19, 13.38%), book (10, 7.04%), and trade journals (3, 2.11%). The majority of the retrieved documents were published in English (131, 92.25%), followed by Japanese (7, 4.93%). Other languages include Portuguese, Romanian, Russian, and Turkish that each only contributed to less than 1% of the total retrieved documents. This shows the role of English as the main language to disseminate knowledge on Society 5.0 among the international research community.

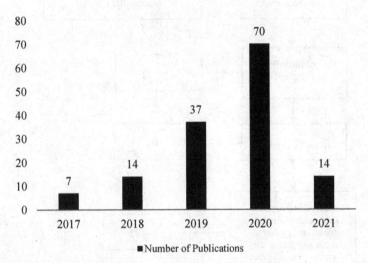

Fig. 2. Number of published documents per year on Society 5.0 retrieved from the Scopus database

We calculated citation metrics for the retrieved documents by using Harzing's Publish or Perish. For the publication period between 2017 to February 2021, the retrieved documents received a total of 275 citations, 68.75 cites/year, and 1.94 cites/paper. We also analyzed the h-index, which measures the quality of research output based on the number of total citations received. The h-index and g-index of the retrieved documents were 7 and 13, respectively.

3.2 Research Subject Area

Scopus database allocates relevant subject areas to the documents in their indexing list. The top 10 research subject areas in the Scopus database are listed in Table 1. *Computer Science* and *Engineering* ranked first and second with total publication (TP) of 61 and 59, respectively. After that, *Social Sciences* ranked third with TP of 43, followed by *Business, Management, and Accounting* with TP of 28. Apart from publications from the apparent areas, extensive research works have been done in other disciplines due to the interaction of several industries. From the Scopus database, we observed *Mathematics* with TP of 22, and *Economics, Econometrics and Finance* with TP of 17.

Table 1. Top 10 subject areas covered by Society 5.0

Subject area	Total Publication (TP)	Percentage %
Computer Science	61	42.96
Engineering	59	41.55
Social Sciences	43	30.28
Business, Management and Accounting	28	19.72
Mathematics	22	15.49
Economics, Econometrics and Finance	17	11.97
Decision Sciences	15	10.56
Energy	13	9.15
Environmental Science	13	9.15
Earth and Planetary Sciences	11	7.75

Another interesting observation that can be concluded from Table 1 is the wide coverage of Society 5.0 that include other research disciplines such as *Decision Sciences, Energy, Environmental Science,* and *Earth and Planetary Sciences.* There are also subject areas categorized by Scopus that are not listed in Table 1 that accounted for less than 7% of total publications namely: *Materials Science, Physics and Astronomy, Chemical Engineering, Arts and Humanities, Medicine, Psychology, Agricultural and Biological Sciences, Neuroscience,* and others. This also indicates how research studies on Society 5.0 integrate interdisciplinary areas to solve real-life problems for various industrial applications.

3.3 Geographical Distribution of Publications and Leading Institutions

Our bibliometric analysis shows that the publications on Society 5.0 originated from 41 different countries. However, Fig. 3 only shows the top 20 productive countries as we excluded countries that contributed to only one publication. Our analysis revealed that Japan is currently ranked first in term of the number of publications (n = 39), followed by Indonesia (n = 24), and the United States (n = 9).

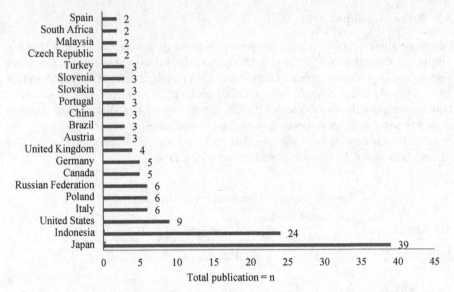

Fig. 3. Worldwide distribution of Society 5.0 publications from countries with more than one publication, 2017 – February 2021

Based on the dataset, we also identified the top 10 leading institutions with the highest number of publications. The University of Tokyo and Hitachi, Ltd is currently ranked first and second, with total publication (TP) of 7 and 4 documents, respectively. Keio University (Japan, TP = 4) ranked third, followed by Nagoya University (Japan), Univerza v Mariboru (Slovenia), Silesian University of Technology (Poland), National Institute of Advanced Industrial Science and Technology (Japan), Bina Nusantara University (Indonesia), Fachhochschule des Mittelstands (Germany) and Universidade da Beira Interior (Portugal). By identifying the leading research organizations, researchers who intend to venture into Society 5.0 research domain can reach out to these organizations for collaboration opportunities and technical expertise.

3.4 Key Authors and Intellectual Structure of Society 5.0 Knowledge Base

Keyword co-occurrence analysis was used to analyze the intellectual structure of the present Society 5.0 knowledge base and to identify emerging topics in this research domain that have received the utmost attention from scholars. Similar to co-citation analysis, keyword co-occurrences analysis deciphers the similarity between the frequently used index and authors keywords in the literature. The relationship between two keywords is strengthened when there are more co-occurrences between the two keywords [5]. Therefore, current topics related to Society 5.0 can be determined, and potential future research direction can be predicted. For this study, we conducted a separate analysis of author keyword and index keyword co-occurrences. We also compared the network visualization maps produced by both analyses. As Society 5.0 is relatively a recent field of study, we set the keyword threshold = 2 for better visualization of keywords network. In comparison to the index keyword determined by Scopus, we found out that the author keyword co-occurrence analysis revealed a lesser number of key-words (keyword display = 36) (Fig. 4). The frequency of the occurrence is indicated by the size of the nodes. Each node is clustered using different colours, according to the co-occurrence network of multiple keywords. Network cluster maps of index and author keywords consist of the most highly used keywords in this research domain. Our analysis shows that Society 5.0 is closely interconnected with "*artificial intelligence*", "*Internet of Thing*" (IoT), "*cyber-physical systems*", "*big data analytics*", and "*smart society*". Besides, Fig. 4 also shows connections between Society 5.0 and the United Nation's Sustainable Development Goals (SDGs) as indicated by the keyword "*SDGs*", "*sustainability*" and "*sustainable development*". Mapping of the author key-words also revealed interconnection between the keyword "*Society 5.0*" and "*covid-19*" in the retrieved dataset.

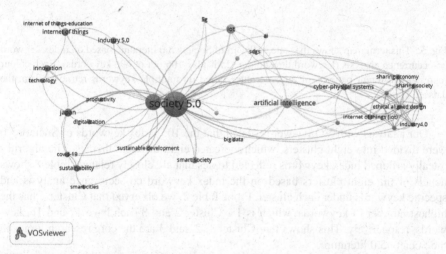

Fig. 4. Network visualization map of the author keywords (keyword threshold = 2; display 36). Each colour represents different patterns of co-occurrences based on multiple keywords retrieved from the dataset.

Alternatively, the index keyword co-occurrence map (Fig. 5) shows 105 keywords display. Based on this result, we inferred that co-occurrence analysis using index key-words produced a clearer understanding of the current state of the art of Society 5.0 in comparison to author keywords co-occurrence analysis. However, the description of an article's content is more accurate with the use of the authors' keyword [6]. The index keywords of different clusters were presented in various colours.

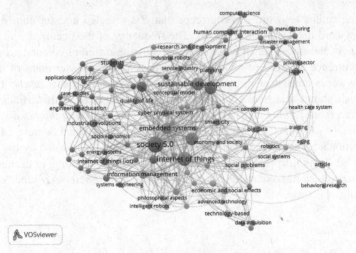

Fig. 5. This term map shows the state of the art of Society 5.0 literature based on index keyword co-occurrence analysis (keyword threshold = 2; display 105 out of 696 keywords). Each colour represents different patterns of co-occurrence based on multiple keywords retrieved from the dataset.

Our analysis with VOSviewer revealed that the 105 index keywords of Society 5.0 were divided into eight clusters, which indicated eight different themes. The algorithmically grouped index keywords reflected topics that are closely related. Table 2 shows details of the eight clusters based on the index keyword co-occurrence analysis and specific keywords under each cluster. From Table 2, we observed that Cluster 1 has the highest number of keywords, which is 18. Cluster 2 and 3 each have 17 and 16, keywords, respectively. This shows that Cluster 1, 2, and 3 are the core research topics in the Society 5.0 literature.

Table 2. Eight clusters of Society 5.0 based on index keyword co-occurrence analysis

Cluster	Color	Number of keywords	Selected keywords
1	Red	18	Artificial intelligence; computer science; computers; cost-effectiveness; decision making process; disaster management; government; higher education; human activities; human computer interaction; innovation; integrated approach; Japan; manufacturing; physical world; policy making; private sector; research and development

(continued)

Table 2. (*continued*)

Cluster	Color	Number of keywords	Selected keywords
2	Green	17	Application programs; case-studies; computation theory; customer satisfaction; decision making; education computing; education technology; education challenge; electronic commerce; engineering education; human machine interface; innovative learning; instructional designs; ITS applications; learning systems; man-machine systems; students
3	Blue	16	Energy efficiency; energy management system; energy systems; engineering; industrial management; industrial revolutions; information and communication; Internet of Things (IoT); productivity; renewable energy resource; science and technology; smart power grids; Society 5.0; socio-economics; standardization; system engineering
4	Yellow	14	Advanced technology; conceptual model; economics and social effects; Europe; knowledge management; manufacture; Poland (Central Europe); research work, sales, social development; technology-based; virtual worlds; visualization; well-being
5	Purple	11	Aging; article; behavioral research; economic development; health care system; human; human experiment; robotics; social problems; social systems; training
6	Sky blue	10	Authentication; competition; digital technologies; industrial robots; industry 4.0; planning; quality of life; robot programming; service industry; sustainable development
7	Orange	10	Cyber physical system; economy and society; embedded systems; industrial economics; information management; intelligent robots; intelligent systems, philosophical aspects, smart society, smart system
8	Maroon	9	3D printers; big data; data acquisition; data analytics; Internet of Things (IoT); Internet of Things; signal processing; smart city; social computing

Figure 6 shows a temporal overlay on the keyword occurrence map (keyword threshold = 2, display = 105), which connects keywords to the document's publication date. Therefore, researchers can determine the evolution of research terms periodically [5]. The nodes in darker shades (e.g., blue) indicates topics that were published earlier than those in lighter shades (e.g., yellow). The most recent 'hot' topics are represented by yellow nodes such as "*quality of life*" [11] and "*economic and social effect*" [12, 13].

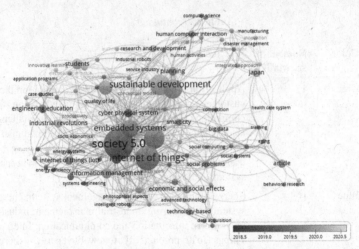

Fig. 6. Overlay visualization of index keyword co-occurrence analysis. Temporal overlay on keyword occurrence map (keyword threshold = 2, display = 105) shows the evolution of research terms on Society 5.0. Overlay visualization by VOSviewer shows that circles with cold colours (e.g., blue) represent research topics with an older average publication year and the circles with hot colours (e.g., yellow) shows the terms with a more recent average publication year. (Color figure online)

4 Discussion

This bibliometric review revealed a substantial knowledge base on Society 5.0 consisting of 142 Scopus-index documents published from 2017 to February 2021. We identified eight clusters of research themes in Society 5.0, which represent the current research direction. Our analysis shows that the intellectual structure of the knowledge base on Society 5.0 is primarily driven by IR 4.0 technologies such as the Internet of Things (IoT), big data analytics, and artificial intelligence (AI) to build smart cities integrated with cyber-physical systems. Due to the COVID-19 pandemic, the role and impacts of IR 4.0 are exponentially growing as many sectors were badly impacted due to the pandemic. Even though there is still a lack of empirical data to support this claim, reviews by Acioli et al. (2021) [8], Amaldi-Enchendu and Thopil (2020) [9] and Safraz et al. (2021) [10] provide some insights on the future research directions. The COVID-19 pandemic has triggered manufacturers globally to leverage advanced IT technologies such as AI, IoT, and robots [10].

Keyword co-occurrence analysis has been used to study intellectual structure in various research domains by many researchers. Kalantari et al. (2017) compared author keyword and KeyWords plus to examine big data research trends [19]. Analyzing literature retrieved from the Scopus database for documents published in 1994–2018, Udomsap and Hallinger (2020) used keyword occurrence analysis to conceptually structure the sustainable construction knowledge base [20]. The evolution trend of research topics as shown in the overlay visualization of index keyword co-occurrence analysis map (see Fig. 6) and steady growth in publication numbers suggest that research topics on Society 5.0 are progressively receiving attention from scholars. The maturity of a research field is assessed by these criteria: well-codification of literature, high accessibility to published documents, clear distinction with other research areas, vigorous research methods/approaches and research paradigm, high citation matrix (that indicate impacts on research community), and industrial applications [18]. Based on these criteria and referring to our findings presented previously, we deduced that Society 5.0 research domain is still under-researched and requires further attention from the academic community globally.

Our analysis also shows the role of the university as an important stakeholder towards developing Society 5.0. Besides solely focusing on teaching and academic research, the university has also embraced the third mission of the university, which is the commercialization of Intellectual Property Rights (IPR) [15]. One of the classic examples is the university-industry partnership between the University of Tokyo and Hitachi Ltd with the establishment of Hitachi-UTokyo Laboratory (H-UTokyoLab) [16]. Inclusive of the University of Tokyo and Hitachi, Ltd, 50% of the top 10 leading institutions with the highest total number of publications were based in Japan. This reflects Japan's standing as the pioneer and leader in developing Society 5.0.

This study is limited as it only used the Scopus database for the bibliometric review. Besides, it only presents the description of retrieved literature and keyword co-occurrences analysis. For future study, it is recommended to include other databases such as Web of Science (WoS) and Dimension.oi. In addition, it is also suggested to conduct other bibliometric indicator analyses such as bibliographic couplings and co-citation analysis for a more comprehensive study.

References

1. Japan Business Federation (Keidanren): Toward the Evolution of ESG Investment, Realization of Society 5.0, and Achievement of SDGs - Promotion of Investment in Problem-Solving Innovation, Keidanren, Tokyo (2020)
2. Polat, L., Erkollar, A.: Industry 4.0 vs. Society 5.0. In: Durakbasa, N.M., Gençyılmaz, M.G. (eds.) ISPR 2020. LNME, pp. 333–345. Springer, Cham (2021). https://doi.org/10.1007/978-3-030-62784-3_28
3. Ranjbar-Sahraei, B., Negenborn, R.: Research positioning & trend identification: a data-analytics toolbox. (Version 2.2 ed.) The Delft University of Technology (2017). http://aida.tudelft.nl/toolbox/aida-booklet
4. van Eck, N.J., Waltman, L.: Software survey: VOSviewer, a computer program for bibliometric mapping. Scientometrics **84**, 523–538 (2010). https://doi.org/10.1007/s11192-009-0146-3
5. Zupic, I., Čater, T.: Bibliometric methods in management and organization. Organ. Res. Methods **18**(3), 429–472 (2015). https://doi.org/10.1177/1094428114562629
6. Zhang, J., Yu, Q., Zheng, F., Long, C., Lu, Z., Duan, Z.: Comparing keywords plus of WOS and author keywords. J. Assoc. Inf. Sci. Technol. **67**, 967–972 (2016). https://doi.org/10.1002/asi.23437
7. De Wit, A., Shaw, R., Djalante, R.: An integrated approach to sustainable development, National Resilience, and COVID-19 responses: the case of Japan. Int. J. Disaster Risk Reduc. **51** (2020). https://doi.org/10.1016/j.ijdrr.2020.101808
8. Acioli, C., Scavarda, A., Reis, A.: Applying Industry 4.0 technologies in the COVID–19 sustainable chains. Int. J. Prod. Perform. Manage. vol. ahead-of-print No. ahead-of-print (2021). https://doi.org/10.1108/IJPPM-03-2020-0137

9. Amadi-Echendu, J., Thopil, G.A.: Resilience is paramount for managing socio-technological systems during and post-Covid-19. IEEE Eng. Manage. Rev. **48**(3), 118–128. https://doi.org/10.1109/EMR.2020.3013712.

10. Sarfraz, Z., Sarfraz, A., Iftikar, H., Akhund, R.: Is COVID-19 pushing us to the Fifth Industrial Revolution (Society 5.0)? Pakistan J. Med. Sci. **37**(2) (2021). https://doi.org/10.12669/pjms.37.2.3387

11. Fachrunnisa, O., Adhiatma, A., Tjahjono, H.K.: Spiritual welfare creation for knowledge workers in Society 5.0: a conceptual model. In: Barolli, L., Poniszewska-Maranda, A., Enokido, T. (eds.) CISIS 2020. AISC, vol. 1194, pp. 300–306. Springer, Cham (2021). https://doi.org/10.1007/978-3-030-50454-0_28

12. Umamah, N., Marjono, S., Hartono, F.P.: Teacher Perspective: Innovative, Adaptive, and Responsive Instructional Design Aimed at Life Skills, IOP Conference Series: Earth and Environmental Science, Volume 485, Second International Conference on Environmental Geography and Geography Education (ICEGE), East Java, Indonesia, 28–29 September 2019 (2020)

13. Liliasari, S., Amsad, L.N., Wahyudi, A.: Innovative chemistry education: an alternative course models in the disruption era. Journal of Physics: Conference Series, Volume 1731, Mathematics and Science Education International Seminar (MASEIS) 2019, Bengkulu, Indonesia, 5 October 2019 (2021)

14. Mashur, R, Aditya, H.P.K.P., Ashoer, M., Hidayat, M., Gunawan, B.I., Fitriyani, F.: Moving from traditional to Society 5.0: case study by online transportation business. 유통과학연구 **17**(9), 93–102 (2019). https://doi.org/10.15722/JDS.17.9.201909.93

15. Ranga, M., Etzkowitz, H.: Triple helix systems: an analytical framework for innovation policy and practice in the knowledge society. Ind. Higher Educ. **27**(4), 237–262 (2013)

16. Deguchi, A., et al.: What is Society 5.0? In: Hitachi-UTokyo Laboratory (H-UTokyo Lab.) (eds.) Society 5.0, pp. 1–23. Springer, Singapore (2020). https://doi.org/10.1007/978-981-15-2989-4_1

17. Shiroishi, Y., Uchiyama, K., Suzuki, N.: Society 5.0: for human security and well-being in Computer, vol. 51, no. 07, pp. 91–95 (2018). https://doi.org/10.1109/MC.2018.3011041

18. Keathley-Herring, H., Van Aken, E., Gonzalez-Aleu, F., Deschamps, F., Letens, G., Orlandini, P.C.: Assessing the maturity of a research area: bibliometric review and proposed framework. Scientometrics **109**(2), 927–951 (2016). https://doi.org/10.1007/s11192-016-2096-x

19. Kalantari, A., et al.: A bibliometric approach to tracking big data research trends. J. Big Data **4**(1), 1–18 (2017). https://doi.org/10.1186/s40537-017-0088-1

20. Udomsap, A.D., Hallinger, P.: A bibliometric review of research on sustainable construction, 1994–2018. J. Clean. Prod. **254** (2020). https://doi.org/10.1016/j.jclepro.2020.120073

Determinants of the Adoption of Virtual Team Collaboration as a Mode of Knowledge Transfer within Innovation Driven Organisations

Marius Anno van der Meulen[1](✉) and Hanlie Smuts[2]

[1] Graduate School of Technology Management, University of Pretoria, Pretoria, South Africa
[2] Department of Informatics, University of Pretoria, Pretoria, South Africa
`hanlie.smuts@up.ac.za`

Abstract. Society 5.0 seeks to resolve social and economic imbalances through the integration of the virtual world and the physical world. Amid the COVID-19 pandemic the need and possibilities hereof has become so much clearer. This paper aims to shed light on the factors affecting the adoption of virtual team collaboration within innovation driven companies, as their primary mode of knowledge transfer. By getting insight into these factors, we will be on our way to enable individuals, companies and governments to promote effective adoption of virtual team collaboration. This in turn can reduce the knowledge gap that exists in developing post-colonial countries, by enabling knowledge to be better transferred between industries within the country and from outside the country. This paper provides an in-depth coverage of the existing literature starting by looking into knowledge transfer as a management principle, then looking at the innovation of virtual team collaboration itself and finally at the social system, an innovation driven organisation, into which the innovation will be adopted. The findings are then applied to the Diffusion of Innovation theory's Innovation-Decision Process. By understanding these key determinants, organisations may utilise this guidance in the application of virtual team collaboration (VTC) as a mode of knowledge transfer when considering innovation.

Keywords: Society 5.0 · Virtual team collaboration · Innovation driven organisation · Knowledge transfer · Knowledge management · Diffusion of innovation · Innovation-Decision Process

1 Introduction

In the age we live in, remote work, long-distance communication and virtual collaboration is becoming more of a reality every day, driven by the rapid improvements of the technologies that enable this [1, 2]. The capability to make use of the available technologies, to effectively replace face-to-face collaborating teams, can be a competitive advantage to any organisation driven to innovate [3]. Companies have the opportunity to collaborate across continents and share knowledge in this way [3]. However, not only companies can benefit from these innovations, but also educational institutions, such as

A. Gerber and K. Hinkelmann (Eds.): Society 5.0 2021, CCIS 1477, pp. 105–115, 2021.
https://doi.org/10.1007/978-3-030-86761-4_9

Universities, can collaborate across borders and share and create knowledge not limited to a single country's viewpoint [4]. Countries that are leading the charge in innovation can become more and more competitive on a global scale.

In contrast to this, the outlook for African countries is not entirely the same [5]. After reaching political independence, African countries have not quite achieved full independence from their overseas powers. In the context of technology, Africa and, for this study, South Africa (SA) is still very much dependent on developed countries for technology and South Africa is continuously in a game of catch-up. SA makes great use of industrial work, but not that much on technology development. Through this dependence, SA can be construed as a technology colony with a knowledge transfer gap between the industrial sector and design and development sectors [5].

Bridging the knowledge transfer gap would mean to create the availability of a scientific or technology skill base within the design and development stage of the technology life cycle in industry [5]. In this creating exposure opportunities for indigenous knowledge workers at all stages of the technology life cycle. Enabling them to add value to technologies at earlier stages of the life cycle [5]. This in turn, shifts the SA industry towards a service and knowledge work industry [6], which places the intellectual property in SA [5]. This will enable SA to export the technology from SA and have the financial stem of the technology within SA [5]. Through VTC technology's ability to remove traditional boundaries such as time or geographical location VTC can happen on a global scale and can increase the competitive advantage of companies in SA and increase their operational flexibility [7]. Companies can break the communication barriers of time and distance and make use of VTC to do so [1]. A study into what determines the adoption of VTC by companies in SA, can possibly play a role in closing this knowledge transfer gap that is currently present in SA.

Therefore, this paper aims to add to the body of knowledge of knowledge transfer as well as present an informative document sheading light for companies on how VTC can be diffused and better adopted to decrease the current knowledge gap. This is done by exploring answers to the question: *"What are the determinants of the adoption of VTC as a mode of knowledge transfer within innovation-driven companies operating in SA?"* An understanding of the key determinants may enable organisations to consider VTC.

The following section (Sect. 2) provides and in-depth overview of the literature followed by the methodology applied in Sect. 3. Sect. 4 presents the exploration of an adoption model and the final section (Sect. 5) concludes the paper.

2   Background

The little research and development that is done in SA, is at tertiary institutions and very little of that is retained in the country, but rather transferred, at an early stage to the more fertile technology centres or "hubs" overseas. Very little research gets transferred to development and thereafter manufacturing within the borders of SA. This creates a knowledge transfer gap within the industry technology life cycle [5]. Knowledge transfer can be improved, in and into SA through virtual team collaboration (VTC). The need for better knowledge transfer arises on the level of a larger social system, namely the country. But for this need to become addressed, it needs to become the need of multiple smaller social systems, such as companies or industries, in the larger social systems [8]. With improved adoption of virtual team collaboration, as an innovation, in organisations in SA, it might be possible to bridge this gap in knowledge transfer.

In the remainder of this section, an overview of knowledge transfers aspects, virtual team collaboration and innovation driven organisations are presented.

2.1 Knowledge Transfer

Knowledge can be described as information that has been processed by an individual [9]. Knowledge is either tacit or explicit [10]. Tacit knowledge refers to the concrete know-how and physical skills that one might attain through experience and repetition of certain tasks. It involves parallel processing complexities of current problems at hand, to develop a subjective understanding based on one's own values. In contrast to this, explicit knowledge is objective, discretely recorded knowledge that can be understood in a linear fashion upon consumption [10].

There are six knowledge management processes identified from literature that play an essential role in the transfer of knowledge. *Knowledge discovery and detection*, to recognise and categorise knowledge. *Knowledge organisation and assessment*, to ensure successful identification, retrieval and understanding of knowledge [11]. *Knowledge sharing*, which is an obvious part of knowledge transfer, but which is an incredibly important part and a critical competency any organisation needs to develop [9, 11]. *Knowledge reuse* of created knowledge, needs to be properly managed, since for a lot of companies this also is a source of competitive advantage [12]. *Knowledge creation* is implemented through practice, collaboration, interaction and education [10]. *Knowledge acquisition* meaning knowledge obtained from external sources [13].

Nonaka [10] observed that it is through continuous iterations of communication between individuals that ideas get developed into knowledge. This communication happens in communities of interaction such as work teams. In this study it is proposed that VTC can be used to extend the reach of these communities, by allowing inputs from overseas sources, at the inception stage [8, 14]. At the same time, this deviation from the norm of communication creates challenges to the effective transfer of knowledge.

Knowledge is one of the linchpins of an organisation's competitive advantage and the foundation for a lasting advantage as it cannot be easily transferred or replicated outside the organisation [15]. Knowledge is the justified belief or understanding of information on a subject that is obtained through previous experience and that enables an entity to take more effective action [1, 16]. Individuals form ideas in their heads and according to Nonaka [10] this is exactly where they remain unless validated through social interaction and knowledge transference. This interaction creates shared meaning within an organizational context and shapes the collective interpretation of events [17].

2.2 Virtual Team Collaboration

According to Townsend, Demarie [6, p. 18], virtual teams (VTs) can be defined as "groups of geographically and/or organisationally dispersed co-workers that are assembled using a combination of telecommunications and information technologies to accomplish an organizational task. A slightly more recent definition of virtual teams states that it is a team that functions, through using technology in various degrees to collaborate, across locational, temporal and relational boundaries [18]. Virtual teams rarely, if ever, meet in a face-to-face setting". Although it was found that virtual teams are a more popular topic in research it was decided to differentiate between VTs and VTC, where finding VTC adoption determinants will be the aim of this study. Adding on to the definition of virtual teams, virtual team collaboration is the method of knowledge transfer between VT team members. Virtual team work has a lot of advantages and disadvantages for team members and although virtuality has sometimes been found to impede the performance of teamwork, this is not a unanimous finding as there are ways to mitigate negative effects of virtuality [3]. Mbatha, Ocholla [19] found that the use of information communication technology tools, and it is assumed by association VTC as well, is limited and underdeveloped in African countries. The companies that might need this most are especially the small to medium enterprises (SMEs) who are located in a single location, struggling to expand past certain physical borders [20].

Individual knowledge is legitimized by social interaction [10] it thus stands to reason that knowledge transfer should often occur within a team context. But the way we collaborate in teams can also be altered to include virtuality. Which might increase or decrease the efficiency with which this happens through the necessary tools and structures [2, 17, 21]. Virtual team collaboration is discussed through the dimensions of virtuality, tools and success factors to the effective use of VTC. Larson and Dechurch [22] define virtual collaboration as "remote communication through digital tools". Knowledge collaborations happens through activities between two or more people using a structured platform which enables them to achieve these objectives [1]. Add a dimension of virtuality on to that and you can infer that VTC is the method or design of knowledge transfer inherent in the way these VTs function. VTs are often temporary and only last for a predetermined time, which can have a negative effect on the members of such a team and does not give them a chance to build a shared meaning [17, 23] or social capital [1]. This is why it is proposed to use VTC as a primary mode of KT to improve the possibility of shared meaning building in VTs as they will be constantly in use and virtual social spaces can be structured as a necessary part of these companies [1]. The perceived ability to build shared meaning in temporal teams can possibly affect the adoption of VTC. In addition to this VTs should meet occasionally to improve these social structures, so an organisation's abilities to enable this occasionally over large distances can also determine whether the adoption of VTC will remain in place for an organisation [17, 24].

Among the challenges of using virtual team collaboration or working in virtual teams is the intercultural differences between members if the teams are geographically dispersed [17]. Cultural differences create a lack of shared meaning in a life world level. This means that there are differences in how we automatically interpret information based on previous experiences. Creating this shared meaning based on other levels usually takes effort in any organisation and is easier to do in person [17]. South Africa is in a unique position of great multiculturalism, which means the individuals are better adapted towards cultural differences [25].

2.3 Collaborative Tools

The improvements of collaborative technologies is what has enabled us to move in any instance from traditional face-to-face collaboration to different levels of virtuality over the years [26]. Collaborative technology is an overarching term used to describe tools such as wikis, blogs, podcasts, chat platforms, video conferencing, enterprise social media, messaging or emailing applications and file sharing platforms [22, 26]. And for a team to effectively use these tools, they need a certain level of information communication technology (ICT) competency and efficacy or self-efficacy. This self-efficacy can be a barrier to the adoption of VTC but can also be improved through training in these tools. So sequentially an organisation's perceived ICT training ability can also influence whether they decide to adopt VTC or not [27].

This said, VTC is media dependant, as collaboration in VTC is mediated through technologies, this makes them technology dependant [26, 27]. So a necessary requirement for VTC is some form of groupware technology, giving it the knowledge repositories and functionalities to create shared-objects-of-work amongst participants [17]. This space should allow for articulation of work, construct meaning around objects and agreements around how meanings will be assigned [17]. This technology should enable all the KT processes to be successful. VTC tools serve as a form of group memory enabling the re-use of knowledge by current members or induction of new members into what has been done [26].

The knowledge, skills, abilities and other (KSAO) characteristics of individual team members also influence the performance of a virtual teams [3] and whether members are perceived to have these KSAOs can be assumed to influence the decision to adopt or reject VTC. These KSAOs include for example: knowledge of media transfer, communication skills, willingness to trust others and share knowledge [28], ability to work with people from other cultures and self-, time-, and project management abilities [3].

Collective KSAOs are important in any team, whether virtual or face-to-face and are for example cognitive emergent states of shared mental and transactive memory, affective mental states of cohesion and trust, and behavioural integration processes [22]. One of necessary characteristics to the performance of VTs, whether for individuals or the collective is the ICT efficacy and the training processes around the use of ICT [29]. How easily the technology can be implemented and adapted to the organisational structures also determines whether it will be adopted and used on a continuous basis.

The use of VTC as primary mode of transfer has certain perceived pros to its adoption by an organisation. It gives an organisation access to worldwide markets and can bring together experts and their knowledge regardless of location. It also has pros to the individual within a team like flexible hours and reduced traveling times. It however also has disadvantages to it such as difficulty working with the technology, asynchronous communication in different time zones, new industry and organisational norms need to be established, and cross-cultural challenges across different countries or provinces. Some of the mentioned benefits can also become hindrances where a VT member working from home struggles to draw the line between work and their personal life causing conflict and mistrust in teams [7]. The perceived benefits and disadvantages to the adoption on both an individual and organisational level is believed to influence the adoption decision of VTC [3].

2.4 Innovation Driven Organisations

Van De Ven [30] defines innovation as "the development and implementation of new ideas by people who over time engage in transactions with others within an institutional order". Described differently, innovation relates to the adoption or rejection of an idea that is perceived to be new. For this study, the adoption of VTC as primary mode of knowledge transfer will be studied through companies that is believed to include the idea of continually innovating processes as a part of their competitive strategy. This is because these companies are most likely to have previously adopted or rejected VTC or might plan to do so in the future. An organisation's innovativeness is thus already an antecedent to the adoption of any innovation [8], especially one that has a chance of increasing the interconnectedness of individuals in an organisation, which by itself will perpetuate innovativeness [8, p. 326].

Innovation should ideally also be at the frontend of an organisation's operations, rather than reactive to its environment [10]. Innovativeness is structured and defined by organisational leadership [22]. This consistent and endured innovativeness is an indicator of behavioural change. Where innovation champions for VTC are either opinion leaders within an organisation or part of the decision-making unit, innovation adoption is more likely to happen [8, 31]. Diffusion and adoption of innovation needs to happen within a social system [8, p. 27]. The reasons for studies into innovation is either for marketing reasons or for strategic organisational management reasons [31], and this study aims to study adoption of innovation for both, but through the strategic management view of why an organisation would adopt VTC. It studies the adoption of innovation within an external social system of a country and through a study unit of an organisation.

Among the possible influences on an organisation's innovativeness is leadership and how agile, responsive and transformational it is [22]. Another factor is the organisational culture and willingness to embrace initiatives [32]. How the decision making is done within the organisation can also determine whether or not an innovation will be adopted, in other word how much power is in the hands of a small number of people can possibly negatively or positively affect the adoption of innovations [33]. Complexity of organisations (the level of experience and expertise) has been found to be positively correlated to innovativeness. Formality and interconnectedness within companies has been found to negatively affect the innovativeness of a company. Organisational slack (having more resources than needed) has been found to be positively correlated to innovativeness, along with the organisational size [33]. An organisation that sees itself as entrepreneurial might also be prone to risk taking and it can be proposed that this might also influence its innovativeness [34]. An innovation also needs to fit into the organisational systems as is, without too much adaption [8].

For an organisation to be seen as an innovation driven organisation in this study, it thus has to constantly adopt new processes and exert innovative behaviour over a large period of time [31]. Ruvio, Shoham [35] confirmed 5 constructs that can also be used to measure an organisations innovativeness, and which will also be used along with traditional measure of number of innovations adopted over time. These are: *Creativity*, the focus of an organisation to adopt or creating new ideas. *Organisational openness*, an organisational ability to flexibly respond to new ideas or industry changes. *Future orientation*, which is a temporal measure of how prepared an organisation is for future environmental changes and its positioning in perspective to these changes. *Risk taking,* the measure of how willing managers are to make large risky resource commitments, considering the possible gains or losses relating to these risks. *Pro-activeness,* an indication of a organisations pursuit of business opportunities to overcome inertia. Organisations with higher levels of innovation adopt more [35].

3 Methodology

The purpose of our research is to identify the key determinants organisations may consider in the application of VTC as a mode of knowledge transfer. design science where the research aim is on utility [36]. We followed a design science approach where the research aim is on utility, i.e. key determinants in this instance [37, 38]. In particular, we applied the design science research conceptual framework proposed by Hevner et al. [39] that consists of 3 aspects: environment, knowledge base and research.

Firstly, *environment* refers to people, organisations and technologies defined as business needs through organisational strategies, organisational structures, as well as roles and characteristics of people working within the organisations. Secondly, the *knowledge base* points to the scientific foundations such as frameworks, constructs or models, as well as methodologies such as data analysis techniques and measurement. *Research* is then conducted based on two complementary phases, develop and build, and justify and evaluate, guided by the articulated business need and anchored in applicable knowledge from the knowledge base.

The design artefact, in our study the determinants of the adoption of VTC as a mode of knowledge transfer, contributes in its application to the context where the business need was identified. By applying the proposed framework for information systems research, a research project addresses the utility of a new artefact and presents the evidence in support of the research project outcomes. Hence, the research problem, the artefact and its utility must be presented in such a manner that the implications for both research and practice are clear.

The scientific foundation that guided our study is Rogers' [8] innovation-decision process (IDP) i.e. the process an individual or decision making unit goes through sequentially when making a decision to adopt an innovation or not [8]. The phases of this process include knowledge, persuasion, decision, implementation and confirmation. They are described by Rogers in his book Diffusion of Innovation [8], as:

- **Knowledge.** When the unit learns of the existence of the innovation and seeks to reduce the initial uncertainty about it through outlets such as mass media.
- **Persuasion.** When the unit evaluates the knowledge it gathered to form an opinion on the innovation.
- **Decision.** When the decision to start implementing it takes place and the innovation is groomed for implementation and if possible, it is used on a trial basis.
- **Implementation.** Comes after the decision and trial when the innovation is put into practice, but the user is still uncertain and needs assistance.
- **Confirmation.** When the unit seeks for reinforcement on the efficacy of the innovation and whether it should not discontinue its implantation.

The process is also illustrated along with the generic adoption determinants in Fig. 1.

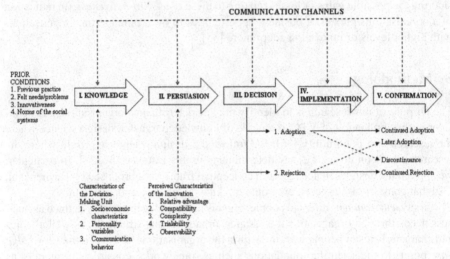

Fig. 1. Rogers's visualisation of the Innovation-Decision Process [8, p. 185]

By applying this Innovation-Decision Process, we consider the key determinants of adopting VTC as knowledge sharing mechanism.

4   Exploring the Key Determinants of Adoption of Virtual Team Collaboration for Knowledge Sharing

In order to directly relate the background knowledge to the adoption of VTC in Innovation Driven Organisations specifically, this paper proposes to view the process through a window of the three domains of research. These domains are the social system within which the adoption takes place, the Innovation Driven Organisation in this case. The management principle of knowledge transfer and finally the innovation, VTC, itself which is adopted from an external environment. Finally, it is also suggested that the adoption of the innovation be viewed through the looking glass of the Innovation-Decision Process. Figure 2 is an illustration of the how these different factors contribute to the determinants to adoption.

Figure 3 shows the proposed mapping between the theory in Sect. 2 of this paper and the DOI model. These are only the primary determinants extracted from the theory and not an exhaustive list.

In Fig. 3 the authors compared the existing literature found in section two and placed the primary determinants from the literature into the different stages of the Innovation-Decision Process as defined in the DOI theory. This was based on the context of the theory and where it was found to be most applicable, starting with prior determinants that affected the decision even before the organisation gathered any knowledge on the innovation and ending with the confirmation stage.

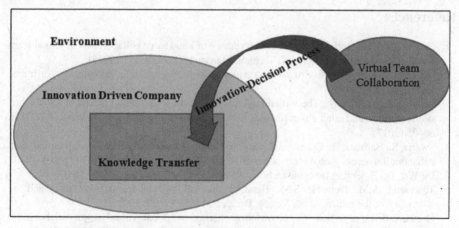

Fig. 2. Proposed interaction between adoption affecting factors (author contribution)

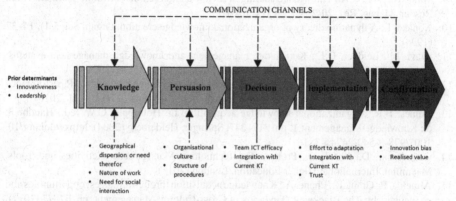

Fig. 3. Proposed DOI mapping for adoption of VTC as KT mode (adapted from Rogers [8, p.185])

5 Conclusion

The paper shows multiple dimensions of factors affecting the adoption of VTC as a primary mode of knowledge transfer. These factors whether implicit or explicit can improve the way future research sees the adoption of this innovation.

By applying the information contained in this paper prospective adopters of VTC can see what to take into account when making their decisions. Companies and governments can promote the adoption of this innovation better than before and developers designing VTC tools can create a better product by taking this information into account.

Further to the research methodology and particular design science framework followed, this paper still lacks the application of industry knowledge through a possible longitudinal or cross-sectional study, which will be the next step to an ideal and practical view of what would determine the adoption of VTC as knowledge sharing mechanism.

References

1. Gao, S., et al.: Factors affecting the performance of knowledge collaboration in virtual team based on capital appreciation. Inf. Technol. Manag. **17**(2), 119–131 (2015)
2. Hacker, J.V., et al.: Trust in virtual teams: a multidisciplinary review and integration. Australas. J. Inf. Syst. **23** (2019)
3. Schulze, J., Krumm, S.: The virtual team player: a review and initial model of knowledge, skills, abilities, and other characteristics for virtual collaboration. Organ. Psychol. Rev. **7**(1), 66–95 (2017)
4. Swartz, S., Barbosa, B., Crawford, I.: Building intercultural competence through virtual team collaboration across global classrooms. Bus. Prof. Commun. Q. **83**(1), 57–79 (2020)
5. De Wet, G.: Emerging from the technology colony: a view from the South (2010)
6. Townsend, A.M., Demarie, S.M., Hendrickson, A.R.: Virtual teams: technology and the workplace of the future. Acad. Manag. Perspect. **12**(3), 17–29 (1998)
7. Horwitz, S.K., Santillan, C.: Knowledge sharing in global virtual team collaboration: applications of CE and thinkLets. Knowl. Manag. Res. Pract. **10**(4), 342–353 (2012)
8. Rogers, E.M.: Diffusion of Innovations. Simon and Schuster, New York (2010)
9. Wang, S., Noe, R.A.: Knowledge sharing: a review and directions for future research. Hum. Resour. Manag. Rev. **20**(2), 115–131 (2010)
10. Nonaka, I.: A dynamic theory of organizational knowledge creation. Organ. Sci. **5**(1), 14–37 (1994)
11. Alavi, M., Leidner, D.E.: Knowledge management and knowledge management systems: conceptual foundations and research issues. MIS Q. **25**(1), 107–136 (2001)
12. Forsgren, N., Sabherwal, R., Durcikova, A.: Knowledge exchange roles and EKR performance impact: extending the theory of knowledge reuse. Eur. J. Inf. Syst. **27**(1), 3–21 (2018)
13. Gaines, B.R.: Organizational knowledge acquisition. In: Holsapple, C.W. (ed.) Handbook on Knowledge Management 1, pp. 317–347. Springer, Heidelberg (2004). https://doi.org/10.1007/978-3-540-24746-3_16
14. Cetindamar, D., Phaal, R., Probert, D.: Technology Management: Activities and Tools. Macmillan International Higher Education, London (2016)
15. Almeida, P., Grant, R., Phene, A.: Knowledge acquisition through alliances: opportunities and challenges. In: The Blackwell Handbook of Cross-Cultural Management, pp. 67–77 (2017)
16. Chhim, P.P., Somers, T.M., Chinnam, R.B.: Knowledge reuse through electronic knowledge repositories: a multi theoretical study. J. Knowl. Manag. **21**(4), 741–764 (2017)
17. Bjørn, P., Ngwenyama, O.: Virtual team collaboration: building shared meaning, resolving breakdowns and creating translucence. Inf. Syst. J. **19**(3), 227–253 (2009)
18. Martins, L.L., Gilson, L.L., Maynard, M.T.: Virtual teams: what do we know and where do we go from here? J. Manag. **30**(6), 805–835 (2004)
19. Mbatha, B.T., Ocholla, D.N., Roux, J.L.: Diffusion and adoption of ICTs in selected government departments in KwaZulu-Natal, South Africa. Inf. Dev. **27**(4), 251–263 (2011)
20. Tesar, G., Vincze, Z.: Motivating SMEs to Cooperate and Internationalize: A Dynamic Perspective. Routledge, New York (2017)
21. Gibson, C.B., Cohen, S.G.: Virtual Teams that Work: Creating Conditions for Virtual Team Effectiveness. Wiley, San Francisco (2003)
22. Larson, L., Dechurch, L.A.: Leading teams in the digital age: four perspectives on technology and what they mean for leading teams. Leadersh. Q. **31**(1), 101377 (2020)
23. Chamakiotis, P., et al.: The role of temporal coordination for the fuzzy front-end of innovation in virtual teams. Int. J. Inf. Manag. **50**, 182–190 (2020)
24. Baker, J.: The technology–organization–environment framework. In: Dwivedi, Y.K., Wade, M.R., Schneberger, S.L. (eds.) Information Systems Theory, pp. 231–245. Springer, New York (2012). https://doi.org/10.1007/978-1-4419-6108-2_12

25. Singh, P., Rampersad, R.: Communication challenges in a multicultural learning environment. J. Intercult. Commun. **23**, 1404–1634 (2010)
26. Raghupathi, V.: Changes in virtual team collaboration with modern collaboration tools. i-Manager's J. Inf. Technol. **5**(2), 5–13 (2016)
27. Majchrzak, A., et al.: Technology adaptation: the case of a computer-supported inter-organizational virtual team. MIS Q. **24**(4), 569–600 (2000)
28. Alsharo, M., Gregg, D., Ramirez, R.: Virtual team effectiveness: the role of knowledge sharing and trust. Inf. Manag. **54**(4), 479–490 (2017)
29. Lin, C.-P., Chiu, C.-K., Liu, N.-T.: Developing virtual team performance: an integrated perspective of social exchange and social cognitive theories. RMS **13**(4), 671–688 (2017). https://doi.org/10.1007/s11846-017-0261-0
30. Van De Ven, A.H.: Central problems in the management of innovation. Manag. Sci. **32**(5), 590–607 (1986)
31. Subramanian, A., Nilakanta, S.: Organizational innovativeness: exploring the relationship between organizational determinants of innovation, types of innovations, and measures of organizational performance. Omega **24**(6), 631–647 (1996)
32. Fuller, M.A., Hardin, A.M., Scott, C.L.: Diffusion of virtual innovation. ACM SIGMIS Database **38**(4), 40 (2007)
33. Lundblad, J.P.: A review and critique of Rogers' diffusion of innovation theory as it applies to organizations. Organ. Dev. J. **21**(4), 50 (2003)
34. Gabriel, M.L.D.D.S., Da Silva, D.: Diffusion and adoption of technology amongst engineering and business management students. Int. J. Innov. **5**(1), 20–31 (2017)
35. Ruvio, A.A., et al.: Organizational innovativeness: construct development and cross-cultural validation. J. Prod. Innov. Manag. **31**(5), 1004–1022 (2014)
36. Venable, J., Pries-Heje, J., Baskerville, R.: FEDS: a framework for evaluation in design science research. Eur. J. Inf. Syst. **25**, 77–89 (2016)
37. Kuechler, B., Vaishnavi, V.: A framework for theory development in design science research: multiple perspectives. J. Assoc. Inf. Syst. **13**(6), 395–423 (2012)
38. van der Merwe, A., Gerber, A., Smuts, H.: Guidelines for conducting design science research in information systems. In: Tait, B., Kroeze, J., Gruner, S. (eds.) SACLA 2019. CCIS, vol. 1136, pp. 163–178. Springer, Cham (2020). https://doi.org/10.1007/978-3-030-35629-3_11
39. Vaishnavi, V., Kuechler, B.: Design research in information systems (2004). http://desrist.org/design-research-in-information-systems/

An Indoor Farming Framework for Decision Support Towards Food Security in Society 5.0

Amoré van Zyl⊙ and Hanlie Smuts(✉)⊙

Department of Informatics, University of Pretoria, Pretoria, South Africa
hanlie.smuts@up.ac.za

Abstract. One of the key aspects outlined in the Sustainable Development Goals (SDGs), is food security. The discourse around food security recognizes that resources such as water and land are finite, and the agenda to end hunger remains a major challenge. Furthermore, the objective of Society 5.0, to integrate digital technologies and a human-centered society to foster economic advancement and the resolution of social problems, augmented the reasons to address food security. Therefore, the purpose of this paper is to consider indoor farming as an agricultural technology capable of producing more food using fewer resources, as opposed to traditional farming, that is enabled through targeted capital investments. We developed an Integrated Farming Framework (IFF) with the aim to provide decision support to guide potential investors in indoor farming. Ten key aspects were identified and mapped to the Technology-Organization-Environment (TOE) framework, identifying a fourth construct, societal context. These constructs include the basic elements required for investors to consider financing in indoor farming projects. By applying the IFF, investors will be able to consider their investment options holistically.

Keywords: Society 5.0 · Sustainable development goals · Food security · Human-centered society · Indoor farming · Investment · Decision support

1 Introduction

In 2020, the impact of the COVID-19 pandemic resulted in a significant increase in the number of people experiencing chronic hunger, adding up to 132 million to the already 690 million people ($\approx$8.9% of global population) experiencing malnutrition and hunger globally [1]. This brings the achievability of eradicating hunger by 2030 as per the SDGs into question, calling for bolder actions on a global scale [2, 3]. The 2020 report on the *State of Food Security and Nutrition in the World* raises the need for modern and innovative approaches to address the growing social challenges in sustainable manners [1].

By seeking to employ technology in a more human-centered manner towards addressing social challenges, Japan's Government introduced Society 5.0 in 2016 as part of their growth strategy [4, 5]. The concept of Society 5.0 builds on the Information Society (Society 4.0) and promotes the development of information networks to create value, by centering the use of technology and the digital transformation around advancing a human-centered society [5]. At the core of Society 5.0 lies the use of innovation and the technological advancements from Industry 4.0, such as artificial intelligence (AI), robotics and big data, to address social challenges including challenges addressed by the SDGs [5]. One of the seventeen (17) SDGs, number two (2), aims to zero hunger by achieving food security and improving nutrition through several global intervention actions, including the promotion of sustainable agriculture [6–8]. As it is the goal of Society 5.0 to enhance society through a close collaboration with technology (i.e. AI and autonomous systems), it is necessary to determine the holistic impact Society 5.0 may have on chronic social problems such as hunger.

This paper aims to contribute to the body of knowledge of Society 5.0 within the context of SDGs by considering the following research question: *"How can an Indoor Farming Framework (IFF) be applied towards decision support for food security in Society 5.0"*. Through the systematic review of available Society 5.0 and indoor farming literature, the paper proposes an IFF aimed at providing potential investors with key consideration for investing in indoor farming with the objective of addressing food insecurity.

In the next section (Sect. 2), an overview of the literature is provided, followed by the research approach in Sect. 3. The data analysis and findings are presented in Sect. 4, with Sect. 5 proving the research contribution of an IFF. Finally, the paper is concluded in Sect. 6.

2 Background

Food insecurity, unlike Society 5.0, is not a novel idea. In 1798, Thomas Malthus predicted food production will be superseded by population growth and reiterated his hypothesis in 1826 stating that *"population has this constant tendency to increase beyond the means of subsistence"* [9, 10:14]. Although the definition of food (in)security has evolved over the last century, hunger remains a persistent social challenge globally [1, 7]. The paper aims to determine to what extent the Society 5.0 approach can be applied in finding solutions for global food insecurity in a sustainable manner. Sect. 2 provides an overview of Society 5.0 and food security, followed by an introduction into indoor faming, and information system frameworks capable of providing decision support to potential investors in the agricultural sphere.

2.1 Overview of Society 5.0

Society 5.0 principles aim to resolve modern social challenges by merging the real world with the virtual world in a manner where humans or society remain at the center [5]. Following the Information Society (Society 4.0), where technology advances have been extensive, Society 5.0 intends to guide the mobilization of innovation and technology to ensure a sustainable future, balancing economic and social advancement [5, 11]. This human-centered approach allows for additional value creation in products and services by addressing gaps and social problems through the connection of technologies and the physical space in a sustainable manner. This goal aligns with the United Nation's SDGs to promote action towards a sustainable future for all [12]. AI, big data, the internet of things (IoT), and robotics are some of the technologies utilized to create social value and address digital divides [13].

On the other hand, the challenges of implementing such lofty goals include ethical concerns, for instance privacy and security in both the physical and digital space, and barriers to technological adoption [5]. In addition, a super-smart society (Society 5.0) requires an extensive level of technological transformation that will allow for tackling of social challenges [3, 13]. Where diversity, social inclusion, cultural balance, innovation, and global perception promote acceptance of technology through positive experiences [14]. To address these challenges, a conscious and purposeful process is required to create a sustainable future through societal evolution.

2.2 Overview of Food Security

Napoli [15] and Kruzslicika [7] provide a thorough background of the evolution of food security and its definition, highlighting the core aspects associated with food security with the progression of time [7, 15]. Although food security is a difficult concept to define and measure, the Food and Agriculture Organization (FAO) defines food insecurity as *"A situation that exist when people lack secure access to sufficient amounts of safe and nutritious food for normal growth and development and an active and healthy life"*, opposed to food security defined as *"when all people, at all times, have physical and economic access to sufficient, safe and nutritious food which meets their dietary needs and food preference for an active and healthy life"* [15:7–9, 16, 17]. Subsequently, food security considers more than just the **availability** of food, it requires a holistic improvement to the entire food value chain, including **stability, accessibility,** and **affordability** as well as the safety and nutritional value of produced food and how it is **utilized** [15, 16].

To mitigate the significant impact of the COVID-19 pandemic on the agriculture and food sector, the FAO is imploring swift global action [2, 6]. The FAO has provided several policies and strategies to establish resilient food systems in areas where food insecurity persists. One of these strategies, the Twin-Track Approach, aims to address the key areas of food insecurity by combining rural development with sustainable agriculture [16, 18]. By fostering sustainable agriculture, social and environmental sustainability can be promoted alongside economic growth. Therefore, sustainable agriculture has the potential to mitigate environmental, social, and economic challenges [19, 20]. In support of this, Kruzslicika [7] also highlights the important role sustainable agriculture and the responsible use of resources play in working towards food security [7]. However, to establish sustainable agriculture and promote rural development, funding and support is required, especially in low-income regions [18, 21]. As the world population continuous to grow and consumption patterns shift, the demand for food increases, adding to the increasing resources requirement that put agricultural systems under great pressure [22]. The increase in resource requirements alone, escalates the food crises further, as food production and distribution are further burdened [22]. Considering the plight of Society 5.0 to address social challenges, one innovative approach to producing food with minimum resource requirements, whilst minimizing natural interferences (i.e. rainfall and sunlight), is found to be Controlled Environment Agriculture (CEA), otherwise known as indoor farming [23–27].

2.3 Indoor Farming

Constraints on natural resources, such as water, requires agricultural practices to find sustainable avenues of producing more food with less resources to play its role in addressing food security [20]. It is the objective of sustainable agriculture to conserve and protect resources while meeting the social needs and not compromise the ability to produce adequately for future agricultural needs [7, 8, 20]. The application of indoor farming technology has evolved significantly in recent years, providing farmers with the ability to produce crops with minimum resources and space, while simultaneously reducing the use of harmful pesticides and fertilizers [23, 24]. In addition, indoor farming complements already established urban and rural farming systems using technologies such as IoT and AI [23, 24, 28].

There are several types of indoor agriculture, ranging from tunnel farming that requires minimum technological input to highly autonomized and controlled systems such as container farming [23, 24, 28–31]. The growing environment (i.e. vertical farms) and growing methods (i.e. hydroponics) require varying levels of technologies [28, 29]. A CEA approach to indoor food productions allows for the utilisation of technology to optimise growing conditions for crops and extend growing season [26, 27, 32]. These enclosed structures provide farmers with the option to control variables such as humidity, temperature and nutrient solutions through the utilisation of a variety of technology and information systems [26, 31, 32]. Although this form of sustainable indoor farming is resilient to various climate conditions, there is still a risks and costs that must be accounted for during the development and design of these projects [23]. As a result of the high start-up cost of indoor farming initiatives, exposure to the market is limited [23]. However, indoor farming may serve to address high operating cost such as fertilisers, transport and water [26]. Regardles of the initial cost associated with indoor farming, Sulser et al. [33] emphasised that investment in agricultural sphere is essential to achieve results in reducing food insecurity [33]. Furthermore, Antornaras and Kostopoulos [8] highlights the crucial role private investors play in the development and implementation of practical and scalable sustainable agricultural solutions addressing social challenges such as food insecurity [8, 23]. To guide investors in the process of investing in the diffusion of farming technology, decision support frameworks can be used as described in the next section.

2.4 Decision Support Frameworks

Petry et al. [34] notes that innovation, usually associated with the contribution of new resources and knowledge, in the agricultural sphere typically relates to the increase in production, crop quality and improved production processes [34]. When considering the principles of Society 5.0, technology must be diffused within the social system through a process of information flow to advance the spread and acceptance of technology [13]. Where a decision support framework is an information system solution to support problem solving and complex decision making [27, 35, 36]. Tornatzky and Fleischer's Technology-Organisation-Environment (TOE) framework is one such information system model that facilitates the adoption of innovation [37]. The framework consists of three constructs that consider what may influences the process of technology adoption in organisations [37, 38]. Where the technology contexts considers the available technology for adoption as well as what is already established within the organisation [38]. Secondly, the organisational context considers the organizational structure, size and communication processes [36]. The final construct, environment, looks at elements such as market structures, infrastructure and external support, including governmental regulations [38].

Although TOE frameworks have been used in other sectors to develop a decision support system that looks at the adoption of sustainability initiatives throughout the value chain and the systems lifecycle, there is little reference to the application of the diffusion framework applied in the agriculture sphere found in literature [38, 39]. The framework considers the technological, organizational, and environmental context wherein the system lies and highlights decision factors for the adoption of specific technologies within the sector. It should be noted that the adoption of innovation and knowledge transfer in the agricultural sphere is influenced by several factors [40]. Diederen et al. [40] also note that market position and access to information is one of the contributing factors to the adoption of innovation [40].

3   Research Approach

The goal of this paper is to provide potential investors with a decision support framework for investing in indoor farming with the objective of addressing food insecurity. To establish this decision support framework that supports investors in the agricultural sphere, a systematic literature review (SLR) is used to identify the key considerations or themes for investing in indoor farming. Where a SLR identifies, evaluates and synthesizes the existing body of knowledge produced by practitioners, researchers, and scholars to answer the stated research question [41]. The SLR follows a clearly defined replicable protocol to conduct a comprehensive search over various databases and grey literature (i.e. technical reports) [41, 42]. Strings of keywords were used to search specific and inclusive peer-reviewed literature published in various approved academic databases as well as to search for grey data published in technical reports found using the Google search engine. Keywords and phrases included "Society 5.0", "food (in)security", "SDG", "sustainable agriculture", "indoor agriculture and farming", "investing in indoor farming", and "innovation and technology diffusion", as well as derivatives thereof. Strings of keywords were also used to refine and focus the literature search, although predominantly sources from 2016 onwards were included, as this was the year when Society 5.0 was introduced. However, older literature is also included to address long standing social challenges and agricultural practices. The total number of articles and technical reports that match the key terms are indicated in Fig. 1.

Although the initial search identified 824 papers and reports, a screening process was applied to refine the search against specific criteria. Papers and reports were excluded if they were found to be duplicates, non-English publications, not relevant to the research question or were unobtainable. After the application of the initial screening process, 174 papers and reports were selected. The detailed screening process of the prospective papers found that 153 documents were excluded based on exclusion criteria such as unrelated context and studies not addressing the research question. During further iterations of framework development, three (3) sources were additionally included in the final SLR.

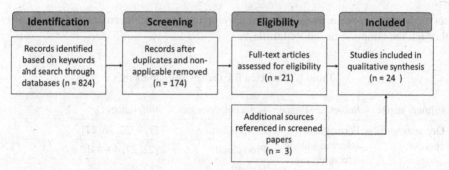

Fig. 1. The number of reports and papers found on databases and grey-literature sources

4 Data Analysis and Findings

The paper aims to develop a conceptual framework that will provide potential investors with key considerations for investing in indoor farming to sustainably address food insecurity. Key considerations have been grouped using a process of thematic analysis as shown in Table 1 [43]. The first column indicates the primary themes as context elements, while the second column indicates the secondary theme as mapped from the TOE framework. The third column provides key considerations, and the final column indicates the applicable references.

Themes were identified by considering the Tornatzky and Fleischer's TOE framework structure as a baseline. However, several themes derived from the SLR could not be mapped according to the TOE framework. These themes address the social challenges associated with food insecurity and were included through the addition of a new primary theme, social context (shaded grey).

The first primary themes emerging from the SLR relates to the *organizational context* of indoor farming. Within the organizational context, consideration is given to secondary themes that link the indoor farming value chain, both formally and informally, as well as the organizational size, communication processes and logistical elements. Where elements to consider before investing in any agricultural sector include a range of interlinking components that stretch from preproduction to the point of sale of the food produced indoor. Secondly, the *environmental context* serves as the second primary theme where the industry's characteristics, legal regulations and practices, as well as technological infrastructure are considered. These considerations, both physical and human related, play a significant role in the feasibility of indoor farming investment. The third primary theme is identified as the *technological context*, that emphasizes the influence of innovation diffusion and the availability of technological features on the successful adoption of indoor farming. Considerations include the availability of technology and the organizational characteristics such as the organizational ideals, resources, and investment budget. In addition to the traditional structure of a TOE framework, the shortfall of social construct consideration is included to produce an extended IFF framework to address the final primary theme. Furthermore, the extension of the framework allows for the alignment with SDGs and Society 5.0 principles. Hence, the *social context* serves to address the aspects of social development and achievement of food security through the adoption of indoor farming.

Table 1. Extracted IFF themes and sub-themes

Primary theme	Secondary theme	Key considerations	References
Organizational context	Formal and informal linking structure	Pre-production	[7, 8, 22, 26, 27]
		Production	[22, 27, 40, 44]
		Harvest	[22, 27]
		Processing	[22, 27, 40, 44]
		Distribution, packaging & handling	[22, 23, 27, 40]
		Point of sale	[22, 26, 27]
		Disposal/End of life	[27]
	Communication processes	Regulations & Government	[8, 23, 40, 45]
		Associations	[8, 31]
		Community	[8, 26, 40]
		Business development	[8, 27, 33, 40]
		Suppliers & Service providers	[8, 27, 33]
		Target market	[26, 33, 40]
	Size	Farm size	[26, 40]
		Location/Climate	[8, 23, 26, 27, 31, 32]
		Labor requirement	[23, 26]
		Harvest size	[26]
		Investment cost	[8, 23, 26, 27, 31, 33]
Environmental context	Industrial characteristics and market structure	Consumer	[23, 26]
		Market structure	[26, 27]
		Competitors	[26]
		Suppliers & Service providers	[8]
		Investors & Stakeholders	[8, 26, 27, 40]

(continued)

Table 1. (*continued*)

Primary theme	Secondary theme	Key considerations	References
	Technology support infrastructure	Crop technology	[3, 8, 26, 27]
		Level of farming technology	[23, 26, 27, 31, 32, 40]
		ICT & IS	[3, 14, 26, 32, 44]
		Skill development & training	[8, 23, 26]
		Data management	[3, 14, 27, 32, 44]
		Maintenance & Upgrades	[26, 31]
	Government and international standards and regulations	Quality assurance	[27, 31]
		Food Safety	[26]
		Health & Safety	[8]
		Community relations	[8, 26, 40]
		Technology	[40]
		Inputs (i.e. Seeds, fertilizer, etc.)	[7]
		Water, Energy & Waste Management	[7, 23, 27, 32]
		Site & Facility management	[26, 45]
		Financial & Business management	[26]
		Certification	[8, 23, 45]
Technological context	Availability	Inputs (i.e. Seeds, fertilizer, etc.)	[3, 8, 26, 27, 46]
		Indoor farming structures & material	[23, 26, 40]
		Farming technology	[3, 23, 26, 27, 46]
		Information systems	[3, 14, 26, 27]
	Characteristics of the organization	Resources	[26, 40]
		Budget (time/cost)	[27, 32, 40, 46]
		Ideals	[26, 27, 40]
		Production goals	[8, 46]
		Skilled labor	[8, 23, 40]

(*continued*)

Table 1. (*continued*)

Primary theme	Secondary theme	Key considerations	References
Societal context	Social development	Heritage/Culture	[26]
		Tenure	[26]
		Women development	[7, 47]
		Education	[7, 8, 26, 40]
		Extension services	[7, 32]
		Self-reliance	[7, 8, 26, 46, 47]
	Food security	Access	[1, 7, 16–18, 23, 26, 31, 32, 48]
		Availability	[1, 7, 16–18, 26, 33, 48]
		Utilization	[1, 7, 8, 16–18, 44, 48]
		Stability	[1, 2, 7, 16–18, 44, 48]
		Sustainability	[5–8, 23, 26, 27, 46]

Ten secondary themes were mapped to create the four primary themes namely organizational context, environmental context, technological context and the societal context. In the next section we discuss the primary and secondary themes and how it contributes to proposing an IFF in more detail.

5   A Conceptual IFF Model

From the analysis in Table 1, combining the themes from literature and by mapping the key considerations to TOE, the existing TOE framework has been enriched to create an IFF. This IFF model aims to provide potential impact investors with key considerations for investing in sustainable indoor farming.

The conceptual IFF in Fig. 2 derived from the raw data in Sect. 4 is created across the four constructs, namely technology, organization, environment, and social context. Despite the arrangement of the TOE framework structure around the adoption of technology, the organizational context provide the base around which the remaining constructs are centered. The *organizational context* observes the characteristics of the farm, considering the structure, scope, and size as well as the communication processes. These considerations provide potential farmers with a set of key considerations that guide the decision-making process for investing in indoor farming technology. Themes identified in Sect. 4 were aligned with the skeleton structure of the TOE framework, highlighting variables potential investors need to take into account prior to investing in an indoor farm. When considering the informal and formal links in an organization (the farm), attention should be given to the complete life cycle of the indoor farm, from preproduction elements that include the preparation of facilities, information systems, pesticides and seeds, up to the logistics and management associated with marketing and the sale of produced food. Furthermore, the market players that serve to support the core farming activities include the government, employees, nonprofit organizations (NPO), associations and business membership which need to be established. Also, investors need to consider the available support network as well as the size of the farm. As the size of the organization refers to more than the farm size, consideration must be given to the location, harvest size, investment cost, and required workforce.

The *environment context* does not only consider the market structure and industrial characteristics but also the technology support infrastructure and associated regulations and standards underlining the production of food. Investors are to consider the distance to consumers, competitors' operations and products, market structure, and suppliers as well as stakeholders in the indoor farm. The infrastructure for supporting technology is another essential consideration that emphasizes the necessity of understanding how effectively various forms of technology can be used to support food production. Crop technology (i.e. increased nutrient content), information systems, training, data management and maintenance are some of the considerations associated with the environmental technology support infrastructure. Finally, the organizational environment needs to look at the underlying regulations, standards and governmental objectives addressing food safety, community relations (i.e. labor laws), health and safety, facility and site management, production input (i.e. seeds and fertilizers), water and electricity use, financial management and farming certification.

Conversely, the *technological context* considers the availability of the technology to be adopted as well as the organizational characteristics. For indoor farming to be diffused in the traditional agricultural space, the availability of suitable inputs (i.e. seeds, nutrients and growth mediums), indoor farming structures and materials, farming technologies and information systems need to be considered. The investor is encouraged to align these considerations with the characteristics of the organization itself, looking at the resources, budget, ideals, production goals and the availability of skilled labor, including the farmer.

The IFF model strives to provide potential investors with a complete range of considerations for the adoption of indoor farming as a potential solution to sustainably addressing food insecurity through impact investment. Hence, consideration is given to social aspects not addressed in traditional TOE frameworks. The *social context* is concerned with two main themes, social development and food security. Where social development addresses factor such as tenure, education, extension services, women upliftment, as well as heritage and culture protection to promote self-reliance. On the other hand, the food security theme emphasizes the four pillars of food security (access, availability, utilization, and stability) and the sustainability thereof. *Access* does not solely refer to access to food but, also access to markets, assets, labor, guarantees and institutions, while *availability* considers the land, production, and market investments available to the investors and the community. When considering the *utilization* of food, the knowledge of nutrition, food preparation, food safety and storage processes are essential to effectively address food security challenges by ensuring that available food is nutritionally sufficient. The final pillar, *stability*, requires the investor to look at diversifying crops and labor, risk management, security and safety as well as promoting peaceful relations among governance and communities. All these factors need to be considered with sustainability in mind, to ensure social and economic challenges are addressed for the future by supporting the environment.

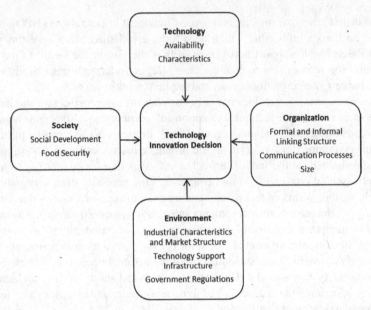

Fig. 2. Conceptual indoor farming framework for decision support towards food security.

6 Conclusion

Although the international community have committed to the agenda set out by the SDGs to end hunger, food insecurity remains a major challenge. With the human-centered nature of Society 5.0 and the objective to achieve sustainable food security, effective targeted investments in agriculture are required. Indoor farming is an agricultural technology capable of producing more food using fewer resources in comparison to traditional farming methods. The purpose of this paper is to present a conceptual framework that will provide decision support towards improving food security. This proposed IFF contains four main constructs derived from a two-step process of SLR and thematic analysis. These constructs include the basic elements from the TOE framework with an extended primary construct that considers the social context of investing in indoor farming for addressing food insecurity. The primary constructs include technology, environment, organization, and social context with underlying key considerations. By applying the IFF, investors will be able to consider a broad range of holistic elements associated with indoor farming investment to mitigate the risk of incurring unplanned expenditure, legal restraints, operational and technological restrictions, as well as social and cultural problems. Furthermore, investors using the IFF as a decision support tool will be required to consider far reaching impacts prior to investing capital to ensure a successful operational indoor farm capable of supporting food security goals.

This extended framework serves as a conceptual model that can be validated through further research to align the framework model with real-world scenarios.

References

1. FAO: The state of food security and nutrition in the world 2020 (2020)
2. Nguyen, K.: 2020 State of Food Security and Nutrition in the World Report: Rising Hunger and COVID-19 Present Formidable Challenges (2020)
3. Charania, I., Li, X.: Smart farming: agriculture's shift from a labor intensive to technology native industry. Internet of Things **9**, 100142 (2020)
4. Gladden, M.E.: Who will be the members of society 5.0? Towards an anthropology of technologically posthumanized future societies. Soc. Sci. **8**(148), 1–39 (2019)
5. Fukuyama, M.: Society 5.0: Aiming for a New Human-Centered Society **2**, 47–50 (2018)
6. Chishala, B.H., Mofya-Mukuka, R., Chabala, L.M., Kuntashula, E.: Zero hunger. In: Gill, J.C., Smith, M. (eds.) Geosciences and the Sustainable Development Goals. SDGS, pp. 31–51. Springer, Cham (2021). https://doi.org/10.1007/978-3-030-38815-7_2
7. Kruzslicika, M.: Food security through sustainable agriculture. Agric. Econ. Rural Dev. **11**, 195–202 (2014)
8. Antonaras, A., Kostopoulos, A.: Stakeholder agriculture: innovation from farm to Store, pp. 125–147 (2017)
9. Maisonet-Guzman, O.E.: Food security and population growth in the 21st century. E-Int. Relat. **18**, 1–10 (2011)
10. Malthus, T.R.: An Essay on the Principles of Population, J. Johnson, London (1826)
11. Guarda, D.: Society 5.0: What Is It & How to Achieve a Human-Centered Society, Intelligent HQ, Tunbridge Wells
12. United-Nations: Transforming Our World: the 2030 Agenda for Sustainable Development.
13. SAP: Society 5.0: Overcoming Societal Challenges and Co-creating the Future Through Digitalisation and Unity in Diversity. Breda University, Germany (2020)
14. Shiroishi, Y., Uchiyama, K., Suzuki, N.: Society 5.0: for human security and well-being. Computer **51**, 91–95 (2018)
15. Napoli, M., Muro, P., Mazziotta, M.: Towards a Food Insecurity Multidimensional Index (FIMI) (2011)
16. FAO: Food Security. FAO Agriculture and Development Economics Division, Rome (2006)
17. FAO: Declaration on World Food Security and World Food Summit Plan of Action. World Food Summit, Rome (1996)
18. FAO: Reducing poverty and hunger: the critical role of financing for food, agriculture and rural development. In: International Conference on Financing for Development, Mexico (2002)
19. Umesha, S., Manukumar, H.M., Chandrasekhar, B.: Sustainable Agriculture and Food Security (2018)
20. Cambay, S., Singh, C.: Biofortification: A Sustainable Strategy for Enhancing Grain Micronutrients, in Sustainable Agriculture for Food Security Concepts and Approaches, pp. 151–168 (2017)
21. Kadiresan, K.: Ending global hunger need not cost the earth – if we invest now (2020)
22. Deloitte: The food value chain: a challenge for the next century (2015)
23. Qiu, J., Bayabil, H.K., Li, Y.: Indoor Vertical Farming Systems for Food Security and Resource Sustainability, in School of Forest Resources and Conservation. EDIS, University of Florida, Gainesville (2020)
24. Dempsey, P.: A high-yield indoor farming system ideal for the city, in Farmer's Weekly (2020)
25. Avgoustaki, D., Xydis, G.: Indoor vertical farming in the urban nexus context: business growth and resource savings. Sustainability **12**, 1965 (2020)
26. Benke, K., Tomkins, B.: Future food-production systems: vertical farming and controlled-environment agriculture. Sustain. Sci. Pract. Policy **13**(1), 13–26 (2017)

27. Li, L., et al.: A decision support framework for the design and operation of sustainable urban farming systems. J. Clean. Prod. **268**, 121928 (2020)
28. Kateman, B.: Is the future of farming indoors? Forbes (2020)
29. Stein, E.: What Is Indoor Farming? Center of Excellence for Indoor Farming (2020)
30. GreenAgri: Controlled Environment Agriculture. Western Cape Government - Agriculture
31. McCartney, L., Lefsrud, M.G.: Protected agriculture in extreme environments: a review of controlled environment agriculture in tropical, arid, polar and urban locations. Appl. Eng. Agric. **34**(2), 455–473 (2018)
32. Shamshiri, R., et al.: Advances in greenhouse automation and controlled environment agriculture: A transition to plant factories and urban agriculture. Int. J. Agric. Biol. Eng. **11**(1), 1–22 (2018)
33. Mason-D'Croz, D., et al.: Agricultural investments and hunger in Africa modeling potential contributions to SDG2 – Zero Hunger. World Dev. **116**, 38–53 (2019)
34. Petry, J.F., et al.: Innovation and the diffusion of technology in agriculture in floodplains in the State of Amazonas. J. Contem. Admin. **23**(5), 619–635 (2019)
35. Dulčić, Ž, Pavlic, D., Silic, I.: Evaluating the intended use of decision support system (DSS) by applying technology acceptance model (TAM) in business organizations in Croatia. Procedia. Soc. Behav. Sci. **58**, 1565–1575 (2012)
36. Poit-Lepetit, I., Florez, M., Gauche, K.: Understanding the determinants of IT adoption in agriculture using an integrated TAM-TOE model: a bibliometric analysis. In: EAAE Seminar: Governance of Food Chains and Consumption Dynamics: What Are the Impacts on Food Security and Sustainability? France (2019)
37. Awa, H.O., Ukoha, O., Emecheta, B.C.: Using T-O-E theoretical framework to study the adoption of ERP solution. Cogent Bus. Manag. **3**(1), 1196571 (2016)
38. Tsetse, A.: Barriers to government cloud adoption. Int. J. Manag. Inf. Technol. **6** (2014)
39. Hwang, B.-N., Huang, C., Wu, C.H.: A TOE approach to establish a green supply chain adoption decision model in the semiconductor industry. Sustainability **8**, 168 (2016)
40. Diederen, P., van Meijl, H., Wolters, A.: Modernisation in Agriculture: What Makes a Farmer Adopt an Innovation? (2003)
41. Gough, D., et al.: An Introduction to Systematic Reviews. Systematic Reviews. SAGE, London (2012)
42. Piper, R.J.: How to write a systematic literature review: a guide for medical students. University of Edinburgh (2013)
43. Fugard, A., Potts, H.W.W.: Thematic analysis. In: Atkinson, P., et al. (eds.) Qualitative Analysis, SAGE Publishing, London (2019)
44. Kabir, A.Z.M.T., et al.: IoT based low cost smart indoor farming management system using an assistant robot and mobile app. In: 2020 10th Electrical Power, Electronics, Communications, Controls and Informatics Seminar (EECCIS) (2020)
45. Diehl, J.A., et al.: Feeding cities: Singapore's approach to land use planning for urban agriculture. Glob. Food Secur. **26**, 100377 (2010)
46. Mok, W.K., Tan, Y.X., Chen, W.N.: Technology innovations for food security in Singapore: a case study of future food systems for an increasingly natural resource-scarce world. Trends Food Sci. Technol. **102**, 155–168 (2020)
47. Agarwal, B.: Gender equality, food security and the sustainable development goals. Curr. Opin. Environ. Sustain. **34**, 26–32 (2018)
48. FAO: Fighting poverty and hunger. In: What Role for Urban Agriculture (2010)

Does Board Composition Taking Account of Sustainability Expertise Influence ESG Ratings? An Exploratory Study of European Banks

Silke Waterstraat[1]([⊠]) [iD], Clemens Kustner[1], and Maximilian Koch[2]

[1] University of Applied Sciences Northwestern Switzerland, Basel, Switzerland
silke.waterstraat@fhnw.ch
[2] University of Applied Sciences Northwestern Switzerland, Windisch, Switzerland

Abstract. In the context of the European Green Deal, the European Commission opened a consultation on the realignment of corporate governance with key aspects of a sustainable economy in late 2020. Based on the understanding that board composition is considered a key factor to promote sustainable business management (EU Commission and EY 2020), the European Commission is considering enforcing legislative measures regarding sustainability expertise on boards. Why sustainability expertise on boards drives sustainability forward is substantiated by different theories, such as the resource dependency theory, human capital theory, agency theory and social psychological theory (Carter et al. 2010). Academic literature in the area of ESG performance in relation to board characteristics most widely uses the variables (gender) diversity, the share of independent directors, board size and the existence of a sustainability committee (Birindelli et al. 2018). The impact of sustainability expertise on ESG performance has not been studied so far. This study examines if the number of board directors with sustainability expertise and sustainability leadership have a positive effect on the ESG ratings of EURO STOXX Banks 30. Results indicate that sustainability expertise on boards and sustainability leadership with major European banks is still rather low. Encouraging results could be found supporting the hypotheses.

Keywords: Sustainability · Board composition · Banks

1 Introduction

Following legislative measures, such as the European Green Deal [3] and the communication on the COVID19-recovery plan [4], the European Commission opened a consultation in late 2020 on the realignment of corporate governance with key aspects of a sustainable economy. The consultation aimed to find views and inputs from different stakeholders on topics being part of the United Nations Sustainability Development Goals (SDGs), such as board compensation to be complemented by longer-term goals including sustainability risks and opportunities, directors' duties regarding the balancing

© Springer Nature Switzerland AG 2021
A. Gerber and K. Hinkelmann (Eds.): Society 5.0 2021, CCIS 1477, pp. 129–138, 2021.
https://doi.org/10.1007/978-3-030-86761-4_11

of interests of a broad range of stakeholders with rather short-term oriented shareholders, sustainability expertise on boards, pollution and many more [4].

To increase sustainability expertise on boards, the options the European Commission is considering range from soft to hard law, e.g., from promoting the consideration of sustainability related expertise in the nomination process up to a new EU directive requiring companies to consider sustainability criteria in the board nomination process [3]. The consultation period ended on 8 February 2021 and raised several stakeholder reactions highlighting disadvantages of potential legislative measures on board composition [6, 16, 17].

2 Theoretical Background, Literature Review and Hypotheses

2.1 Theoretical Background and Literature Review

The United Nations Global Compact initiative reports that it "is now firmly acknowledged by researchers, investors and executives that corporate sustainability is key to long-term profitability and viability of most, if not all, companies" [23, p. 4].

Board composition is considered a key factor to promote sustainable business management and a focus on the long-term [3, 10, 28], with other factors such as alignment of the interests of the company and directors' duties, shift of investors' focus to the long-term and board renumeration also playing an important role [3]. Currently, the number of appointed directors with sustainability expertise is still limited [27]. This applies to both board committees focusing on sustainability as well as independent advisors [3, 27]. Studies [9, 26] found that only a quarter of a sample of international companies covered had one director with ESG, ethics or social responsibility experience and out of more than 600 US companies, only 19% had a board member with sustainability expertise.

Why sustainability expertise on boards drives sustainability forward is substantiated by different theories, such as the resource dependency theory, human capital theory, agency theory and social psychological theory [5]. These theories aim to explain how external resources of the organization (resource dependency theory [22]), e.g., the board of directors, and their education and experiences (human capital theory [8]), their degree of independence (agency theory [7]) and diversity (social psychological theory [25]) may influence the behavior and performance of the organization.

Further empirical research has shown the importance of the role of the board in identifying and working with management on ESG issues [30] given the reputational impact, the public, investor and stakeholder relations dimensions and the impact on the bottom line [21, 27]. Research results suggest that directors and selected employees educate themselves on ESG issues relevant for the company [21]. In this context, it is acknowledged that "the absence of relevant knowledge and expertise inside the board might significantly undermine a board's capacity to identify and discuss sustainability risks and impacts" [3, p. 3].

Academic literature on ESG performance in relation to board characteristics most widely uses the variables (gender) diversity, the share of independent directors, board size and the existence of a sustainability committee [30]. Diversity encompasses different perspectives such as age, gender, nationality, race as well as different backgrounds and experiences – including sustainability expertise [3]. Diversity drives sustainability forward, as it promotes vision and strategies in both economic [3] and extra-financial areas [10, 28]. Various researchers with a focus on gender representation show a positive impact of female board participation on ESG performance [20, 31] or financial performance [11, 18, 20], a positive impact related to specific circumstances such as firms with weak governance [32, 34] or an inverted U-shape relation [30]. Others found no impact on financial performance [5, 8, 33]. The independence of board members serves as well as catalyst for firms to promote social responsibilities in their business activities [15, 24, 31]. According to Birindelli et al. (2018) other studies did not find this link, leading to an overall inconsistent set of research findings regarding this variable.

Some researchers have found the positive impact of sustainability and/or governance committees on ESG ratings in the Gulf region [31] and for European banks [30], which is the usual board characteristic to study sustainability expertise. So far, it has not been explored if besides the existence of a sustainability committee, the sustainability expertise of board members has an impact on ESG performance. Neither on a regional nor on an industry level. The WBCSD (2020) considers banks one of the industries which should along with other high-risk sectors focus on the duties of directors regarding ESG issues. The banking sector - through its financial intermediary function – is one of the key sectors to promote the transition to a more sustainable economy [30]. Therefore, this study focuses on the impact of sustainability expertise on the ESG ratings of European banks. Results can contribute to the discussion whether legislative action in the area of board composition and sustainability expertise might foster sustainable business management in Europe's largest banks.

2.2 Hypotheses

Resource dependence theory and human capital theory provide a sound theoretical basis why sustainability expertise could influence the behavior or organizations towards sustainability. The agency theory and social psychological theory provide a less clear reasoning. Theory and empirical studies [30, 31] do suggest that the link between sustainability expertise and ESG performance is positive.

To test whether a law on a quota for sustainability expertise on board would make sense and impact the sustainability practice in firms, the following main hypothesis has been formulated:

Hypothesis 1: The number of board directors with sustainability expertise has a positive effect on the ESG ratings of EURO STOXX Banks 30.

The second hypothesis takes account of the fact that the consultation does not differentiate between the board of directors or executive board. Following Alm and Winberg (2016) who studied the impact of female leadership on firms' financial performance, sustainability leadership will be measured with either the Chairperson or the CEO having a sustainability-oriented profile on the firm's website.

Hypothesis 2: Sustainability leadership has a positive effect on the ESG ratings of EURO STOXX Banks 30.

3 Data and Methodology

3.1 Data

Data on ESG ratings and further financial data has been collected from Thomson Reuter's DataStream. Data on board of directors' composition collected from Thomson Reuter's DataStream and is manually complemented from corporate websites. Data includes major European banks from the EURO STOXX Banks 30 index and consists of 30 banks. Following recent studies [5, 30, 31] a 5-year panel dataset (from 2015–2019) has been constructed. The overall sample consists of 1375 director-firm-year observations, after deletion for missing values.

The ESG performance rating from Thomson Reuters has been used following recent studies [30] as dependent variable to test the hypotheses. The study is focusing on the impact of sustainability expertise on ESG ratings of European banks; therefore, the independent variables of primary interest are sustainability expertise on board level (SUSTEXP) and sustainability leadership (SUSTLEAD). Following previous research [5, 30], different types of control variables were used, e.g., the share of women on the board of directors (WBOD), the share of independent directors (BODIND), board size (BODS) and the existence of a sustainability committee (SUSTCO). In line with previous research [5, 30] additional control variables are added, which might influence the ESG rating. These are bank size (BANKSI), return on equity (ROE), leverage (LEV) and country-specific variables which are measured through the development of the economy (GDP) (see Table 1).

Table 1. Measurement of independent/control variables

Independent variable	Measurement	Exp. relationship with ESG rating	Sources
SUSTEXP	Proportion of directors with sustainability expertise divided by the total number of directors on the board	Positive	Ceres (2015)
SUSTLEAD	Dummy variable that is equal to 1 if the bank has a Chairperson or CEO with sustainability profile, 0 otherwise	Positive	Alm and Winberg (2016)
WBOD	Total number of women on the board of directors divided by the total number of board members	Positive	Arayassi et al. (2020), Rao et al. (2017)
BODIND	Percentage of independent board members divided by the total number of board members	Positive/negative	Arayassi et al. (2020), Garas et al. (2017)
BODS	Percentage of independent board members divided by the total number of board members	Positive	Birindelli et al. (2018)

(*continued*)

Table 1. (*continued*)

Independent variable	Measurement	Exp. relationship with ESG rating	Sources
SUSTCO	Dummy variable that is equal to 1 if the bank has a sustainability committee, 0 otherwise	Positive	Birindelli et al. (2018)
BANKSI	Total assets (Euro) of the bank	Positive	Tamini et al. (2017), Carter et al. (2010)
ROE	Bank's net income divided by the value of its total shareholders' equity	Positive/negative	Setó-Pamies (2015)
LEV	Tier 1 Capital as percentage of total assets (proxy for the Basel 3 leverage ratio)	Positive	Helfaya and Moussa (2017)
GDP	Gross Domestic Product (GDP) per capita based on purchasing power parity (PPP)	Positive/negative	Fernandez-Feijoo et al. (2014)

3.2 Methodology

The hypotheses have been tested regarding the effect of the independent variables on the ESG rating. Following the methodology of recent research [5, 30, 31], panel data analysis is used to control for omitted and/or unobserved variables. The choice of fixed effects (with respect to random effects) model can also partly mitigate endogeneity issues (Woolridge 2014).

Natural logarithmic transformations of the numerical (non-index) variables of the board size, GDP and bank size have been performed to better approximate a normal distribution and overcome a possible problem of heteroskedasticity [30]. The OLS fixed effects regression model is estimated as:

$$y = \beta_0 + \beta_1 X_{i,t} + \varepsilon_{i,t}, t = 1, 2, 3, 4, 5 \tag{1}$$

where y is the dependent variable, the ESG rating, β_0 is the constant, the variable X, e.g., the variables of interest, are the different board characteristics as per Table 1, ε is independent disturbance, i stands for the individual bank, and t stands for the years covered by the data sample.

Following previous research [5, 7, 18, 34] the OLS fixed effects regression model is complemented by a Hausman's specification test to test whether X is a truly endogenous variable [37]. The respective 2SLS regression model is estimated as follows:

$$x = \alpha_0 + \alpha_t A + \varepsilon_i \tag{2}$$

where x is the dependent variable, the ESG rating, α_0 is the constant, the variable A, the different board characteristics as per Table 1, ε is independent disturbance, i stands for the individual bank, and t stands for the year covered by the data sample.

4 Results

4.1 Descriptive Statistics

Table 2 shows the descriptive statistics for the dependent and independent variables. The descriptive statistics include the mean, standard deviation, the minimum and the maximum. The mean of ESG ratings of the banks in the sample is 63%, with a minimum of 29% and a maximum of 88%. The average ESG score is in line with previous research [30]. Sustainability expertise on boards shows a mean of 13% and a maximum of 57%, which is a rather low value. Sustainability leadership, e.g., a CEO or Chairperson with sustainability experience, exists with a rather low number of 12% of the companies in average. The share of woman on boards and the proportion of independent directors on boards stand at 30% and 62%, respectively. The share of woman on boards remains rather low but seemed to increase compared to previous research findings [30]. The share of independent directors is in line with previous research [30]. In average, 15% of the banks have a sustainability committee.

Table 2. Descriptive statistics for the dependent and independent variables

Variable	Mean	Standard deviation	Minimum	Maximum
ESG rating	0.63	0.15	0.29	0.88
Sustainability expertise	12.88	13.29	0	57.14
Sustainability leadership	0.12	0.33	0	1
Woman on the board of directors	30.14	10.87	0	50
Board independence	62.35	24.3	18.75	100
Board size	2.62	0.32	1.79	7.68
Sustainability Committee	0.15	0.36	0	1
Bank size	5.81	1.16	2.89	7.68
Return on equity	7.81	10.72	−26.18	106.9
Leverage	8.49	8.18	3.61	43.07
GDP per capita, PPP	10.76	0.21	10.46	11.40

4.2 Correlation Results

Table 3 provides a pair-wise correlation matrix showing important relationships between the main independent variables of the study. A multicollinearity problem usually arises when the correlation between two variables exceeds 0.9 [5]. In this correlation matrix the highest correlation measured is between bank size and leverage. Therefore, we can conclude that we have no problem of collinearity [35]. The relationships show that more women on the board and the existence of a sustainability committee are associated with

Table 3. Correlation matrix

Variable	SUSTEXP	SUSTLEAD	WBOD	BODIND	BODS	SUSTCO	BANKSI	ROE	LEV	GDP
SUSTEXP	1									
SUSTLEAD	.094	1								
WBOD	.260**	−.175	1							
BODIND	.218*	.021	.132	1						
BODS	−0.403**	.057	.134	−.49**	1					
SUSTCO	.510**	.185*	−.035	−.058	−.141	1				
BANKSI	.178*	−.146	.309**	−.360**	.407**	.079	1			
ROE	−.083	−.079	.067	.122	−.032	−.032	−.093	1		
LEV	.202*	−.101	−.161	.108	−.466**	.416	−.592**	.038	1	
GDP	−.056	−.263**	.119	.228*	−.119	.057	−.088	.008	−.073	1

[***p < 0.01, **p < 0.05, *p < 0.1]

higher levels of sustainability experience. In addition, the existence of a sustainability committee is associated with sustainability leadership.

The result of the fixed effects regression is presented in Table 4. The results show that one of the independent variables of primary interest, sustainability leadership, is statistically significant at the 10% significance level. Sustainability expertise is not statistically significant at none of the significance levels. However, it shows that there is a significant negative relationship between the board size and the ESG rating. This contradicts previous research, where a positive relation between board size and ESG performance was found [30]. A non-significant negative result has been found for the share of independent board members current result, where current findings are inconclusive [30]. A negative relationship was found by Walls et al. (2012), Hannifa and Cooke (2005) and others [30].

Table 4. Fixed effects regression results

Variable	Regression coefficient	Robust standard error
SUSTEXP	.118	.160
SUSTLEAD	.095*	.054
WBOD	.163	.163
BODIND	−.050	.079
BODS	−.117*	.063
SUSTCO	.007	.42
BANKSI	.013	.024
ROE	.001	.001

(continued)

Table 4. (*continued*)

Variable	Regression coefficient	Robust standard error
LEV	.003	.003
GDP	−.220**	.093
Constant	2.974***	1.073
R−squared	.519	.130
Regression Model	1.140***	1.392

[***p < 0.01, **p < 0.05, *p < 0.1]

The result of the Hausman's specification test shows an R^2 of .1725, an F-value of 4.6375 and a p-value of .0019. Regression coefficients for SUSTEXP and SUSTLEAD of .411 (standard error .133) and .129 (standard error .067) with statistical significance at the 1% and 5% level, respectively.

5 Conclusion

The fixed regression model and the Hausman's specification test show a significant relationship between the variable sustainability leadership and ESG rating. In addition, the Hausman's specification test, shows a significant relationship between sustainability expertise on boards and the ESG ratings from Thomson Reuters Datastream.

In summary, data based on the sample of EURSTOXX 30 Banks and Thomson Reuters Datastream could reveal that sustainability expertise and sustainability leadership positively impact the ESG rating of the banks. While these results are based on a sample of the largest European banks, results are limited to those and need to be interpreted in this context.

Further studies might consider to including additional ESG rating data providers, such as Morningstar (Sustainalytics), Bloomberg, S&P given the different ESG rating methodologies applied by the before-mentioned agencies. The company sample might be expanded to additional banks in Europe and to more high-risk and lower risk sectors and industries, in order to gain a broader picture and an understanding if a hard law or a soft law on in the European Union would foster sustainability in European firms.

References

1. European Commission: 2019 Report on equality between women and men in the EU. 25 March 2021 (2019). https://ec.europa.eu/info/sites/info/files/aid_development_cooperation_fundamental_rights/annual_report_ge_2019_en.pdf. Accessed 21 Feb 2021
2. European Commission: Press release: 11 December 2019: The European Green Deal sets out how to make Europe the first climate-neutral continent by 2050, boosting the economy, improving people's health and quality of life, caring for nature, and leaving no one behind (2019). https://ec.europa.eu/commission/presscorner/detail/en/IP_19_6691. Accessed 21 Feb 2021

3. European Commission, EY: Study on directors' duties and sustainable corporate governance (2021). https://op.europa.eu/en/publication-detail/-/publication/e47928a2-d20b-11ea-adf7-01aa75ed71a1/language-en. Accessed 21 Feb 2021

4. European Commission: Can research and innovation save the day? A fair green and digital recovery from COVID19. Report July 2020 (2020) https://ec.europa.eu/info/publications/can-research-and-innovation-save-day_en

5. Alm, M., Winberg, J.: How Does Gender Diversity on Corporate Boards Affect the Firm Financial Performance? (2016) https://core.ac.uk/download/pdf/43561419.pdf. Accessed 25 Mar 2021

6. Association française de la gestion financière – AFG : Cover Letter for AFG's response to the sustainable corporate governance consultation (2021). https://www.afg.asso.fr/wp-content/uploads/2021/02/2021-02-08-afg-contribution-sustainable-corporate-governance-consultation.pdf. Accessed 8 Feb 2021

7. Carter, D.A., Simkins, B.J., Simpson, G.W.: Corporate governance, board diversity and firm value. Fin. Rev. **38**, 33–53 (2003)

8. Carter, D.A., D'Souza, F., Simkins, B.J., Simpson, G.W.: The gender and ethnic diversity of US boards and board committees and firms. Corp. Govern. Int. Rev. **18**(5), 396–414 (2010)

9. Ceres: View from the top: How corporate boards can engage on sustainability performance (2015). https://www.ceres.org/sites/default/files/reports/2017-03/ceres_viewfromthetop.pdf. Accessed 25 Feb 2021

10. Ferrero Ferrero, I., Fernández Izquierdo, M.Á., Muñoz Torres, M.J.: Integrating sustainability into corporate governance: an empirical study on board diversity. Corp. Soc. Responsib. Environ. Manag. **22**(4), 193–207 (2015)

11. Fan, P.S.: Is Board Diversity Important for Firm Performance and Board Independence? – An exploratory study of Singapore Listed Companies. The Monetary Authority of Singapore, MAS Staff Paper No. 52 (2012)

12. Fernandez-Feijoo, B., Romero, S., Ruiz-Blanco, S.: Women on boards: do they affect sustainability reporting? Corp. Soc. Responsib. Environ. Manag. **21**, 351–364 (2014)

13. Helfaya, A., Moussa, T.: Do board's corporate social responsibility strategy and orientation influence environmental sustainability disclosure? UK evidence. Bus. Strat. Environ. **26**, 1061–1077 (2017)

14. Setó-Pamies, D.: The relationship between women directors and corporate social responsibility. Corp. Soc. Responsib. Environ. Manag. **22**, 334–345 (2015)

15. Garas, S., ElMassah, S.: Corporate governance and corporate social responsibility disclosures: the case of GCC countries. Crit. Perspect. Int. Bus. **14**(1), 2–26 (2018)

16. IPE Nordic Investment Forum: EC's sustainable governance play: Asset owners wary of potential snags (2021). https://www.ipe.com/ecs-sustainable-governance-play-asset-owners-wary-of-potential-snags/10050702.article .Accessed 15 Feb 2021

17. Norges Bank Investment Management – NBIM: European Commission consultation on sustainable corporate governance - Letter to the European Commission (2021) https://www.nbim.no/en/publications/consultations/2020/european-commission-consultation-on-sustainable-corporate-governance/. Accessed 23 Mar 2021

18. Reguera-Alvarado, N., de Fuentes, P., Laffarga, J.: Does board gender diversity influence financial performance? Evidence from Spain. J. Bus. Ethics **141**(2), 337–350 (2015). https://doi.org/10.1007/s10551-015-2735-9

19. Tamimi, N., Sebastianelli, R.: Transparency among S&P 500 companies: an analysis of ESG disclosure scores. Manag. Decis. **55**(8), 1660–1680 (2017)

20. Arayssi, M., Dah, M., Jizi, M.: Women on boards, sustainability reporting and firm performance. Sustain. Acc. Manag. Policy J. **7**(3), 376–401 (2016)

21. Silk, D.M., Katz, D.A., Niles, S.B.: ESG and Sustainability: The Board's Role. Harvard Law School Forum on Corporate Governance. https://corpgov.law.harvard.edu/2018/06/29/esg-and-sustainability-the-boards-role. Accessed 31 Mar 2021
22. Terjesen, S., Sealy, R., Singh, V.: Women directors of corporate boards: a review and research agenda. Corp. Govern. Int. Rev. **17**(3), 320–337 (2009)
23. United Nations Global Compact: A New Agenda for the Board of Directors: Adoption and Oversight of Corporate Sustainability. https://www.unglobalcompact.org/library/303. Accessed 24 Feb 2021
24. Rao, K., Tilt, C.A., Lester, L.H.: Corporate governance and environmental reporting: an Australian study. Corp. Gov. **12**(2), 143–163 (2012)
25. Westphal, J.D., Milton, L.P.: How experience and network ties affect the influence of demographic minorities on corporate boards. Adm. Sci. Q. **45**(2), 366–398 (2000)
26. World Business Council for Sustainable Development – WBCSD: The state of corporate governance in the era of sustainability risks and opportunities. Internet: https://www.wbcsd.org/Programs/Redefining-Value/Business-Decision-Making/Governance-and-Internal-Oversight/Resources/The-state-of-corporate-governance-in-the-era-of-sustainability-risks-and-opportunities. Accessed 23 Feb 2021
27. World Business Council for Sustainable Development – WBCSD: Board directors' duties and ESG considerations in decision-making (2020). https://www.wbcsd.org/Programs/Redefining-Value/Business-Decision-Making/Governance-and-Internal-Oversight/Resources/Board-directors-duties-and-ESG-considerations-in-decision-making. Accessed 23 Feb 2021
28. Zang, J.Q., Zhu, H., Ding, H.: Board composition and corporate social responsibility: an empirical investigation in the post Sarbanes-Oxley era. J. Bus. Ethics **114**(3), 381–392 (2013)
29. Baltagi, B.H., Long, L.: Alternative ways of obtaining Hausman's test using artificial regressions. Statist. Probab. Lett. **77**(13), 1413–1417 (2007)
30. Birindelli, G., Dell'Atti, S., Ianuzzi, A.P., Savioli, M.: Composition and activity of the board of directors: impact on ESG performance in the banking system. Sustainability **10**(12), 4699 (2018)
31. Arayssi, M., Jizi, M., Tabaja, H.H.: The impact of board composition on the level of ESG disclosures in GCC countries. Sustain. Acc. Manag. Policy J. **11**(1), 137–161 (2020)
32. Francoeur, C., Labelle, R., Sinclair-Desgagné, B.: Gender diversity in corporate governance and top management. J. Bus. Ethics **81**, 83–95 (2008)
33. Mateos de Cabo, R., Gimeno, R., Nieto, M.J.: Gender diversity on European banks´ boards of directors. J Bus. Ethics **109**, 145–62 (2012)
34. Adams, R.B., Ferreira, D.: Women in the boardroom and their impact on governance and performance. J. Financ. Econ. **94**, 291–309 (2009)
35. Wooldridge, J.M.: Introduction to Econometrics. Hampshire, Cengage (2015).
36. Walls, J.L., Berrone, P., Phan, P.H.: Corporate governance and environmental performance: Is there really a link? Strateg. Manag. J. **33**, 885–913 (2012)
37. Daryanto, A.: EndoS: an SPSS macro to assess endogeneity. Quant. Methods Psychol. **16**(1), 5–70 (2020)

The Smart City: Analysis of Application Areas and Their Potential in an International Context

Lea Wipraechtiger[(✉)] [iD] and Marc K. Peter[(✉)] [iD]

School of Business, University of Applied Sciences and Arts Northwestern Switzerland FHNW, Olten, Switzerland

lea.wipraechtiger@students.fhnw.ch, marc.peter@fhnw.ch

Abstract. With the continuous growth of the world's population, increased pollution levels, global warming, resource scarcity, lack of physical and social infrastructure, hyper-urbanization as well as changes driven by the fast-advancing technology sector, there is a need for fresh input to the strategic development of cities. In the battle for cost-effectiveness and ensuring environmental stability, it is of utmost importance that cities alter their strategies and approaches to achieve higher efficiency in all domains. This study includes the identification of a smart city's application areas and will investigate whether they work in practice in a cross-country comparison of smart cities. A best practice framework that includes successful smart city application areas and their potential including a holistic strategy is provided based on a solid literature foundation and validated by empirical research. The findings of this research suggest that a holistic strategic approach of a smart city's application areas contributes to achieving its maximum potential through a government that not only makes data publicly available, but also sets the right framework for modern business models, and thinks comprehensively to deploy resources where they are most needed.

Keywords: Smart city definition · Urbanization · Smart city application areas · Smart city best practice framework

1 Introduction

The world's population is growing fast and by 2030 there will be approximately 8.5 billion people on this planet, representing a rise of ten percent over twelve years [1]. The future is urban and hence, it is assumed that ten years from now, almost two-thirds of the world's population will live in cities. Today, 55% of the world's population lives in cities [2]. In 2018, three times as many people from less developed regions were estimated to live in cities compared to more developed regions; 3.2 billion versus 1.0 billion [2]. The sustainable growth of the economy, society, and the environment leads to higher long-term growth of cities. This is due to a set of reasons; for instance, more births than deaths in urban areas; migration from rural areas and from abroad to urban areas; and the development of rural areas into urban areas [3]. Urbanization, however, has brought positive aspects, inter alia, poverty reduction, economic growth, technological

© Springer Nature Switzerland AG 2021
A. Gerber and K. Hinkelmann (Eds.): Society 5.0 2021, CCIS 1477, pp. 139–150, 2021.
https://doi.org/10.1007/978-3-030-86761-4_12

and other innovations, a skilled workforce because of better education, gender equality, and participation [4].

Cities are among the most prominent players in generating economic growth. People foster innovation along with wealth. While only two percent of the planet's surface is occupied by cities, they are responsible for seventy percent of global CO_2 emissions. Increasing urban growth is accompanied by an unequal consumption of physical and social resources. Cities rely heavily on traditional systems to provide resources – which is unsustainable in the long-run.

Further challenges that are faced by the world and more specifically by cities include people that need to be moved around and need to be safe; housing that ought to be available for everyone; measures which must be taken to combat unemployment; as well as energy supplies that must be secured, and environmental problems that ought to be tackled [5]. Furthermore, the acceleration of high-technology innovation continues and leads to faster, better, and cheaper products [6]. Undoubtedly, digital transformation triggers changes in entire industries as well as societies [7]. Therefore, it is not only governments and businesses that need to respond adequately, but also cities.

This study aims to understand the organization of smart cities that apply new solutions because of the significant demographic shift and urbanization. This study focuses on the constitution as well as the application areas of successful smart cities. Moreover, it tries to identify these cities' leverage drivers, their views on a holistic strategy and how they can reach their maximum potential.

2   Smart Cities and Villages

The numerous definitions of the term 'smart city' in the literature vary widely. Many definitions include the use of data and new technologies, usually information and communication technologies, as a means to optimize the operational efficiency of a city. The goals are to improve the citizens' quality of life through a well-connected infrastructure along with overcoming environmental challenges and achieving economic growth [8]. A smart city takes advantage of the Internet of Things, a network of connected devices that can communicate and exchange data. The collected data is usually stored in the cloud – in other words, it is connected with the internet. As a first insight, it can be said that the Internet of Things and data analysis support a city in the evaluation of their improvement potential [9].

The fact that there is neither a universal definition for the concept of a smart city nor a single template of it leads to confusion [10]. Another factor of possible confusion is the usage of other similar terms, such as a digital or intelligent city. A so-called digital city focuses on technological features. A digital city's concept aims to create the basis for interaction and sharing of people's experience and knowledge as well as creating public spaces on the internet for residents and visitors [11]. An intelligent city, on the other hand, primarily comprises of functions of research, technology transfer, product development and technological innovation as a hotbed of innovative industries [12]. It uses top-down approaches with a focus on technology [13]. For an intelligent city to become a smart city, the aspect of people must be added.

Furthermore, there are smart villages. A village consists of one or various human settlements that create a community. The community uses innovative solutions to improve its resilience while leveraging local assets and opportunities. Active participation of the community is needed to develop and implement the strategy of improving their economical, social, and environmental conditions with the help of digital technology [14]. Many human resources can be found in every village. Using them efficiently can bring significant benefits. The impact of information and communication technologies in a small city's traditional life is likely to be greater in terms of the domestic economy as well as social life [15]. In a digital village, technology is integrated into the everyday lives of citizens as they are provided with digital solutions and services [16]. Smart villages are also self-sufficient as well as sustainable [17].

Moreover, urban growth and the indispensable economic growth of a city prompt governments to act more environmentally friendly and use fewer natural resources. A green city is predominantly characterized by its environmental performance, to maximize social as well as economic benefits [18]. Overall, as some definitions focus only on environmental aspects, others include socio-economical, environmental and infrastructure elements, policies, information and communication technologies [19].

The components of a smart city as identified in the literature provided input for the questionnaire for field research. A definition of *smart city* validated by research will be provided in Sect. 4.2.

3   Research Methodology

This research seeks to identify the contribution of a holistic strategic approach of a smart city's application areas to reach its full potential in an international context. Given the study's explanatory nature, a qualitative method will be employed through semi-structured interviews, supplemented by secondary data. A deductive approach to theory is adopted since it is based on existing literature. The analytical technique that will be applied is pattern matching logic [20–23]. To achieve data triangulation and thus, strengthening the construct validity of the research, four interviews per case, i.e., per smart city, were completed.

The paradigm of postpositivism appears as the sources, as types of data and theories are diversified and thus, triangulation is created. In the critical theory, the objectively analyzed data is transferred into a comprehensible way; however, it cannot be ruled out that a subjective view, shaped by the researcher's reality, influences the presentation of the results. The context is significant. Therefore, constructivism occurs in the present study. Furthermore, a participatory approach takes place while conducting interviews with experts from the cities under research [22, 24–26].

The method selected is case study because of the research question's character along with the lack of necessity of control over behavioral events; and the fact that the focus of the research is on contemporary events [20]. The qualitative case study research design chosen is a multiple-case study with the same context and theoretical replication logic and a single type of embedded units of analysis. The context is the smart city's holistic strategic approach in order to reach its maximum potential based on the analysis of three analyzed cities. The replication logic is theoretical because the cases are expected to reach distinct results due to different starting positions and approaches. The qualitative method, or the constructivism paradigm [13], will be applied due to the aim to gain in-depth insights into specific cases as well as for contextualization [26]. The embedded units of analysis are constitution, active domains, and leverage drivers.

Independent rankings from 2019 of smart cities [27–29] were utilized in order to identify the three most successful smart cities. Based on these rankings, the top three cities (and those analyzed in this study) were London, Singapore, and Vienna. Four interview participants per city (i.e., P1 to P12), based on their relevance of job titles to the study, were interviewed (Table 1). Given the location of participants in multiple countries, the interviews were conducted via online conferencing platforms between July and September 2020. The interview questionnaire was based on the key concepts identified in an extensive literature review. The average length of the interviews was 52 min with the shortest being 37 min and the longest 95 min. The majority of the results is compatible. However, a difference in the cities' focus was observed: London's emphasis is on digitalization through data and collaboration; Singapore stresses the importance of technology; and Vienna puts sustainability at the center. The interviews, although small in number, provided a rich and comprehensive insight.

Table 1. Interview participants.

City	Participant	Function	Organization
London	P1	Chief Digital Officer	London City Hall
	P2	Lead for Energy Systems	Greater London Authority
	P3	Transport Engineer	Consultancy firm
	P4	Industry Principal in Mobility	Frost & Sullivan
Singapore	P5	Technology Solution Provider	Center for Pioneering Cities
	P6	Government Relations Manager	Autonomous vehicle firm
	P7	Consultant in Technology	Consultancy firm
	P8	Head of Energy Innovations	Commercial firm
Vienna	P9	Consultant for City and Sustainable Planning	Consultancy firm for innovative cities
	P10	Deputy Office Manager and Consultant for Urban Planning	Office of the Vice Mayor (City Councilor for Urban Development, Transport, Climate Protection, Energy Planning and Citizen Participation)
	P11	Head of Innovation	Consultancy firm (mobility solutions)
	P12	Head of Smart City	Urban Planning and Development

As previously mentioned, data collected from this study was analyzed through the analytical strategy and technique of pattern-matching logic. Causal inferences were created based on comparisons of patterns established prior to the data collection with patterns yielding from the findings [21, 23]. Each case was analyzed on its own with specific analytical generalization. In a second step, the empirical patterns that emerged across the cases were compared. Similarity and difference across the cases based on the theoretical foundation (e.g., secondary data) were again compared to the empirically generated cross-case patterns. Further patterns were concluded from juxtaposing as well as cross-case analysis of the interviews. The application of these approaches aimed at developing internal and external validity [20, 22].

4 Findings

The analyzed cities differ heavily in various aspects. The population in London, for instance, is 8.96 million [30] whereas Singapore has a population of 5.64 million [31] and Vienna 1.9 million [32]. However, they all have a migration rate between 29.1–35.7% [33]. Singapore has the highest population density but the lowest unemployment rate [31] whereas Vienna has the lowest crime rate but the highest unemployment rate [34].

Even though the three cities differ with regard to their size, culture, etc., they have many points in common in regard to understanding the concept of and being a successful smart city.

4.1 Constitution

The research identified two commonalities in the constitution of the three smart cities. The first similarity is the role of government: It is crucial in the process of building a smart city, such as the planning of a citizen-centric strategy, adapting regulations and laws for modern business models, distributing resources fairly, and improving infrastructure, where necessary. Hence, it is not about the political structure per se, but rather about the action of the government to create the right framework for the city to develop into a smart city and be able to prosper. The second commonality is the strategy itself. There must be an overarching smart city strategy that includes long-term goals to guarantee that every domain is working towards the same objectives and that financial resources are directed appropriately [21, 35, 36]. For the reason that the strategy includes the city as a whole, it has to be holistic [27].

Moreover, the cooperation and collaboration between the departments can be widened and strengthened thanks to such a goal-setting elaborated strategy [36]. Research shows that success factors in building a holistic smart city strategy is the presence of a project team and the definition of realistic goals [36, 37, 40, 41, 44–46]. Only with a solid strategy, a city can embark on its transformational journey to become a smart city.

4.2 Application Areas

A smart city's main application areas that derived from the literature and were validated by the field research are holistic strategy, government, technology, data, infrastructure, citizens, mobility, education, health, environment & sustainability, quality of life, and economic development. According to the fieldwork, the government is the most important application area, followed by citizens, data, technology, and environment and sustainability. Four cohesions result from the fieldwork, namely data, innovation, government, and mobility.

An in-depth literature review combined with the examination of the empirical results led to the following definition of a smart city: *A smart city follows a governmental developed data-based holistic strategy that focuses on investments in technology, infrastructure, healthcare, and education, which in turn fuels innovation and sustainable economic development in an environmentally friendly context, resulting in high quality of life.*

4.3 Leverage Drivers

Four leverage drivers were identified in all three cities that enable a smart city to take advantage of its full potential. The first leverage driver is data. In all cities, data is publicly available. This helps to increase the public understanding of the city's activities and it further boosts the innovation and start-up sector [36, 37, 40, 41, 44, 47]. The second aspect is the inclusion of a holistic strategy. By establishing a comprehensive strategy, the collaboration of departments is almost guaranteed. The strategy serves as a reference point not only for the government and the departments but also for other stakeholders such as the citizens. It is important to monitor the strategy and to adapt it, if necessary. This also supports the notion that the city can further develop sustainably. Thirdly, another area in common is mobility. London, Singapore, and Vienna have advanced mobility systems. This is an important driver as it enables flexibility at the same time as reducing traffic. There are many other benefits to smart mobility, including safety, connectivity, reliability, cleanliness, convenience, fewer emissions, and less time consumption [36–43, 48]. The last leverage driver that can be identified in all cities is citizen-centricity. It is crucial to put the citizen at the center; social inclusion should be the primary goal of a smart city. It is vital to involve citizens to create a better quality of life for them. High quality transport services for the public, disruptive technologies that allow citizens to be involved in decision-making, an advanced healthcare system, and sustainable solutions are only some examples of how the smart cities analyzed engage their citizens [35–46]. By combining and implementing the first three leverage drivers, it is crucial to focus on the fourth leverage driver 'citizen-centricity' to ensure their receptivity amid changes.

4.4 Potential

The evaluated responses of the interviewees revealed that data are essential to reach a city's full potential. Without data, a city can neither develop professionally nor sustainably [35, 38, 44]. It is important to focus on the big picture and then prioritize [26]. Plan and set goals, monitor them and act accordingly [37, 40, 41, 43]. A holistic strategy is a "must" for a city that aims to become a smart city and in order to reach its maximum potential [39, 41–43, 45].

Furthermore, a government should have laws and policies which are business-friendly, as well as development plans that boost the overall progress of the city [38–40, 45, 46].

International exchange is important for benchmarking and for adapting the strategy so that the city ultimately reaches its full potential [40]. The significance of interactions is tremendous as cities can help each other, and simplicity should be embraced as there are already many great innovations just waiting to be used [36].

4.5 Holistic Strategic Approach

With a holistic strategic approach, goals become understandable to all stakeholders, and it will be easier to collaborate. It is also recommended to provide sub-strategies for each sector with more detailed targets. A holistic strategy also assists to direct financial resources accordingly and to assign the funds appropriately to the relevant domain [36, 37]. Finally, the topics that shall be covered by a smart city strategy include design thinking, data handling, open innovation, and technology usage [37].

The holistic strategy should have long-term goals to allow cooperation and collaboration between the various departments and municipal companies. Contrary to sectoral strategies that include short-term objectives that help to promote, support and implement into a certain area [36].

4.6 Strategy Replication

Reviewing a strategy or parts of from other cities can help to benchmark, to obtain a better understanding of good practices as well as to adopt and adapt the current strategy, but not for replicating the same strategy [37, 40, 45]. Because every city is different, it is therefore difficult and nearly impossible to replicate a strategy [41]. Cities with similar prerequisites can copy strategies, however, adjustment is always necessary as "no one size fits all" [38].

The digitalization of data and their usage to improve the infrastructure (as derived from the fieldwork) is an area that can be replicated more easily. The city of London has five principles that are most likely replicable in different cities [44]:

1. Design: Things should be designed better according to principles.
2. Data and connectivity: It should be thought about how data is shared to solve problems effectively.
3. Fix the plumbing: The infrastructure ought to be up to date before going a step further.
4. Talent: People's and society's digital maturity, as well as a strong labor market, are key.
5. Collaboration: Institutions that are right to collaborate with others and that form links need to be ensured.

For a city to replicate a strategy and to transform itself into a smart city, many obstacles must be faced, such as a city's political structure and the financial situation [35, 39, 42].

5 Best Practice Framework

As mentioned previously, every city is very distinct. Nevertheless, the conceptual framework allows derivations that led to a best practice framework which was validated by the field research (Fig. 1). There are three main parts, namely enablers, goals, and results.

The enablers can be seen as the foundation of a smart city. The four dimensions that enable a smart city (a holistic strategy, data & technology, infrastructure and citizen-centricity) to reach its maximum potential are closely interlinked and mutually reinforcing. Without this group, it is nearly impossible to build and sustain a smart city. The basis of the enablers is the holistic strategy. Field research identified that without a solid strategy, the city lacks a roadmap, it is running the risk of duplicating work, and it becomes very difficult to achieve the desired result. Data & Technology help not only to establish the strategy but also to monitor and improve it. In addition, infrastructure is viewed as an enabler since it is a key element of a city. The engagement of citizens is indispensable when implementing the strategy because they need to be involved and motivated for change. Only when these four components are established, the smart city goals can be achieved.

The four main goals include education, mobility, innovation, and health. These four pillars should be managed smartly. The fulfillment of these goals leads to the earlier defined results. One of the results is environment & sustainability. A smart city should be environmentally conscious and function sustainably. Furthermore, economic development is important as it provides employment and business which are both necessary for a city to operate and finance itself. And lastly, a higher quality of life – not only for citizens but also for visitors – is the greatest result that should be aimed to be achieved as a city is built for its citizens.

The framework is shaped by the government and its institutions, as both the literature and field research provided evidence for the important role it plays. Government needs to set the right framework and goals for the particular city that include appropriate laws and regulations that allow a transformation of the city. Also, the international exchange between the smart city government and other countries and cities can support the transformation. Not only innovation, but also ideas, experiences, and issues can be discussed and shared in order to help each other in the improvement of cities. Since international exchange is not a mandatory element, it is delimited with a dotted line from the core part of the presented framework.

A smart city's concept is comprehensive, as presented in Fig. 1, and with all of its components validated in the field research. The focus, however, differs from one city to another, depending on various elements such as the progress of their transformation, citizens resistance to change, the political situation, financial position, etc.

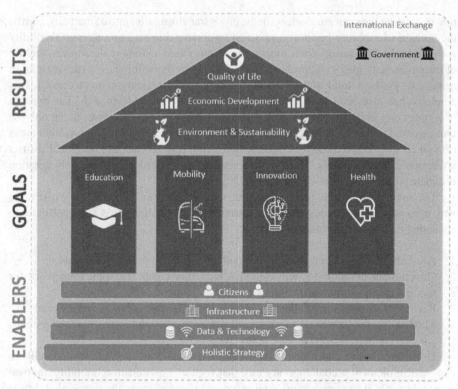

Fig. 1. Smart city best practice framework as derived from the research.

6 Discussion and Conclusion

The research identified two aspects of a successful smart city's constitution. Firstly, the government's fourfold role: Government institutions are strategic planners and with this, they should put their citizens in the center of their activities. The second role is as a framework setter: Government institutions create the right framework for the city's prosperous development, including business-friendly laws and regulations including contemporary business models and support for start-ups. Thirdly, it is dealing as a resource allocator as it plans a fair distribution of resources to all stakeholders. Lastly, the government's role as a renovator includes the renewal of infrastructure wherever necessary.

The second commonality of the smart city's constitution is an overarching strategy that includes long-term goals. Having a holistic strategy facilitates the understanding of all stakeholders and removes the risk of work duplication. Both elements are mentioned multiple times in the literature. This emphasis has been confirmed with the findings from the collected research data.

Regarding the application areas, there is cohesion in four of them. The first includes data storing and harmonizing and to make them publicly available. Secondly, the application area of innovation because of open data availability which fuels innovation.

The third application area, government, is congruent to the results of the commonalities regarding the constitution of a successful smart city. It is important as it plays a key role in creating the right parameters for the city's transformation into a smart city. Lastly, the domain of mobility because it plays an important role as a promoter to flexibility and efficiency. The results from this research imply that a strategy determines the use of resources, anticipates and evaluates risks and shows the willingness to act in order to achieve set goals. A solid strategy is indispensable for a smart city to be successful. This emphasis has also been confirmed with the findings from field research. The concept of a smart city is holistic as it touches many different fields. Therefore, it can only be implemented with a holistic approach. A holistic strategy includes all application areas of a smart city, and it should be broken down into levels, inter alia, the local district government, and the public. Through this methodology, interdepartmental collaboration is enhanced, and resources can be allocated accordingly.

The findings from this research project suggest that four main factors explain the way a holistic strategic approach of a smart city's application areas can contribute to achieving its maximum potential:

1. All-embracing thinking: it will foster collaboration and promote innovation;
2. Government decisions: it will establish laws that create the right framework for modern business models including start-ups;
3. Resources distribution: it allocates resources where they are most needed; and
4. Making data publicly available: it provides transparency and fosters new ecosystems.

However, a smart city requires the workforce which has the capacity and skills to plan and implement a contemporary city that focuses on education, mobility, innovation and health. It requires vision, dedication and in many cases the financial ability to establish a smart city. Further research is recommended to understand the differences between the enablers, goals and results of a best practice smart city and those who are not yet that advanced on their transformation journey. It is suggested that research shall measure the maturity levels of constitution, application areas and drivers to build a better understanding of the success factors of city transformation. With the identified and described Smart City Best Practice Framework, a reference point and navigation aid will support governments in the pursuit of their holistic strategies to advance their cities in the digital age.

References

1. United Nations, Department of Economic and Social Affairs, Population Division: World's Population Prospects 2019, Highlights (2019). https://population.un.org/wpp/Publications/Files/WPP2019_10KeyFindings.pdf
2. United Nations, Department of Economic and Social Affairs, Population Division: World Urbanization Prospects: The 2018 Revision. (ST/ESA/SER.A/420). New York, United Nations (2019)
3. Lerch, M.: International migration and city growth. Population Division Technical Paper. 2017/10. New York, United Nations (2017)
4. Cohen, B.: Urbanization in developing countries: Current trends, future projections, and key challenges for sustainability. Technol. Sci. **28**, 63–80 (2006)

5. Sarkar, A.N.: Significance of smart cities in 21st century: an international business perspective. In: Sarkar, A.N. (ed.) Smart Cities: A Symbiosis of Heritage, Aesthetics, Architecture, Economy, Environment and Modern Lifestyle, pp. 53–82. SSDN Publishers & Distributors, New Delhi (2015)
6. Moore, G.E.: Cramming more components onto integrated circuits. Electronics **38**(8), 114–117 (1965)
7. Peter, M.K., Kraft, C., Lindeque, J.: Strategic action fields of digital transformation. An exploration of the strategic action fields of Swiss SMEs and large enterprises. J. Strat. Manag. **13**(1), 160–180 (2020). https://doi.org/10.1108/JSMA-05-2019-0070
8. Albino, V., Berardi, U., Dangelico, R.M.: Smart cities: definitions, dimensions, performance, and initiatives. J. Urban Technol. **22**(1), 3–21 (2015)
9. Griffith, E.: What Is Cloud Computing? PC Mag. https://uk.pcmag.com/networking-communications-software/16824/what-is-cloud-computing
10. O'Grady, M.J., O'Hare, G.: How Smart Is Your City? https://uk.pcmag.com/networking-communications-software/16824/what-is-cloud-computing
11. Ishida, T.: Digital city Kyoto. Commun. ACM **45**(7), 76 (2002)
12. Komninos, N., Sefertzi, E.: Intelligent cities: R&D offshoring, Web 2.0 product development and globalization of innovation systems. In: Paper presented at the Second Knowledge Cities Summit. Shenzen, China (2009)
13. Letaifa, S.B.: How to strategize smart cities: revealing the SMART model. J. Bus. Res. **68**, 1414–1419 (2015)
14. European Network for Rural Development. Smart Villages Portal. Briefing note. Brussels. https://digitevent-images.s3.amazonaws.com/5c0e6198801d2065233ff996-registration filetexteditor-1551115459927-smart-villages-briefing-note.pdf
15. Khoir, S., Davison, R.M.: iTransformation of a digital village: a community development initiative through ICTs. In: Chowdhury, G., McLeod, J., Gillet, V., Willett, P. (eds.) iConference 2018. LNCS, vol. 10766, pp. 114–119. Springer, Cham (2018). https://doi.org/10.1007/978-3-319-78105-1_14
16. Atieno, L.V., Moturi, C.A.: Implementation of digital village projects in developing countries – Case of Kenya. Br. J. Appl. Sci. Technol. **4**(5), 793–807 (2014)
17. Kar, A., Gupta, M., Ilavarasan, P., Dwivedi, Y.: Advances in Smart Cities. Chapman and Hall/CRC, New York (2017)
18. European Bank for Reconstruction and Development (EBRD): Green City Program Methodology; London: European Bank for Reconstruction and Development (2016)
19. Brilhante, O., Klaas, J.: Green city concept and a method to measure green city performance over time applied to fifty cities globally: influence of GDP, population size energy efficiency. Sustainability **10**(6), 1–23 (2018)
20. Bell, E., Bryman, A., Harley, B.: Business Research Methods. Oxford University Press, Oxford (2018)
21. Saunders, M., Lewis, P., Thornhill, A.: Research Methods for Business Students. Pearson Education, London (2009)
22. Silverman, D.: Doing Qualitative Research: A Practical Handbook. Sage, London (2005)
23. Yin, R.K.: Case Study Research: Design and Methods, 5th edn. Sage Publications, Thousand Oaks (2014)
24. Benton, T., Craib, I.: Philosophy of Social Science: The Philosophical Foundations of Social Thought, 2 edn. Palgrave, Houndsmill/Basingstoke/New York (2010)
25. Guba, E.G., Lincoln, Y.S.: Competing paradigms in qualitative research. In: Denzin, N., Denzin, L. (eds.) Handbook of Qualitative Research, pp. 105–117. Sage, Thousand Oaks (1994)

26. Sławecki, B.: Paradigms in Qualitative Research. In: Ciesielska, M., Jemielniak, D. (eds.) Qualitative Methodologies in Organization Studies, pp. 7–26. Springer, Cham (2018). https://doi.org/10.1007/978-3-319-65217-7_2

27. Zelt, T., Narloch, U., Eikmanns, B., Ibel, J.: The smart city breakaway: how a small group of leading digital cities is outpacing the rest. In: Smart City Strategy Index 2019. Think:Act, navigating complexity. Munich, Roland Berger GmbH (2019)

28. Berrone, P., Ricart, J.E.: IESE Cities in Motion Index, vol. 26 (2019). https://doi.org/10.15581/018.ST-509

29. Bris, A., et al.: Smart City Index 2019. https://www.imd.org/research-knowledge/reports/imd-smart-city-index-2019/

30. Clark, D.: London – Statistics & Facts. https://www.statista.com/topics/3799/london/

31. Pletcher, H.: Singapore – Statistics & Facts. https://www.statista.com/topics/2721/singapore/

32. Lincoln, Y.S., Guba, E.G.: Naturalistic Inquiry. Sage Publications, Newbury Park (1985)

33. CAN: Singapore's population declines to 5.69 million, with fewer foreigners. https://www.channelnewsasia.com/news/singapore/singapore-population-declines-non-residents-citizens-pr-13141862

34. Mohr, M.: Statistiken zu Wien. https://de.statista.com/themen/3459/grossstadt-wien/

35. P3: Personal interview (2020)

36. P12: Personal interview (2020)

37. P2: Personal interview (2020)

38. P4: Personal interview (2020)

39. P6: Personal interview (2020)

40. P7: Personal interview (2020)

41. P9: Personal interview (2020)

42. P10: Personal interview (2020)

43. P11: Personal interview (2020)

44. P1: Personal interview (2020)

45. P5: Personal interview (2020)

46. P8: Personal interview (2020)

47. Bibri, S.E., Krogstie, J.: The emerging data–driven Smart City and its innovative applied solutions for sustainability: the cases of London and Barcelona. Energy Inform. 3(1), 1–42 (2020). https://doi.org/10.1186/s42162-020-00108-6

48. Nikitas, A., Michalakopoulou, K., Njoya, E.T., Karampatzakis, D.: Artificial intelligence, transport and the smart city: definitions and dimensions of a new mobility era. Sustainability 12(7), 2789 (2020). https://doi.org/10.3390/su12072789

Adopting AI in the Banking Sector – The Wealth Management Perspective

Xinhua Wittmann[1,2](✉) 🆔 and Flutra Lutfiju[1]

[1] University of Applied Sciences and Arts, Windisch, Northwestern Switzerland, Switzerland
xinhua.wittmann@fhnw.ch
[2] University of Zurich, Zurich, Switzerland

Abstract. While interest in understanding the impact of Artificial Intelligence (AI) in the real world has been growing, there is limited research on what digital transformation means in the banking sector. The present paper aims to address this gap in the literature by means of a field study based on 11 interviews with wealth managers from across front, middle and back offices in a large Swiss bank. Our analyses suggest bank employees have relatively positive attitudes toward the adoption of new technologies. According to the research, the top three advantages for adopting AI in wealth management are: efficiency, enhanced clients' experience and better customer insight. Yet, AI also brings new challenges to banking. Obstacles identified include process complexity, greater maintenance effort, and increased regulatory requirements. Still, AI is expected to change the banking model to an integrated, hybrid and leaner operation with digital processes that offer front-to-back solutions. With respect to the future of the bank workforce, hiring tech-savvy talent will be crucial. AI will be able to free bank employees from repetitive jobs for more interesting and creative tasks.

Keywords: Artificial Intelligence (AI) · Banking sector · Wealth management

1 Introduction

Since the world entered the Industry 4.0 phase, digital strategy in the financial sector has become a critical element for banks looking to maintain sustainable growth and competitiveness. The application of communication technologies, AI and robotics in banking industry requires different competencies from managers [1]. The clients of today demand better banking experiences in terms of speed, price and digital connectivity. Millennials, who are seen as digital natives, are expected to soon become the largest client population for banks. Therefore, private banking and wealth management have undergone a fundamental transformation through the introduction of AI and financial technology (FinTech).

With the increasing popularity of AI across all industries as well as in the consumer's daily life, there is growing interest in conducting research on the social and ethical dimensions of AI [2, 3]. The opinions collected are mainly from either the digital technology provider side, or the consumer side. Based on empirical studies, researchers

© Springer Nature Switzerland AG 2021
A. Gerber and K. Hinkelmann (Eds.): Society 5.0 2021, CCIS 1477, pp. 151–162, 2021.
https://doi.org/10.1007/978-3-030-86761-4_13

have identified what drives consumers who are early adopters of FinTech products [4]. A more recent study conducted by Aitken et al. (2020), done with a wide range of focus groups that included diverse members of the public, shows that AI in the banking sector can be a double-edged sword. The focus groups appreciated the benefits of AI enhanced services but had concerns about the negative impact of AI on society [5]. While the key to success with AI is human-machine collaboration [6], so far research has largely overlooked the perception of AI from the perspective of bank employees, who have seen their everyday functions change dramatically. The present study addresses the gap in the literature through qualitative research at a large bank. Our rationale for choosing the wealth management business unit to provide the research context is two-fold. First, AI is expected to play a crucial role in wealth management in the future [7]. It is therefore essential to understand how AI is going to change the wealth management operation model. Second, but equally important, is to analyse how wealth managers and the rest of the banking workforce perceive the opportunities and risks of using this new technology, as the application of AI can only reach the potential of its full advantages if it is accepted and welcomed. The objectives of this research are to understand the impact of AI on the wealth management operation model and identify the key opportunities and challenges for the banking workforce. To this end, the findings of this study will contribute to the current literature of our understanding of how and why a new technology is perceived to be useful. For practitioners, the study results are evidence of certain potential applications of AI in the banking sector in general, as well as the implications for wealth management in particular.

In the next session we will briefly review the general operation model of wealth management, discuss the impact of digitalization, and look at several AI use cases in the banking sector. Thereafter, we will describe our research design and method. In Sect. 4, the field research results will be presented and analysed. In the final section, we will summarise our research findings, highlight the limitations of the present study, and outline future research avenues.

2 Wealth Management and the Use of AI

Until about 20 years ago, the 200-year-old wealth management industry had been growing steadily under pretty much the same operation models. Since the financial crisis of 2008–2009, the financial services sector has been under growing pressure to adapt to fast-changing business environments, demanding client needs, higher expectations of shareholders and new regulatory requirements. More recently, wealth managers have experienced considerable headwinds. In 2018, global high net worth grew only by 4%, quite low compared to previous years. Because of lower growth in assets under management, increased fee pressures and volatile markets, the business valuations of wealth management firms dropped by more than 20% in 2018 [8]. Furthermore, higher regulatory requirements have led to more focus and resources directed toward risk and compliance. In essence, moderate economic growth, increased emphasis on risk and regulation aspects, and higher capital requirements have affected the traditional operation models of wealth management [9, 10].

Wealth management, in general, is defined by the provision of financial advice to clients with respect to maintaining, transferring and enhancing their wealth. The typical business comprises core banking services, including liquidity management, lending products, brokerage, and financial and non-financial advisory in fields such as real estate, commodities, alternative investments, offers of discretionary and advisory mandates and wealth planning [11]. The bank's wealth management operation model is usually divided into three organizational units: the front, middle and back offices.

Traditionally, banks have focused on introducing various independent initiatives within each unit, with the aim of improving efficiency and performance [12]. The result of this practice is the duplication of efforts and recourse redundancy. Since the front office contributes to more than 50% of overall costs, to increase efficiency, processes automation of front office operations can enable advisors to spend more time on clients to generate revenue [8]. In fact, applying a digital business model can automate processes across the front, middle and back offices [13]. This will lead to the simplification and the optimization of processes, enabling cost reductions for the bank and increased focus on value-adding tasks for the employee. However, in the short term, this requires upskilling the existing workforce, hiring tech-savvy employees and implementing new technologies [14].

AI is a set of technologies that has the power to make predictions and anticipate future events, including autonomous learning, as well as recognize patterns, make good decisions and communicate with humans [15]. Facilitated by the falling costs of data storage and the increasing speed of connectivity, the banking business is already in the AI-powered digital age. According to a McKinsey report (2020), annually AI can potentially unlock $1 trillion in incremental value for banks [16]. Often cited use cases where AI is applied in the banking sector include:

Credit Scoring. AI is used to improve standardized credit scoring processes. In the past, most banks assessed their credit ratings based on the lender's payment history. Today, banks use data sources, such as mobile phone usage or social media activity, to assess creditworthiness and achieve more accurate loan ratings [17]. Customer data and credit history are also analyzed through a system that applies machine learning algorithms for quicker credit decision-making, thus reducing a bank's default risks and providing higher quality assessment [18].

AI–Powered Fraud Detection. AI is also used for better risk management by using machine learning and huge data points for fraud detection, which leads to a more accurate and earlier estimation of risks [17]. Through risk-forecasting and anti-fraud models, banks can benefit from better control over and anticipation of fraud risks [18].

Robo-Advisory. Based on market data, such as client investment preferences, risk appetite or age, robo-advisory provides automated advice to fulfill clients' needs and reduce the bank's staffing costs [18]. However, since robo-advisory is a novel phenomenon in the wealth management sector, it is relatively unregulated, and thus cost transparency and information on consumer protection are lacking [19]. In addition, protecting client information and cybersecurity are very important when offering automated online advice [20, 21].

Personalized Offerings and Client Retention. A popular AI use case among younger generations is virtual agents such as chatbots, which enhance customer service by the automation of simple requests [17]. Clients benefit from a personalized banking experience, with 24/7 online banking access and the opportunity to interact with chatbots at any time, independent of time zone [22].

Regulatory Compliance in the Financial Sector. Regulatory technology (RegTech) is another high potential area for AI development, such as the automation of Know-Your-Customer (KYC) and anti-money laundering, where the entire onboarding process can be streamlined [23]. The KYC process is often time consuming, labor intensive and costly. Through machine learning, pre-checks on background information can be automated, and ongoing periodic reviews can be performed using other public data sources, such as official registers [17].

According to research from Narrative Science, 32% of financial services firms already use AI technologies, such as voice recognition or predictive analytics [24]. In fact, UBS, a Swiss multinational bank with global largest wealth management, has already numerous robots in place and several processes were already automated. As early as 2016, it has carried out a number of active AI-enabled intelligent automation pilots. Furthermore, UBS has also been exploring how to combine behaviour finance and data science to identify and remedy behaviour biases in the investment process [25].

3   Research Design and Method

One of the often-referred research models for the spreading use of new technology by individuals is the technology acceptance model [26]. According to the model, two factors influence the adoption of technology: perceived usefulness and perceived ease of use. The perceived usefulness is the expected user's subjective estimation that using a particular application system will improve job or life performance, whereas perceived ease of use is defined how much the user expects that a specific system is easy to use and free of effort. Since the focus of our research is to examine how AI adoption in the banking sector impacts the operation model, which also influences work behaviour from the perspective of wealth management, we have selected the perceived changes in operation model as the dependent variable. Furthermore, we investigated how the future of the workforce may look like in an AI-powered work environment. We extended the technology acceptance model (shown in Fig. 1) by taking opportunities as the main variables for perceived usefulness in our conceptual framework. The perceived ease of use includes challenges from technical skills, system safety as well as potential ethical issues. The influence of these two aspects on the operation model of wealth management, which further affects the future of the workforce in terms of employment behaviour and the relationship between the bank and its clients.

Guided by the conceptual research framework, we applied a qualitative research approach. By conducting multiple case studies, each in the same banking context but embedded in different business units according to the wealth management operation model, namely front office, middle office and back office, we were able to collect insightful information for further analysis. Before we contacted interviewees, we conducted a pilot study to test if all the questions we asked were properly understood and if some important relevant questions were overlooked. Based on the feedback from the pilot study, we modified the questionnaires which were used in the interviews. In the field research, we selected 3–4 managers from each unit at director or higher levels with various responsibilities as our first-hand sources to gain insight from both operation and decision-making processes. We assured the sources that all the information they provide would be treated anonymously. The semi-structured interviews combined with open-ended questions were conducted between March and April of 2020. Due to the pandemic, all the interviews were done via Skype. The average interview last about an hour. The online conversations were recorded and thereafter transcribed. With the help of the software ATLAS.ti. we analyzed all answers from the interviews and generated inductive codes which will be presented in Sect. 4.

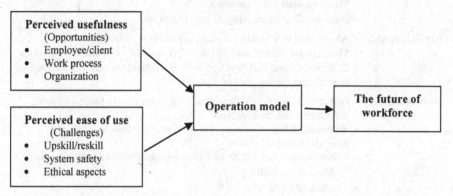

Fig. 1. Conceptual framework of the impact of AI on wealth management (authors).

4   Results and Discussion

This section presents the empirical findings derived from the data collected from the interviews. First comes the within-case analysis for each of the three cases presented, followed by the cross-case analysis, which shows the differences and similarities between the cases.

4.1   Case One: Front Office

The primary activities of the front office include payments, lending and deposits, capital markets, market data and wealth management [13]. Digitizing front-end client interactions and processes can further improve client experiences and reduce costs. Manual tasks, such as client profiling or asset allocation modeling, will be automated, allowing advisors to focus on tailored offerings, advising their clients, and conduct client development [27]. In the bank where we conducted our field research, AI-powered chatbots, machine learning techniques and natural language processing were already in use in the front office. However, most projects are still in a proof-of-concept stage and not yet live.

To improve efficiency, the bank is trying to use AI to automate and streamline processes in client onboarding, by automating checks in existing tools, and in yearly KYC reviews. Based on the four interviews, we summarize the findings from the front office in Table 1.

Table 1. Summary of key findings based on thematic coding of interviews in front office.

Variable	Key findings
Opportunities	• Efficiency (time efficiency for client onboarding) • Client experience and client interaction (through advanced data analytics and better client insights) • Speed (faster execution than humans)
Challenges	• Technical complexity • More regulatory requirements • Buzz-wording (discussing AI but no action)
Operation model	• AI will lead to a mix of self-directed and human-based models • More integrated, efficient and data driven, offer more tailored solutions • Scalability, close collaboration with middle and back offices are the main requirement for integration
Future workforce	• Improved human capabilities enabling employees to focus on more meaningful and creative work • Technical skills are relevant, but for clients the human touch and interaction remain critical • Client-facing roles will be less affected compared to the roles in the middle and back offices • AI can lead to job loss

Our study results show most front office managers are open to adopting AI. This is particularly true for the Millennial generation who enjoy a mix of human and machine in their work. For senior bankers, however, they needed to make more of an effort to catch up with new tech trends and often saw digital transition as a threat. AI should not undermine the importance of '*the human touch and personal interaction with clients*' pointed out by one of our interviewees.

4.2 Case Two: Middle Office

Typical middle office services include trade capturing and settlements, corporate action processing, risk management and reporting regulatory compliance and collateral management [28]. Our research shows that the middle office is clearly focused on robotic process automation (RPA) algorithms, automating simple and repetitive processes such as copy–paste tasks and creating basic reporting. For periodic KYC review, a robot has been built to support the client advisor in performing background checks in the system, one that is connected to the client advisor platform. The research findings from the middle office are summarized in Table 2.

Feedback from the managers we interviewed revealed that they had a generally positive attitude toward new technology in the middle office. Most employees are open

Table 2. Summary of key findings based on thematic coding of interviews in middle office.

Variable	Key findings
Opportunities	• Efficiency (process and cost) • Availability (a robot can run 24/7 and has no sick leave) • Speed and scalability (faster)
Challenges	• Complexity (business process in wealth management) • Operational risk (ethical risk, uncontrollable outcome) • Maintenance effort (technical and human resources)
Operation model	• AI will lead to a leaner organization with fewer people as process will be streamlined and automated from front-to-back • Integrated organization with automated process which lead to cost efficiency, higher accuracy, and faster speed to market requirement for integration
Future workforce	• Improved human capabilities, more expert roles • Technical skills will be relevant, analytical and creativity competence will be important • Some new jobs will be created while some existing ones will disappear

to change and want to develop their skills toward carrying out meaningful tasks and creative work. However, '*The quality, accuracy and reliability of the AI applications must be ensured so that employees trust and accept AI,*' said the manager in the middle office. For AI to succeed at a high level, the bank must have the right workforce, be technologically ready, and provide a stable infrastructure, including proper governance to enable scalability and efficiency.

4.3 Case Three: Back Office

Back office duties include account opening and mortgage loan approvals. As direct interactions with clients are not necessary, back offices are thus usually located in more remote locations due to lower property costs [29]. Traditionally, back office operations have been personnel and paper intensive and mostly conducted manually, because one request may involve several action steps across various departments [29]. Automating back office processes, particularly in operations and risk management, can standardize operations across channels and free up time for employees, which can lead to a 50% increase in client satisfaction and productivity [12]. In the bank where our research was conducted, introduction of investigating robotics and cognitive tools began two years ago, with the focus on basic RPA and automating basic processes using tools such as macros and end-user applications. Thereafter, the focus was on culture change and familiarizing employees with new ways of working. Today, there are several hundred of robots used in operations, most based on RPA. The upcoming evolution will begin with cognitive tools focusing on optical character recognition, where tools can read structured and unstructured text on pages by using natural language processing and chatbots. In risk management, a robot has been built to run scripts, create and send files via file box to the warehouse. However, it will take two to three years to reach a mature level.

Table 3. Summary of key findings based on thematic coding of interviews in back office.

Variable	Key findings
Opportunities	• Efficiency (cost) • Customer insights • Advanced data analytics
Challenges	• Risk from fairness and bias (lack of transparency of an AI model) • Risk from interpretability (lack of auditability of an AI model or difficult to explain why a client did not get the loan because of the machines' decision) • Operational risks (ethical risks)
Operation model	• AI will lead to an integrated operation model • Focus on 'One Bank' spirit by optimizing front-to-back operation • Back office will be operated by fewer but more highly skilled workers
Future workforce	• Improved human capabilities, enable employees to focus on more complex work • Technical skills will be the most relevant • Trend is moving toward hiring data analysts, engineers, and data scientists • Hybrid AI/human workforce, mixed teams consisting onsite and virtual workers

Our takeaway from the back office study (see Table 3) is that thinking along the lines of the 'One Bank' paradigm, having common goals to achieve a more integrated organization, and optimizing front-to-back operations is the key to banking success. Another challenge in the adoption of AI is the lack of technical talent. *'Not only having the right people employed but also having the right infrastructure and a good system landscape in place will be crucial,'* said the head in the back office.

4.4 Cross-case Analysis

According to our results, employees in the front, middle and back offices appear to have generally positive attitudes toward new technologies. Although, a mix of impressions does exist: some feel excited, while others might be afraid to lose their jobs. In general, though, the willingness is there to adopt new tools. In examining the three cases, some differences arise. In the front office, where the focus is on the client, the aim is to use machine learning and natural language processing techniques to understand the client better, get client insights or generate content. Also, digital assistants such as chatbots that can interact with clients for simple client needs play a role. In the middle and back offices, where processes are simpler and more scalable than in the front office, the focus is rather on the automation of simple processes with repetitive tasks in client onboarding or the periodic KYC reviews. While the front office is focused on finding use cases that lead to enhanced client experience and higher sales and profitability, the middle and back offices focus on saving costs and becoming more efficient and agile. To compare:

Table 4. Summary of key findings on similarities and differences between the three cases.

Variable	Similarities	Differences
Opportunities	• Efficiency (time, cost) • Enhanced client experience • Better customer insights	• Scalability of automation • The extend of AI use
Challenges	• Increasing regulatory requirements • Complexity • Maintenance effort • Threat to job	• Operational risks • Legacy structure
Operation model	• AI leads to a more efficient, integrated and leaner operation model • Front-to-back solutions	• Middle office and back office will need fewer workforce but with higher IT skills • Front office will operate in hybrid
Future workforce	• Improve human capabilities enable employees to focus on more complex work • Technical skills are the most relevant; upskilling and reskilling will be crucial	• Different degree regarding job creation • More diverse roles and workforce

5 Conclusion

The present paper is a study on how AI impacts the banking sector. By means of in-depth qualitative field research on wealth management at a large bank, we identified how AI is perceived by managers with respect to opportunities and challenges. In particular, this research also provides an assessment as to how AI will affect intra-collaboration between front, middle and back offices, and how the future banking workforce will be influenced. In reviewing our research, we can draw some preliminary conclusions based on our conceptual framework as shown in Fig. 2.

Wealth management is undergoing a digital transition. The Swiss banking sector has a successful legacy and has proved its resilience over several major crises. However, the Swiss financial sector lags behind key international competitors in terms of digital adoption and adapting to changing business models [30]. Through our analysis, it became clear that bank managers have a relatively positive attitude toward adopting new technologies. Employees also perceive AI as useful if the applications work, the quality of the AI applications is assured, and if they understand how technology helps them to better perform their jobs. AI is meant to create a leaner front-to-back operation process that emphasizes the client's needs. This will lead to a hybrid model, combining self-service to enable clients to access state-of-the-art technologies for basic banking needs combined with human-based high-touch expertise to provide tailored advice. Therefore, AI will create a data-driven culture and only an ethical use of collected data to gain client insights can help offer more tailored solutions and make more accurate risk assessments, which will ensure a sustainable development of the banking sector. From the perspective of future workforce, our study shows AI can substantially free employees from repetitive

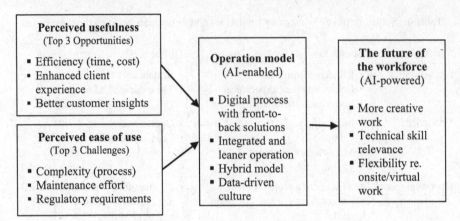

Fig. 2. Applied conceptual framework with key findings from empirical results (Authors).

work for more creative activities. Another advantage of digitalization for the workforce is the flexibility of working remotely. This has best been demonstrated with the pandemic lockdown situation. Without digital means, continuity of the banking business would be in doubt. However, the fear that innovation will cost jobs is justified because digitalization will automate many jobs and integrate what used to be independent units into a whole system. Our research shows that a leaner and AI-powered organizational structure is taking shape, and the crucial factor for the banks will be whether they adopt proactive or reactive approaches to AI.

Though our research findings shed light on how AI impacts the wealth management operation model and the bank workforce, we wish to highlight some of the limitations of the present study. First, our research conclusions are based on 11 interviews from one business area in one bank. To draw general conclusions on how AI is accepted in the banking sector will require more empirical data. Another limitation of the present study is that we did not take organizational culture into account. To what extent the positive attitude toward AI adoption can be attributed to the data-driven culture needs to be further studied. As cross-border banking business becomes more normalized, it is important to keep in mind that if one AI-powered operation model works well in country, that may not necessarily be the case in another national culture and legal environment. Hence, more study on the roles of national culture and leadership in the digital transformation is certainly warranted.

References

1. Mavlutova, I., Volkova, T.: Digital transformation of financial sector and challenges for competencies development. Adv. Econ. Bus. Manag. Res. **99**, 161–166 (2019)
2. Taddeo, M., Floridi, L.: How AI can be a force for good. Science **361**(6404), 751–752 (2018)
3. Mittelstadt, B.: Principles alone cannot guarantee ethical AI. Nat. Mach. Intell. **1**, 501–507 (2019)
4. Chuang, L.-M., Liu, C.-C., Kao, H.-K.: The adoption of fintech service: TAM perspective. Int. J. Manag. Adm. Sci. **3**(7), 1–15 (2016)

5. Aitken, M., Ng, M., Toreini, E., van Moorsel, A., Coopamootoo, K.P.L., Elliott, K.: Keeping it human: a focus group study of public attitudes towards AI in banking. In: Boureanu, I., et al. (eds.) Computer Security. ESORICS 2020. LNCS, vol. 12580. Springer, Cham (2020). https://doi.org/10.1007/978-3-030-66504-3_2

6. Ryder, A.: The key to success with AI is human-machine collaboration, MIT Sloan Manag. Rev. **13** (2021). https://sloanreview.mit.edu/article/the-key-to-success-with-ai-is-human-machine-collaboration/?og=Home+Editors+Picks. Accessed 18 Feb 2021

7. Kobler, D., Frick, J., Stanford, A.: Swiss banking business models of the future - embarking to new horizons. Deloitte Point View **43** (2015). https://www2.deloitte.com/content/dam/Deloitte/ch/Documents/financial-services/ch-en-fs-bank-of-tomorrow.pdf. Accessed 18 Feb 2021

8. Oliver Wyman Wealth Management Report: Global Wealth Managers Out of the pit stop - into the fast lane. https://www.oliverwyman.com/content/dam/oliverwyman/v2/publications/2019/may/Global-Wealth-Managers-2019.pdf. Accessed 18 Feb 2021

9. Lee, M.: How the global wealth management industry is evolving (2018). https://www.ey.com/en_us/wealth-asset-management/how-the-global-wealth-management-industry-is-evolving. Accessed 29 Mar 2020

10. Tschanz, M., Schmitt, C., Hersberger, S., Trautwein, K.: New ecosystems in wealth management and how clients will benefit (2018). https://www.pwc.ch/en/publications/2018/new-ecosystems-in-wealth-management.pdf. Accessed 18 Feb 2021

11. Maude, D.: Global Private Banking and Wealth Management, The New Realities. John Wiley & Sons Ltd, London (2006)

12. Dias, J., Patnaik, D., Scopa, E., van Bommel, E.: Automating the Bank's Back Office. McKinsey & Company, 1–6. https://www.mckinsey.com/business-functions/mckinsey-digital/our-insights/automating-the-banks-back-office. Accessed 25 Feb 2021

13. Genpact Homepage.: Banks reimagine the operating model of the future. https://www.genpact.com/downloadable-content/insight/executive-summary-transforming-banking-operations-through-advanced-operating-models.pdf. Accessed 29 Mar 2020

14. PwC assetmanagement report: Asset & Wealth Management Revolution - Pressure on profitability (2018). https://www.pwc.com/jg/en/publications/pwc_awm_revolution_-_pressure_on_profitability_final.pdf. Accessed 25 Apr 2020

15. WEF publication in collaboration with Deloitte: The new physics of financial services - How artificial intelligence is transforming the financial ecosystem (2018). https://www2.deloitte.com/content/dam/Deloitte/uk/Documents/financial-services/deloitte-uk-world-economic-forum-artificial-intelligence-summary-report.pdf. Accessed 15 Jan 2021

16. Biswas, S., Carson, B., Chung, V., Singh, S., Thomas, R.: AI-bank of the future: Can banks meet the AI challenge? McKinsey & Company, pp. 1–26, September 2020. https://www.mckinsey.com/industries/financial-services/our-insights/ai-bank-of-the-future-can-banks-meet-the-ai-challenge. Accessed 30 Mar 2020

17. Financial Stability Board: Artificial Intelligence and Machine Learning in Financial Services - Market Developments and Financial Stability Implications. Financial Stability Board, November 2017. https://www.fsb.org/wp-content/uploads/P011117.pdf. Accessed 29 Mar 2020

18. He, D., Guo, M., Zhou, J., Guo, V.: The Impact of Artificial Intelligence (AI) on the Financial Job Market Contents. China Development Research Foundation, pp. 1–43, March 2018. BCG-CDRF-The-Impact-of-AI-on-the-Financial-Job-Market_Mar 2018_ENG_tcm9-187843.pdf. Accessed 25 Feb 2021

19. Moulliet, D., Stolzenbach, J., Völker, T., Wagner, I.: Robo-advisory in wealth management: Same name, different game - a look at the German Robo-Advisor landscape (2016). https://www2.deloitte.com/content/dam/Deloitte/de/Documents/financial-services/Robo_No_2.pdf. Accessed 20 Apr 2020

20. Pavoni, S.: Cover story: Wealth management - Robo-Advisors - Wealth management's new robo-reality. The Banker (2015). https://search.proquest.com/docview/1701947492/D5184D 512334B20PQ/2?accountid=15920. Accessed 29 Feb 2020

21. Kaya, O.: Robo-Advisors are the Future of Wealth (2017). https://fintechnews.ch/roboad visor_onlinewealth/robo-advisors-future-wealth-management/11916/. Accessed 29 Feb 2020

22. Digalaki, E.: The impact of artificial intelligence in the banking sector & how AI is being used in 2020. https://www.businessinsider.com/ai-in-banking-report?r=US&IR=T. Accessed 20 Mar 2020

23. Cebula, J.: How AI is shaping the wealth management industry. Investment Week, 12 (2017). https://search.proquest.com/docview/1929354082?accountid=15920%0A. Accessed 20 Mar 2020

24. Narrative Science: The Rise of AI in Financial Services. p. 11 (2018). https://narrativesci ence.com/wp-content/uploads/2018/11/Research-Report_The-Rise-of-AI-in-Financial-Ser vices_2018.pdf. Accessed 25 Feb 2021

25. UBS. Intelligent Automation. A UBS Group Innovation White Paper (2017)

26. Davis, F.D.: Perceived usefulness, perceived ease of use, and user acceptance of information technology. MIS Q. **13**(3), 319–340 (1989)

27. Brown, H., Grillo, J., Kane, E., Kiefer, E., Kurelja, K.: How do you build value when clients want more than wealth? 2019 Global Wealth Management Research Report. https://assets.ey. com/content/dam/ey-sites/ey-com/en_gl/topics/wealth-and-asset-management/wealth-asset-management-pdfs/ey-global-wealth-management-research-report-2019.pdf. Accessed 25 Feb 2021

28. Kutschke, K.: Rethinking the middle office: Solving buy-side challenges with financial technology (2018). https://www.bobsguide.com/guide/news/2018/Mar/13/rethinking-the-middle-office-solving-buy-side-challenges-with-financial-technology/. Accessed 22 Mar 2020

29. TIBCO.: Automating the Back Office -How BPM can help improve productivity in the back office (2011). http://www.redleafco.com/wp-content/uploads/2016/04/wp-automating-the-back-office.pdf. Accessed 30 May 2020

30. Bughin, J., et al.: The Future of Work: Switzerland's Digital Opportunity (2018). https:// alice.ch/fileadmin/user_upload/The-future-of-work-Switzerlands-digital-opportunity.pdf. Accessed 26 Feb 2021

Collaborative Model-Based Process Assessment for Trustworthy AI in Robotic Platforms

Robert Woitsch[1]([X]), Wilfrid Utz[2], Anna Sumereder[1], Bernhard Dieber[3],
Benjamin Breiling[3], Laura Crompton[4], Michael Funk[4], Karin Bruckmüller[5],
and Stefan Schumann[5]

[1] BOC, Vienna, Austria
{robert.woitsch,anna.sumereder}@boc-eu.com
[2] OMiLAB, Berlin, Germany
wilfrid.utz@omilab.org
[3] JOANNEUM RESEARCH – Institute for Robotics and Mechatronics, Klagenfurt, Austria
{bernhard.dieber,benjamin.breiling}@joanneum.at
[4] University of Vienna, Vienna, Austria
{laura.crompton,michael.funk}@univie.ac.at
[5] Johannes Kepler University, Linz, Austria
{karin.bruckmueller,stefan.schumann}@jku.at

Abstract. The use of robots in combination with artificial intelligence (AI) is
a trend with the promises to relieve humans from difficult-, time consuming- or
dangerous work. Intelligent robots aim to solve tasks more efficiently, safer or
partly more stable. Independent of the domain-specific challenge, the configuration of both (a) the robot and (b) the AI currently requires expert knowledge in
robot implementation, security and safety regulations, legal and ethical assessments and expertise in AI. In order to enable a co-creation of domain-specific
solutions for robots with AI, we performed a laboratory survey – consisting of
stakeholder interaction, literature research, proof-of-concept experiments using
OMiLAB and prototypes using a Robot Laboratory – to elicit requirements for an
assistant system that (i) simplifies and abstracts robot interaction, (ii) enables the
co-creative assessment and approval of the robot configuration using AI, and (iii)
ensures a reliable execution. A model-based approach has been elaborated in the
national funded project complAI that demonstrates the key components of such
an assistance system. The main concepts paving the way for a shift from research
and innovation into real-world applications are discussed as an outlook.

Keywords: Robotic · Artificial intelligence · Model-based approaches

1 Introduction

Digital transformation has the potential to create additional value of about 100 trillion $
(in Europe "billion") in the next decade [1]. Industry aims to capitalize this potential by
creating new businesses and improve existing businesses by applying digital technology.
Robotic, AI and the corresponding and enabling key technologies like but not limited

© Springer Nature Switzerland AG 2021
A. Gerber and K. Hinkelmann (Eds.): Society 5.0 2021, CCIS 1477, pp. 163–174, 2021.
https://doi.org/10.1007/978-3-030-86761-4_14

to edge computing, industrial Internet of Things (IoT), block-chain, Big-Data and cloud computing introduce huge business-, social- and technology-potentials. In this paper we address the challenge of autonomous, adaptive or even intelligent robotic systems that promise to (a) be active in dangerous or unhealthy environments, hence relieve human worker from unsafe or unhealthy work, (b) transform or optimize business by either introducing a new form of income or by extending, enlarging or improving an existing business model, (c) reduce volatility by not exclusively relying on human power but relying on human power in combination with supporting robots and the capability to shift some of the workflow between humans and robots.

This paper is based on a one-year survey performed in the national funded project complAI with the aim to: (a) Reduce the complexity and the necessary technological background that is required to realise a robotic application, (b) Empower domain-experts and business managers to co-create innovate new robot scenarios, (c) Enable transparent, audit-proof and compliant solutions "by design" that are assessed and approved according security-, safety-, legal-, ethical- or gender relevant criteria.

Our approach was to develop a model-based assessment tool with the capability to:

1. Introduce a model-based approach using business processes and workflows in order to abstract and hence simplify the complexity of a robot implementation.
2. Enrich the model-based approach with assessment-, approval- and reliability-capabilities to support the generation and execution of compliant workflows at robots.
3. Introduce AI that supports or takes over decision making and enables therefore the introduction of adaptive or autonomous systems.

In the second chapter, we introduce requirements. The main findings are introduced in Sect. 3 – the model-based approach, in Sect. 4 – the assessment criteria, and Sect. 5 – the integration of workflows with assessment criteria. Section 6 lists the downloadable results. Section 7 is a summary with an outlook.

2   Motivation and Use Case Requirements

We started with innovative business models [1, 2] for the hypothetical use case of digital supermarkets, as it enables to (a) identify innovative use cases, without limitations caused by concrete realisation, as well as (b) enable a common understanding with interdisciplinary partners resulting in simplified communication between different technical and professional background as the situation in supermarkets is well known. Based on those high-level ideas we derived concrete use cases like:

- *Workflow creation and abstraction* for robots. Workflows, steering mobile platforms and robots via platform-specific interfaces have been abstracted to become platform-independent workflows defining "artefacts of movements". The more abstract a workflow can be defined; the less technical knowledge is needed.
- *AI for decision making* for adaptive workflows. An adaptive workflow has the capability to change its behaviour either before execution – in case of "pre-binding" – or during execution – in case of "late-binding" – enabling an automated system.

- *Legal and business compliance* of mobile platforms (e.g., self-driving shopping carts) and robot arms (e.g., assembly of products in cold warehouse). This was realised by assessment criteria that have been applied on robot execution models.
- *Assessment of workflows and AI* according legal and business compliance criteria. This was addressed by providing a model-based questionnaire system that links aforementioned workflow models – and abstract workflow models – with AI – semantic lifting and inference as well as rule-based decisions – with a questionnaire model that is extracted out of assessment criteria.

3 Model-Driven Robot Applications

3.1 Introduction into Model-Driven Approach

Conceptual models are used to represent the "system under study" – in our case robots – with the aim to reduce complexity and simplify interaction with the real-world (Fig. 1).

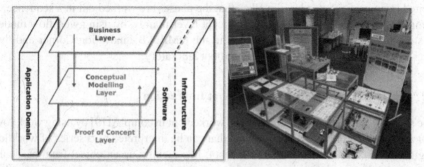

Fig. 1. Introduces the three abstraction layers of the OMiLAB Innovation Corner, of the industrial OMiLAB Innovation Corner at BOC in Vienna is shown in the right part of the figure

We use the OMiLAB innovation corner – introduced above - in order to interlink the (a) business layer that is concerned with creating new business models, (b) the proof-of-concept layer that is concerned with engineering prototypes and (c) the conceptual modelling layer that is concerned with creating organisational models. The OMiLAB Innovation Corner [3] is based on the following principles:

1. **Business Layer:** Focus on Business Model Creation: A business model describes the "rational of how an organisation creates, delivers, and captures value" [4]. The aim is to either improve existing or to generate new business models. This layer therefore provides a high-level overview of the domain, the application scenario as well as the overall eco-system of the organisation. It follows the "Outcome based approach" principle, where digital innovation is always justified by the outcome.
2. **Conceptual Model Layer: Focus on Organisational Model:** Conceptual models are successfully applied in enterprise modelling [5] and information systems [6] and hence capable to describe how the digital solution is applied within an organisation. The digital innovation is therefore described in a technology independent way

using a knowledge-based approach. The knowledge can be interpreted by computer algorithms or by human experts, depending on its model-representation. Hence, we follow the principle to "Invest on use cases and not technology" as the organisational models can be realised with different technologies.

3. **Proof-of-Concept Layer: Focus on Robot Interaction:** Rapid prototyping [7] is "... the idea of quickly assembling a physical part, piece or model of a product". We apply rapid prototyping for both the development of a software application as well as for the development of a physical device. The engineering of rapid prototypes is performed by configuring and integrating pre-packaged features that are provided as services. Instead of fully implementing the prototypes, we apply the "Fail Fast, fail cheap" principle by rapidly composing features in form of services that emulate the main behaviour of the intended solution.

Although the aforementioned layers of the OMiLAB Innovation Corner can be mapped to the three phases of design thinking, "Ideate", "Prototype", and "Test" [8], we explicitly consider that projects either focus on only one or two phases, that phases are visited in no particular order as well as that the phases are worked out in a sequence. In complAI we focused on the proof-of-concept layer mainly, by using workflow models to steer a proof-of-concept robot device in the OMiLAB Innovation Corner and then steer a real-world robot prototype in the robot laboratory.

3.2 Presentation of Workflows for Robot Interaction

The steering of a robot platform hast been worked out in complAI [9] by using workflows that are specified in BPMN notation and that can be interpreted by a series of workflow engines. The concrete movement of a robot, like picking up an object from particular x, y, z coordinates, is implemented as an application interface in form of a method "picking up" with three input variables for x, y and z. This computer program uses platform specific interfaces, in our case these are the dll commands provided by the Dobot Magician, to implement the move of the robot arm to the position x, y, z and start to pick-up the object, in our case to start the suction cup unit with a certain power and a certain amount of time to suck a card that is laying at the corresponding position. All details are provided in the open-source download package [10, 11]. Such a platform-specific command will be exchanged when interacting with the Universal Robot (UR) arm that is used in the laboratory. Hence the movement to pick up an object from a position may be differently implemented but the abstracted move is the same.

This simple sample raises a series of questions like, (a) which tool is used to "pick-up" an object either by grabbing or sucking, (b) is additional information needed for picking and placing like the position when picking and the position when placing, (c) are additional security considerations required like the speed or the power the robot arm moves and the like. Hence, the simple move of an abstract workflow raises several technical and safety relevant questions. In the proof-of-concept environment we aim to free the user from technical questions but focus on issues like picking up an object and placing it. Therefore, we consider this as an "abstraction" to reduce the technical details and enable the focus on other challenges like, who decides what, when and where something is picked up. In a simple form, we can pre-define a fixed sequence of picking-up items and placing them in a fixed order. In case to make the system adaptive and therefore flexible to react on the situation of the environment, we can introduce a sensor that is checking if a certain object is actually available and hence can actually be picked up, or if another object has to be picked up instead. In the following, we describe a layered software stack for executing workflows on a robotic platform, which is further developed from the work presented in [12]. The individual layers can be described as follows: (a) Robots and drivers: Provide hardware specific drivers for individual robots and additional hardware (sensors, etc.). (b) Integration: Provides modules for integrating the underlying hardware, like full body compliance, sensor fusion or robot motion planning. (c) Workflow abstraction: The workflow manager (WFM) provides an execution engine. The state provider collects information of the individual system components and provides it to all other components. (d) Execution: The WFM-API is a re-usable component providing a REST-Interface, which is configured according to the capabilities of the underlying robotic system. In our sample the WFM-API provides methods for executing action sequences like moving the arm to a certain position, relocating the whole platform, or detecting an Augmented Reality-Tag with the camera mounted on the arm's end effector. Similarly, the State-API provides an interface for fetching the current system state from the state provider. (e) User and top-level application: On this layer the user and/or (external) client components can utilize the APIs in order to run or teach robotic applications on the underlying platform.

3.3   AI Integration

The mechanisms to implement and integrate AI in the workflows, are the introduction of adaptive workflows, either pre-binding or late-binding workflows and the introduction of a decision-making component that "binds" the workflow. In our case the "binding" means which values are used for the variables x, y, z, and the decision-making component is either a human who selects which object to pick up next, or an AI component that inferences which object to select next.

In the complAI project, we focused on the model-based aspects and how intelligent decisions related to business [13] can be integrated into the execution models. We based our survey on the assumption that there are tools like image recognition, light-sensors, or weight sensors that can be used to retrieve the necessary information. Our focus was, how to integrate autonomous behaviour in execution models. For that purpose, we propose "decision points" in the execution model, where – potentially – any AI algorithm can be involved to retrieve a decision.

For proof-of-concept purpose, we implemented two approaches in order to decide how to "bind" the workflow. First, we used a rule-based approach following the Decision Model and Notation (DMN) [14] to define "if object a is not available then object b should be taken instead". Such rules can be implemented using a DMN model and the corresponding rule engine that interprets DMN, or it can be programmed in a script, that "if a is not available then object b" should be taken instead. A more sophisticated approach is the semantic lifting of an object with concepts from an ontology. In case this object is not available anymore, a semantic discovery is performed, and the most similar object is used instead. Those AI implementations are provided by ADOxx.org [15]. The demonstration of aforementioned AI-algorithms is considered as a proof-of-concept for showing how AI-algorithms may be integrated into execution workflows. Other AI algorithms may also be integrated to experiment that decisions are either performed by trusted human experts or by a software. The trustworthiness of such a system needs to be ensured, in particular when robot arms or mobile robot platforms autonomously perform movements that need security, safety, legal and ethical reflection. It has to be stated, that independent of the AI-algorithms a certain security level is mandatory and cannot be influenced by AI algorithms for security reasons.

4   Assessment Criteria

4.1   Criteria on Laws and Ethics

Trustworthy AI has grown to become an increasingly important aspect in the quest for ethically sound and legally feasible AI. This has induced many research areas to start thinking about how to (a) build an AI that is trustworthy, and (b) increase the (justified) trust human users put into these systems. And while there are still considerable challenges, especially related to approaches and understandings of trust and trustworthiness, the overall incentive of this quest is not only important, but necessary.

The complAI project [10] addresses some of the practical and theoretical challenges that arise with the realization and implementation of such trustworthy AI. In this, the main task of the ethics team comprised the elaboration of an applicable ethics criteria catalogue. It is important to emphasize the above-mentioned differentiation between trust and trustworthiness. While human agents already – sometimes irrationally and blindly – trust technologies (e.g., navigation systems), a fundamental question is whether the underlying technology is trustworthy [c.f. e.g., 13, 14]. This aspect is echoed in the main objectives of the elaborated criteria.

We began with a more abstract stance on different notions of trust in AI and trustworthiness of AI. Starting from questions concerning expectations towards technologies, over priorizations and values, to ecological and economical objectives, the ethics team put together a set of important key concepts of different disciplines (e.g., law and engineering) who are engaged in the development of trustworthy AI. Some of these elaborated key concepts included i.a. responsibility, risk, danger, ethical corridor, and AI more generally. Based on these concepts, the emerging catalogue focuses on six pillars: (1) The prisonization of the quality of the technical products over the quantitative propagation, (2) Human dignity, (3) The periodization of social wellbeing over economic benefit, (4) Human-centredness of development of AI, (5) Overcoming negative impacts of factual constraints ("Sachzwänge") and impossible backward compatibility ("ausbleibende Rückwärtskompatibilität") so that technological issues do not limit or prefigure human decision making, (6) Risk Management as complex task in technical systems including Robotics and AI.

Those ethical criteria have been refined by aligning with existing literature on trustworthy AI. The catalogue orients itself at some of the key requirements given in the whitepapers and recommendations by the AI HLEG and the ACRAI. These are: Human Agency & Autonomy, Human Oversight, Technical Robustness & Safety, Privacy & Data Governance, Transparency, Diversity, Non-Discrimination & Fairness, Societal &

Environmental Well-Being, Accountability, Responsibility, Values [15–17]. The survey selected the design- and production-level as experimentation filed at which these criteria could (should) be implemented.

In order to specify ethical criteria that (a) address the mentioned principles and values from the project consortium (especially with regards to the established key concepts), and (b) build on the requirements given by the AI HLEG and the ACRAI, the project consortium devised a case study for showing a potentially dangerous interaction situation between human and robot serving as a foundation for the criteria catalogue [10]. An arising example criterion related to the digital supermarket sandbox scenario could then be formulated as follows: (a) General criterion: "Could the AI system affect human autonomy by interfering with the end user's decision-making process in any other unintended and undesirable way?" [c.f. 25] (b) Case-specific: "Does the system stick to the shopping list of the human shopper? Or can it make suggestions according to the shop's incentives?".

This specific criterion is based on the HLEG's requirement on human agency and autonomy and addresses the value of human dignity. With assuring that the human agent's decision and action process are not interfered by the AI, this criterion aims to ensure that the AI does not affect the human agent's autonomy (e.g., by means of manipulation, nudging, or coercion). This means that the human agent's decision environment is not fundamentally changed by the AI, and that the human agent's decision and action can be understood to be the result of a free and autonomous choice.

Summarizing, the criteria given in the catalogue are, first and foremost, an adaption of the criteria given by the AI HLEG and the ACRAI, with the important extension of including the expectations, needs and wants towards values and principles of trustworthy AI, which were established within the project's consortium. These extensions include new learnings on insights, interpretations and understandings, which, so we hope, can be used as a further step towards the development of more trustworthy AI.

Technology and ethics must act within the legal corridor. Especially criminal law plays an important role to avoid damage during the application and, thereby, prevent potential penalties against developers and companies. From a criminal law perspective, several alleged perpetrators can be considered in parallel, in our case the developer/manufacturer as individuals well as the corporation behind them should be protected by a criteria catalogue. Therefor it is particularly important to act with due diligence and predictable in order to prevent subsequent sanctions.

The concept of negligence consists of two additional elements: First, a non-due diligent behaviour (being either an action, or an omission of required action) which actually is causal for the damage, in case of our supermarket robot arm the bodily injury of another person. Second, the predictability of this damage at the time of no-due diligent behaviour. So, the first step for criminal compliant action is to define the standard of due diligent behaviour when developing the robot arm. There is a graduated system of establishing the necessary standard: First, legal ("normative") standards; second, within that normative framework or in case of absence of those rules, professional or social code of conducts (see here the safety and security standards below); finally, in case of missing norms or defined codes of conduct, a comparison to diligent behaviour of (professional) peer groups (we speak about the acting of the "perfect person" in a comparable situation).

Second, due diligence standards require sufficient risks assessment. This includes not only the assessment of existing risks in the application but also the consideration of future dangerous situations. The predictability of potential risks, in general, limits potential accusations of negligent acting. However, especially the implementation of innovative methods and systems demands for supervision of these products. Supervision enables to detect potential risks in process. Thus, supervision forms part of due diligence standards.

Examples of criterion related to the digital supermarket scenario could then be formulated as follows: (a) General criterion to objective acting with due diligence: Is the acting during the development objectively in line with due diligence standards? Are all the standards/leges artis followed? (b) Case-specific: Have all the relevant safety norms been followed in order to avoid that persons are bodily injured? Especially, have ISO 10218-2:2011 and ISO 13482:2014 been followed? (c) General Criterion to predictable risks assessment: Have all the foreseeable/predictable risks emanating from the AI system in action been assessed in the development process? (d) Case-specific: Have all the potential risks been analysed that could result in bodily injury of a person using the arm? Have any possibly dangerous situations been considered that could arise from the user/buyer of the arm?

A total exclusion of risks of liability cannot be guaranteed, but it will limit the risks of sanction and it will contribute to the development of a trustworthy AI system.

4.2 Criteria on Safety and Security

The assessment of a robot application for safety and security always has many application-specific aspects which are hard to generalize. However, in order to establish a criteria catalogue for an initial proof-of-concept, we have used corresponding standards as a basis for our work. In terms of robot safety, we have extracted general guidelines from the ISO-10218-2 [18] "Safety requirements for industrial robots: Part 2: Robot Systems and integration" for stationary robots and ISO-13482 [19] "Robots and robotic devices—Safety requirements for personal care robots" for mobile platforms. We have categorized the requirements and formulated questionnaire questions that can be presented for a later user. Both standards are hard to bring into a machine-readable form since they are not as much checklist formed as others and have many requirements hidden in prosa text. For this proof-of-concept, we have extracted 45 requirements and associated question blocks from ISO-10218-2 and eight such blocks for ISO-13482 (selection of blocks focusing on the safety of the end-product).

For security requirements, we referred to the IEC-62443 [20] "Industrial communication networks - IT security for networks and systems" standards series. It defines requirements and processes for multiple actors involved in developing a secure industrial system, namely the component vendor, the system integrator and the end user. We have specifically used sub-standards 3-3 and 4-2 which define the requirements for the integrator and the component vendor respectively. IEC-62443 defines multiple security levels depending on which kind of attacks a system should be secured against (ranging from incidental manipulation to highly skilled groups with extensive resources). Based on the requirements tables and the associated explanations in the documents, we have formulated example questions for a later questionnaire presented in D5.1 [10].

5   Assistance System to Approve Models

We introduce the model-based assessment assistance system – depicted in the figure below - [11] by linking the different criteria with models that steer robots. After the assessment a digital signature is attached to the models, ensuring quality approval. The experiments faced among others, three key challenges: (1) The model can be checked with regard to legal, ethical and security & safety issues. Essential is the generation of the catalogues and the assessment of models [10]. (2) The modelling of AI and robotics and how assessment ensure compliance [11]. Approved models are signed using hashcodes to avoid fraud, as changes in the models result in a mismatch when comparing the signature. (3) The third challenge is operating compliant models on a robotic platform [9]. Before using the models on the robotic platform their validity can be ensured by means of certification checks. A technical mounting on the robot is necessary that this validation check is performed before starting the execution (Fig. 2).

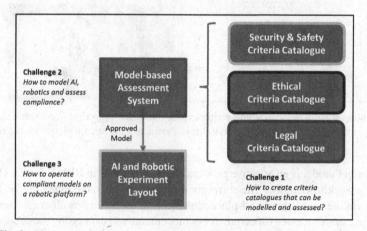

Fig. 2. Depicts the linkage of assessment criteria with the executable workflows

The assessment of a workflow is based on the idea that assessment criteria can be formulated by corresponding safety-, security-, legal- or ethical- experts. Those criteria are then transformed into a semi-structured questionnaire model. The meta model of this questionnaire defines answer types, such as single answers, multiple answers, or textual answers as well as how those answers are then used to calculate a so-called score value. This score indicates if answers to a set of questions can be considered as complaint – green values, not-complaint – red values, or yellow value that are in between and hence need further (expert) investigation. More details on how to link the questionnaire model with the workflow can be found in D4.1 [11] of complAI.

After successfully assessing the workflows, the model is digitally signed using an authentication environment and a digital signature of the model. A cryptographic environment has been designed to ensure that the whole process of developing, assessing, certifying and executing a robot program is secure. This environment has been published in [21]. The verification process is realized in form of a distributed ledger to ensure integrity, authenticity and non-repudiation of the artifacts resulting from the verification process as well as the development process itself. In this context the information shared by the peers is grouped in channels, which ensures privacy of sensitive information as the channel access can be restricted by the use of certificates.

Material for download can be found in [2, 12–14, 19].

6 Available Results

We experimented with the use case where a customer chooses fruits from a mobile app, enter the shop and a pick and place robot already prepared the basket. The challenge is to describe the (a) process of "picking and placing", and (b) decision which fruit to pick. A simple sequence was modelled – as shown below – as a Petri-Net [15] (Fig. 3).

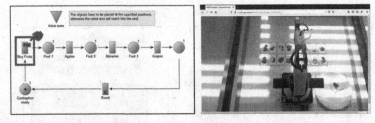

Fig. 3. Shows a Petri-Net describing a simple pick-and-place procedure for a robot arm. Each transition invokes an action from the robot that is shown as a life stream picture on the right

The target model is an adaptive pick-and-place workflow in BPMN format [16] executed by a workflow engine. The corresponding models are in the figure below. In order to transform the simple pick-and-place sequence, we used to a flowchart representation, introducing sub-processes for certain robot movements and expressing the decision pints via user interactions. This enables an explicit demonstration how decisions influence the workflow. In our case the interpretation is based on sensor information which fruits are available and to select the correct choice. This decision point is experimented with a user interaction. The flowchart representation therefore enabled a mock-up of the workflow with adaptive behaviour. The resulting BPMN workflow was implemented on a workflow engine combining the sub-workflows for movements, the orchestration of the movements and the indication of intelligent interaction.

The proof-of-concept engineering of intelligent robot interaction using workflows was based on the following default setting: (a) The pre-packaged Dobot Magician [18] was used to demonstrate the robot arm. (b) The corresponding IoT Adapter – Raspberry-Pi – and corresponding software – Tomcat Web-Application, Dobot Magician interfaces. (c) The pre-installed Modelling Toolkit Bee-Up is used for modelling the Petri-Net, the flowchart and the BPMN processes that accesses the IoT Adapter. (d) A third-party workflow engine was used. The configurations can be downloaded from the complAI ADOxx.org developer space [19] (Fig. 4).

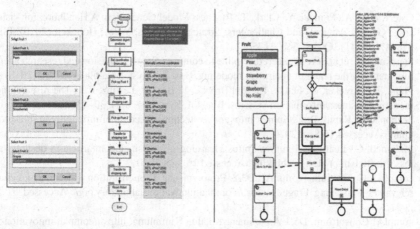

Fig. 4. Introduces a pick-and-place workflow picking up cards with fruit-symbols and introduce dynamic behaviour via sub-processes in form of a flowchart or BPMN workflows

7 Outlook and Next Steps

The paper introduces the co-creation of domain-specific assessment and certification solutions for robots using AI, based on a stakeholder interaction, literature research, experiments within the OMiLAB Innovation Corner and prototypes using a robot.

This model-based approach simplifies the configuration of robots and in addition allow to apply algorithms such as analysis, the management of releasing a model and the integration with AI-algorithms that make a workflow adaptive.

The linkage of a workflow model with so-called assessment criteria that are managed by legal advisors, security experts and ethical advisors enables an eco-system, where experts can cooperate without the need of conceptualization capabilities but by using the modelling-framework that supports the transformation from text to concept models.

When certifying a model – approving that this model passed the technical, legal, security or ethical reviews – this model is then digitally signed to ensure that only certified models are executed on the robot.

Our expectation is that these results support work on higher reliability, governance, risk management and compliance when cyber physical systems act autonomously.

References

1. World Economic Forum, Digital Transformation Initiative. http://reports.weforum.org/dig ital-transformation/wp-content/blogs.dir/94/mp/files/pages/files/dti-executive-summary-201 80510.pdf. Slide 20, Accessed 16 Sept 2020
2. complAI Consortium, D3.1 Spezifikation des Anwendungsfalls. https://complai.innovation-laboratory.org/. Accessed 31 Jan 2021
3. Woitsch, R.: Industrial digital environments in action: the OMiLAB innovation corner. In: Grabis, J., Bork, D. (eds.) The Practice of Enterprise Modeling. LNBIP, vol. 400, pp. 8–22. Springer, Cham (2020). https://doi.org/10.1007/978-3-030-63479-7_2

4. Osterwalder, A., Pigneur, Y., Clark, T.: Business Model Generation: A Handbook for Vision-aries, Game Changers, and Challengers. Strategyzer series. Wiley, Hoboken (2010). ISBN 9780470876411. OCLC 648031756
5. Sandkuhl, K., et al.: From expert discipline to common practice: a vision and research agenda for extending the reach of enterprise modeling. Bus. Inf. Syst. Eng. **60**(1), 69–80 (2018)
6. Frank, U., Strecker, S., Fettke, P., vom Brocke, J., Becker, J., Sinz, E.J.: The research field modeling business information systems. Bus. Inf. Syst. Eng. **6**(1), 39–43 (2014)
7. Techopedia, Rapid Prototyping. https://www.techopedia.com/definition/9093/rapid-protot yping. Accessed 16 Sept 2020
8. Malamed, C.: Learning Solutions. https://learningsolutionsmag.com/articles/a-designer-add resses-criticism-of-design-thinking. Accessed 16 Sept 2020
9. complAI Consortium, complAI D3.2 Prototypische Demonstration sowie Ausarbeitung relevanter Forschung Fragen. https://complai.innovation-laboratory.org/. Accessed 31 Jan 2021
10. complAI Consortium, D5.1 Assessment Katalog Sammlung. https://complai.innovation-lab oratory.org/. Accessed 31 Jan 2021
11. complAI Consortium, D4.1 Modell-basiertes Assistenzsystem. https://complai.innovation-laboratory.org/. Accessed 31 Jan 2021
12. Haspl, T., Breiling, B., Dieber, B., Pichler, M., Breitenhuber, G.: Flexible industrial mobile manipulation: a software perspective. In: Proceedings of the OAGM & ARW Joint Workshop 2019, Steyr, Austria, 9–10 May 2019. https://doi.org/10.3217/978-3-85125-663-5-10
13. Taddeo, M.: Modelling trust in artificial agents, a first step toward the analysis of e-trust. Minds Mach **20**(2), 243–257 (2010)
14. Coeckelbergh, M.: Can we trust robots? Ethics Inf. Tech. **14**(1), 53–60 (2011)
15. AI HLEG: The Assessment List for Trustworthy Artificial Intelligence (ALTAI) for self-assessment, European Commission, Brussels. https://futurium.ec.europa.eu/en/european-ai-alliance/document/ai-hleg-assessment-list-trustworthy-artificial-intelligence-altai. Accessed 21 Dec 2020
16. IEEE, Ethically Aligned Design. https://standards.ieee.org/industry-connections/ec/ead-v1. html. Accessed 21 Dec 2020
17. AI HLEG, Ethics Guidelines for Trustworthy Artificial Intelligence, High-Level Expert Group on Artificial Intelligence, European Commission, Brussels. https://ec.europa.eu/digital-sin gle-market/en/news/ethics-guidelines-trustworthy-ai. Accessed 21 Dec 2020
18. ISO, ISO 10218-2:2011. https://www.iso.org/standard/41571.html. Accessed 11 Nov 2020
19. ISO, ISO 13482:2014. https://www.iso.org/standard/53820.html. Accessed 11 Nov 2020
20. ISA, InTech: New ISA/IEC 62443 standard specifies security capabilities for control system components. https://www.isa.org/intech-home/2018/september-october/departments/new-standard-specifies-security-capabilities-for-c. Accessed 31 Jan 2021
21. Breiling, B., Dieber, B., Pinzger, M., Rass, S.: A cryptography-powered infrastructure to ensure the integrity of robot workflows. J. Cybersecur. Priv. **1**, 93–118 (2021). https://doi.org/10.3390/jcp1010006
22. complAI Webpage. https://complai.innovation-laboratory.org. Accessed 15 Feb 2021

Examining Future Ready Accounting Course (FRAC) Experiences for Non-accounting Students: An Education in Society 5.0 Using Augmented Reality and IoT

S. A. Zainuddin(✉) ⓘD, N. A. M. Nasirⓘ, T. Abdullahⓘ, M. N. H. Yusoffⓘ,
M. R. Yasoaⓘ, S. F. Muhamadⓘ, and N. M. Saidⓘ

Faculty of Entrepreneurship and Business, Universiti Malaysia Kelantan, Kampus Kota,
16100 Kota Bharu, Kelantan, Malaysia
sitiafiqah@umk.edu.my

Abstract. An accounting course today has become an essential syllabus for social sciences students, particularly, in business, management, and entrepreneurship. Since social sciences students are not purely accounting students, learning accounting is proven to be more challenging for them and innovations for the course, including the methods used in teaching the accounting course. This study aims to develop a Future Ready Accounting Course (FRAC) for non-accounting students by using simple augmented reality technology, embedded into the course's teaching and learning method. This study examines the non-accounting students' experiences of applying FRAC in their accounting courses. By using a mixed method approach, questionnaire surveys were conducted to examine the students' experiences towards FRAC revolving three elements of the course, lecturers, and infrastructures or facilities. Since the lecturer teaching FRAC composed one member of the research team, a field observation also carried out to monitor the FRAC's implementation. The results of the study reveal an evidence that an accounting course can indeed be taught in more innovative and attractive ways. In other words, accounting departments would do well to consider the novel contribution made by this study by adopting FRAC to replace the old-fashioned conventional accounting courses. It is noted that the non-accounting students employed in this study were able to feel a new experience in learning an accounting course with the adoption of FRAC. This significantly concludes that FRAC can successfully attract and help non-accounting students to excel in their accounting courses to fulfil the requirements of their degrees.

Keywords: Education for society 5.0 · Future ready accounting curriculum · Augmented reality · Internet of Things

A. Gerber and K. Hinkelmann (Eds.): Society 5.0 2021, CCIS 1477, pp. 175–187, 2021.
https://doi.org/10.1007/978-3-030-86761-4_15

1 Introduction

An accounting course is undeniably no longer limited to only accounting students [3]. This is chiefly because accounting is not a narrow discipline. In other words, the accounting discipline encompasses knowledge beyond the traditional understanding of bookkeeping, debits, and credits. In fact, the accounting field covers wide areas of knowledge that non-accounting students must be equipped with, such as corporate governance [4], earning management [5], risk management [6], and [7] etc. All of these knowledge is ultimately useful for graduates when entering and competing in the employment market. Students equipped with accounting knowledge and skills will find it easier to be employed in comparison to those without [3, 8]. In essence, an accounting course today has become a compulsory or a pre-requisite course for non-accounting students before they are allowed to take advanced courses, depending on their undergraduate programme's specialties or majors. These non-accounting students mostly come from the business, management, and entrepreneurship programmes [9]. These students must therefore grasp the basic functions of accounting knowledge and skills, valuable in helping them manage the financial and non-financial aspects of a business. However, it is noted that some of them have found it difficult to learn accounting [10]. There are many explanations for that, with one outstanding explanation being that the traditional accounting course is 'old fashioned', less attractive, and less engaging for students. Besides, the advent of the Industrial Revolution (IR) 4.0 suggests that technology is ultimately an indispensable tool in optimising outputs, in this case, increasing the innovations and attractiveness of a conventional accounting course. In other words, it is necessary for accounting courses to be embedded with the latest innovations and technologies in order to cover existing loopholes and make the courses more attractive for non-accounting students [9, 11], in particular, those from the Society 5.0. Integration of technology in the teaching and learning method for the course is ultimately necessary as it can encourage students to provide better interest and participation towards the course.

Although the demand for a future-ready curriculum is growing [11, 12], the action taken on improvising and developing the course is proven to be too sluggish. Many studies have been conducted to show the need to develop a future-ready course for students (see [8, 11]). Unfortunately, among those, very few studies have tried to propose relevant processes and methods to develop a future-ready course. The study hence aims to develop a future-ready curriculum, in particular, focusing on an accounting course for non-accounting students.

Evidently, students in the pure sciences disciplines are naturally more technologically-savvy than those in the social sciences disciplines. This is due to the simple fact that technology is a prominent feature in the disciplines of the former. For example, the use of machines to analyse scientific samples and report results of experiments, or the use of artificial intelligence to conduct specific laboratory chores, providing additional mileage to human limitations, all help enhance the familiarity of technology to pure sciences students. For most pure sciences students, laboratories are regarded as their playgrounds, offering a particular excitement and experience in the teaching and learning processes of the pure sciences courses. That subjective value ultimately creates voluntary participation among the students in learning the courses. On the other hand, social sciences students are still largely entrenched in in the traditional ways of teaching and learning the courses. Their exposure to technology are in fact found greater outside of the teaching and learning activities of their courses than inside them. This situation therefore influences the students' commitments, interests and participations in expecting more innovative and attractive social sciences courses. In essence, students from both pure sciences and social sciences must be equipped with technology-based courses to increase their engagement and excitement in their learning experiences [13]. Acknowledging this loophole, this study therefore firmly believes in the need for technology to be embedded into existing social science courses, in particular, the accounting course.

2 Problem Statement

A conventional accounting curriculum currently lacks in its efforts to embed latest technological trends into its syllabus. On top of that, the curriculum also simultaneously fails to equip students with additional set of skills, necessary for students to enhance their employment marketability in the near future. Indeed, it is unfortunate that many students today graduate without being equipped with future-proof skills and sufficient exposures of current trends. This naturally leads to many graduates facing additional challenges in getting a job placement as many employers naturally prefer graduates with better technological and digital knowledge and skills. Hence, this explains the need for students to be supplied with a future-ready curriculum incorporating a greater number of contemporary skills (i.e. digital skills, communication skills, interpersonal skills, etc.) in their learning experiences.

Besides, the year 2020 witnessed an aggressive shift towards digital-based teaching and learning activities. The coronavirus pandemic has impacted every aspect of human life [14], including the education sector. A massive amount of courses around the world are transforming their modes of delivery from that of a non-face to that of a face-to face. In this context, the pandemic has forced the society to follow standard operating procedures to reduce the virus from spreading, for example, through the implementation of social distancing in public places [15]. However, in reality, social distancing has a unique side effect to the traditional activities of teaching and learning. For instance, lectures and tutorials now have to be conducted online through synchronous or asynchronous methods. In the context of accounting courses, this pandemic situation alone proves that the current curriculum is no longer relevant to be practiced and need to be improved or transformed into a future-ready accounting curriculum. In retrospect, the pandemic and the consequential new norms have become the push factors for transforming the conventional accounting curriculum towards one that is forward looking and indeed, future-ready [16].

3 Methodology and Design

Figure 1 shows [1, 2] the Attracting, Informing, Positioning and Delivering (AIPD) framework that has been adapted and modified according to the context of this study. The framework shows that there are four elements regarded as independent variables for the previous study, namely, attracting, informing, positioning, and delivering. The four elements are also called strategic dimensions within the framework. These elements affect the way an 'object' becomes more attractive, dynamic, innovative, trustworthy, and exciting. Based on the current study context, the 'object' here refers to the accounting course. Furthermore, Fig. 1 also implies that an attractive, dynamic, innovative, trustworthy, and exciting accounting course would naturally create positive feedbacks (i.e. positive perception towards the course) from the students.

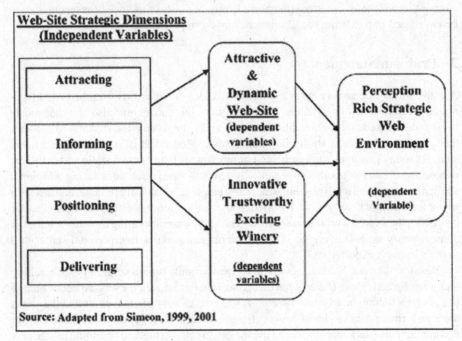

Fig. 1. AIPD framework

3.1 Design of FRAC

In this research, the project design flow in Fig. 2 proposes seven phases of developing and implementing FRAC for students. This design is primarily based on Simeon (1999, 2001) AIPD framework.

Phase 1. In the first phase, the project began with a series of discussions on finding a suitable idea (i.e. innovative and attractive accounting course) for the project. In addition, the discussions were complemented with in-depth readings on the subject matter - the accounting course. The outcome of the discussions and in-depth readings led the research team to an idea that seeks to innovate and restructure existing conventional teaching and learning activities, particularly, for the accounting course. The course needs to be reformed in order to suit current demands arising from rapid technological development, students' preferences, as well as universities' and industries' needs. The idea also reflected the government's aspiration to encourage educational institutions, such as higher learning institutions to produce future-ready curriculums for students in preparing

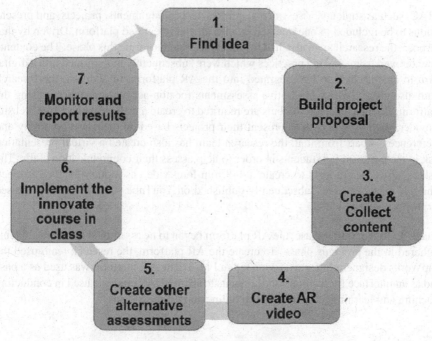

Fig. 2. Project design flow

them to meet the contemporary demands of industries. Upon confirmation of the idea with the research team, the project was named Future Ready Accounting Curriculum (FRAC) for non-accounting students.

Phase 2. In the second phase, more discussions on the agreed idea were performed. The discussions were now focussed on sharing all ideas to build the project's proposal. The project was a strategic collaboration of a research team consisting of lecturers with various knowledge and expertise. The lecturers represent the multiple sub-disciplines of accounting, such as financial accounting, management accounting, financial management, entrepreneurial finance, information technology, business management, social accounting, as well as corporate governance. With a good number of experts working together, the project proposal was prepared and completed within a short period of time. Furthermore, at this stage, the researchers have also started using technology in conducting discussions, segregating tasks and duties to each member in various geographical areas, setting working schedules, and gathering all works in order to form a complete project proposal.

Phase 3. In the third phase, the project proposal was expanded upon completion from the previous phase. Also decided in Phase 3 was the technology employed for the project's innovation. For the purpose of this project, the simple Augmented Reality (AR) technology was used to create an interactive, virtual, and integrated platform containing FRAC contents for both lecturers and students. The AR platform required various contents for

FRAC, such as students' assessments, quizzes, tests, assignments, projects, and presentations to be included in one interactive, virtual, and integrated platform. Driven by that purpose, the research team also had to gather all contents during this phase. The contents were derived from existing practices which were subsequently transformed into a digital form to enable them to be integrated into the AR platform. In addition, the research team also created a few innovative assessments for non-accounting students using the platform. For instance, the students are required to create a website using a free website provider, such as Wix.com to present their projects based on their own creativity and preferences. Apart from that, the research team has also created a virtual presentation task in the platform for students in order to help assess their communication skills. The task requires the students to create a 4–8 min long video as a pitch for their project, which is expected to be subsequently published on YouTube, with an award promised for the most liked video.

Phase 4. In the fourth phase, the AR platform began to be assembled based on contents gathered in the previous phase. To create the AR platform, the research team used the ZapWorks designer platform as depicted in Fig. 3. The AR platform was used as a base and as an interface for lecturers and students to share FRAC contents used in conducting teaching and learning activities in both online and offline classes.

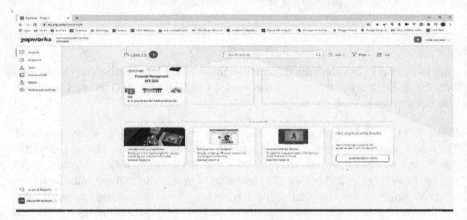

Fig. 3. ZapWorks designer platform

Figure 3 shows the ZapWorks designer platform that was used to create the Zappar Triggers, a components used to incorporate teaching and learning materials into the platform. Once a project from the platform was published, a single user interface appeared and the platform was now ready for use for both students and lecturers. In order to arrive to the interface, students and lecturers needed to scan the Zappar Triggers using the Zappar scanner (Fig. 4) which could be downloaded for free from the Google Play store.

Figure 5 shows the Zappar Triggers needed to be created on the ZapWorks designer platform provided to students and lecturers to enable them to scan the tracker, and enter the platform's classrooms. The trackers also provided access to materials, guidelines,

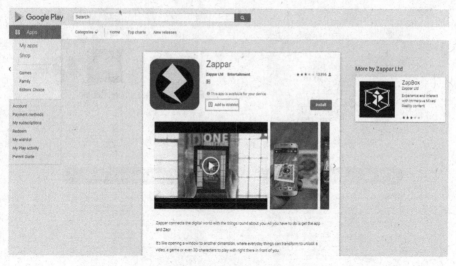

Fig. 4. Zappar scanner

Fig. 5. Zappar triggers

instructions, assessments including quizzes, tests, project reports, videos, lecturer profiles and other materials related to the course, which have been prepared in the ZapWorks Designer Platform beforehand.

The Zappar Triggers must be shared with students by lecturers or FRAC coordinators. They can be shared via the common e-learning platforms provided by the individual university or through social networking platforms such as the class' WhatsApp or Telegram groups. For the purpose of providing better information, the Zappar Triggers could be shared on a piece of poster containing brief information about the course (i.e. FRAC) or they could be also printed on a poster as depicted in Fig. 6 below.

Phase 5. In the fifth phase, other alternative assessments were created for the purpose of blended learning. The assessments were required to be suitable and relevant to FRAC. These included online quizzes, tests, exercises, accounting project reports completed and published on a website (Fig. 7), and presentation videos that are professionally edited, published, and attached on the same website.

Fig. 6. Course poster

Phase 6. The sixth phase saw the implementation of FRAC in accounting classes. Students who were learning via FRAC were expected to experience more interactive and fun learning activities.

Phase 7. In the final phase, the students' responses, feedbacks and recommendations were subsequently gathered and examined. Figure 8 shows the students' responses from

Fig. 7. Student project website

the distributed questionnaire surveys. The descriptive analysis and results of the surveys are illustrated comprehensively in Fig. 9.

A	B	C	D	E	F	G	H
NAMA	KOD_PRO	NAMA_PR	KOD_KUR	NAMA_KU	KATEGORI	MARKAH	JAWAPAN_SOALAN_TERBUKA
MOHD. N	SAL	SARJANA	AFT1043	ASAS PER	A	4	Sangat mudah difahami
MUHAMM	SAB	SARJANA	AFT1043	ASAS PER	A	5	kefahaman utama yang saya perolehi melalui kursus ini adalah cara pengiraan akaun sesebuah syarikat dan dapat r
MUHAMM	SAB	SARJANA	AFT1043	ASAS PER	A	4	inovasi pensyarah dalam pengajaran dan pembelajaran kursus ini dengan menunjukkan slide dan video.
ARIFF BIN	SAL	SARJANA	AFT1043	ASAS PER	A	5	Memahami dengan jelas
LOO CHUM	SAL	SARJANA	AFT1043	ASAS PER	A	5	Menjalankan kelas tutorial dengan menggunakan Google Meet disebabkan kesemua pelajar berada di tempat yan
LOO CHUM	SAL	SARJANA	AFT1043	ASAS PER	A	4	Kemudahan yang lengkap
LOO CHUM	SAL	SARJANA	AFT1043	ASAS PER	A	4	Mempunyai sedikit masalah kerana kursus asas perakaunan lebih memerlukan keterangan yang banyak daripada p
DARVESH	SAB	SARJANA	AFT1043	ASAS PER	A	5	Kepentingan dan aplikasi akaun
MARUN R.	SAL	SARJANA	AFT1043	ASAS PER	A	5	dapat memahami lebih lanjut dan secara teliti perkara-perkara yang mengandungi dalam subjek ini
WAN NUR	SAB	SARJANA	AFT1043	ASAS PER	A	4	intelektual dan mempunyai pelbagai kemahiran untuk melakukan kelas walau pelbagai rintangan yang perlu di ha
LEE ZHENC	SAB	SARJANA	AFT1043	ASAS PER	A	5	online kelas
FATIN SUH	SAB	SARJANA	AFT1043	ASAS PER	A	5	pengiraan yang betul dan teknik pembukaan akaun yang betul
ILHAM NU	SAR	SARJANA	AFT1043	ASAS PER	A	4	saya memahami subjek asas perakaunan ini sangat penting dalam kehidupan seharian. la mengajar kita bagaimana
ILHAM NU	SAR	SARJANA	AFT1043	ASAS PER	A	4	Pensyarah sangat berinovasi dalam membuat sesuatu perkara serta mempunyai pelabagai alternatif kepada pelaja
NUR ANTA	SAL	SARJANA	AFT1043	ASAS PER	A	5	sangat baik
SARAH AN	SAL	SARJANA	AFT1043	ASAS PER	A	5	Its good because my lecturer will post the notes and more information where we able to answer it. The notes that
AINNUR IF	SAB	SARJANA	AFT1043	ASAS PER	A	5	tentang akaun lebih mendalam
ILLY AAINI	SAL	SARJANA	AFT1043	ASAS PER	A	5	Kefahaman utama adalah saya mengetahui pengiraan dalam prinsip perakaunan.
NUR AMIR	SAB	SARJANA	AFT1043	ASAS PER	A	4	Membantu dalam proses memahami pelajaran dengan lebih berkesan
NUR FATIH	SAL	SARJANA	AFT1043	ASAS PER	A	5	baik
NUR ASHII	SAB	SARJANA	AFT1043	ASAS PER	A	5	Sangat terbaik
SALWA BII	SAL	SARJANA	AFT1043	ASAS PER	A	5	menggunakan pengetahuan dan fahaman untuk menjana ilmu ke arah penyelesaian masalah berkaitan bidang per
SALWA BII	SAL	SARJANA	AFT1043	ASAS PER	A	4	Platform seperti e-learning ini sangat bagus kerana memudahkan pelajar dan pensyarah memberi tugasan kepada
MUHAMM	SAB	SARJANA	AFT1043	ASAS PER	A	3	baik
NUR SOLIF	SAB	SARJANA	AFT1043	ASAS PER	A	5	Sangat membantu

Fig. 8. Students' responses, feedbacks and recommendations (in Malay language)

4 Analyses, Results and Discussions

Observations performed during classes and after the course was completed show how FRAC has successfully transformed traditional accounting teaching and learning activities into one interactive course for students. Students were reported as becoming more motivated and committed towards the course's requirements. Furthermore, they also became more guided, compliant and skillful when assigned more technical activities using technology and applications. These results are certainly in line with the FRAC Course Learning Outcome (CLO), intended to equip students with digital, interpersonal, communication, and entrepreneurial skills.

Meanwhile, Table 1, and 2 illustrate responses gathered from 411 non-accounting students after they experienced FRAC throughout one semester. Item Number 2 and 5 in Table 1 show the highest mean score which were 4.5 each. The score indicates that information about the scope of the course's contents were not only accurate, but were also clearly distributed and explained to the students in beginning of the course. The scope of the course' contents is also the most crucial part which guides and tells the students their directions throughout the course, as well as the level of preparation they are required to have before commencing the course.

Table 1. Students' evaluation on course of FRAC

A. Course		Mean score 4.4
1	This course increases my interest to study the related field much deeper	4.4
2	This course has a proper scope of content	4.5
3	This course contains important skills, concepts and information	4.4
4	This course helps my intellectual development	4.4
5	There is a course briefing in the early semester	4.5
6	Teaching activities help the inculcation of soft skills	4.3
7	Assessment results are informed to students in a reasonable time	4.4
8	Generally, I am satisfied with this course	4.4

Table 2 shows students' responses on the infrastructures and facilities during FRAC's implementation. The overall mean scores show that most students gave a 4.1 out of 5.0 rating for this key element of the course. Item Number 6 has the highest mean score with 4.2, referring to the students' satisfaction with the teaching and learning facilities provided in the course.

Figure 9 shows the students' course grade analysis for FRAC. It was found that 314 out of 411 non-accounting students scored A+ to A−, or approximately 76.40% of the total number of students, in their experiences with FRAC. Meanwhile, the average mark obtained among the students was 80 out of 100 with a standard deviation of 10.

Table 2. Students' evaluation on infrastructure and facilities of FRAC.

C.. Infrastructures/facilities		Mean score 4.1
1	Class environment and physical facilities provided support the teaching & learning activities of this course	4.1
2	ICT facilities (internet, laboratories, and software) provided support the teaching & learning activities for this course	4.1
3	Space provided supports individual and group learning for this course	4.1
4	Resources available for this course in the library are adequate	4.1
5	Teaching aids (microphone, LCD, screen, etc.) provided are satisfactory	4.1
6	In general, I am satisfied with the teaching and learning facilities provided for this course	4.2

Based on the observations and lecturers' reports, the one student who obtained a fail for the subject, did not in fact participate in FRAC since the beginning and has made an intention to drop, thus never having had a full experience of FRAC.

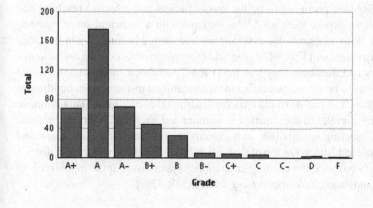

Grade	Total
A+	68
A	176
A-	70
B+	46
B	31
B-	7
C+	6
C	4
C-	0
D	2
F	1

Fig. 9. Students course grade analysis.

This finding is parallel to findings of other studies that conclude embedding technologies in the teaching and learning activities leads to an upward shift in the students' performance [17, 18].

5   Conclusions, Limitations and Recommendations

In summary, FRAC is a suitable and desirable course for the Generation Alpha students (also known as the Society 5.0 students) who are easily captivated by a comprehensive integration of technology in various aspects of life, most particularly, in education. Indeed, this study has produced a novel output for students, lecturers, as well as education providers in the area of accounting. The novel invention not only improved and built on the traditional accounting teaching and learning activities, but also encouraged the level of students' commitment, participation and understanding towards the course. However, in addressing limitations for the study, there are definitely plenty other promising new technologies out there that can be used to provide innovations for the course, such as the Internet of Things (IoT) and Big Data, worth to be explored in future researches. Furthermore, this study can also be replicated for other academic courses and not only limited to accounting courses. As regards to recommendations, this study has proposed a few for students, lecturers, education providers and the Ministry of Education alike. With regards to students, FRAC is an indispensable tool to enhance the students' interests and motivation in learning an accounting course as it provides an interactive learning experience, especially to the Generation Alpha (Gen Alpha) students who are typically technology savvy. Meanwhile, with respect to lecturers, FRAC will be found to be a sophisticated teaching method in teaching an accounting course, especially, to the Gen Alpha students. FRAC is promised to be the most efficient and effective teaching and learning alternative to expose the Gen Alpha students with a sufficient set of contemporary accounting skills alongside the disciplinary knowledge in finance. On the other hand, education providers will find FRAC a stellar example to other courses and schools. As for the Ministry of Education, they will find FRAC perhaps, as one example of best practice or guidelines to be recommended to most educational institutions in building an innovative curriculum and transforming existing traditional curriculums. This initiative is also undoubtedly parallel to the practice recommended by the Ministry to promote innovations in the existing universities' curriculums to suit the current landscape and fulfil demands of the industries. On top of that, FRAC is also aligned with the Ministry's current aspiration to enhance the existing educational system to adapt competitively to a plethora of demands and challenges arising from the IR 4.0.

Acknowledgments. The authors acknowledge Faculty of Entrepreneurship and Business, Universiti Malaysia Kelantan for the facilities. Special thanks to those who contributed to this project directly or indirectly especially to my family, office-mate and accounting team-mate.

References

1. Simeon, R.: Evaluating domestic and international Web-site strategies. Internet Res. **9**(4), 297–308 (1999)

2. Simeon, R.: Evaluating the branding potential of web sites across borders. Mark. Intell. Plan. **19**(6), 418–424 (2001)
3. Roska, V., Martincevic, I., Sesar, V.: Accounting education for better employment-case study in Croatia. In: Economic and Social Development: Book of Proceedings, pp. 312–330 (2018)
4. Nasir, N.A.B.M., Ali, M.J., Ahmed, K.: Corporate governance, board ethnicity and financial statement fraud: evidence from Malaysia. Account. Res. J. **32**(3), 514–531 (2019)
5. Nasir, N.A.M., Ali, M.J., Nawi, N.C.: Studies on earnings management and financial statement fraud in corporate firms. Res. World Econ. **10**(2), 15–19 (2019)
6. Zainuddin, S.A., et al.: Risk management as governmentality in organization. Int. J. Eng. Res. Technol. **13**(12), 4439–4449 (2021)
7. Zainuddin, S.A., et al.: Risk management: a review of recent philosophical perspectives. PalArch's J. Archaeol. Egypt/Egyptol. **17**(9), 1931–1944 (2020)
8. Maali, B., Al-Attar, A.M.: Accounting curricula in universities and market needs: the jordanian case. SAGE Open **10**(1), 1–12 (2020)
9. Bakar, M.A.A.A., Amirul, S.M., Ripain, N., Ab Fatah, N.S., Bosi, M.K.: A preliminary analysis of non-accounting students perception towards introductory accounting course among private institution in Sabah. Malays. J. Bus. Econ. Spec. Ed. **2**, 1–11 (2019)
10. Abbott, J.I., Palatnik, B.R.: Students' perceptions of their first accounting class: implications for instructors. Account. Educ. **27**(1), 72–93 (2018)
11. Andiola, L.M., Masters, E., Norman, C.: Integrating technology and data analytic skills into the accounting curriculum: accounting department leaders' experiences and insights. J. Account. Educ. **50**, 100655 (2020)
12. Bowles, M., Ghosh, S., Thomas, L.: Future-proofing accounting professionals: ensuring graduate employability and future readiness. J. Teach. Learn. Graduate Employab. **11**(1), 1–21 (2020)
13. Alaboudi, A., Alharbi, A.S.: Impact of digital technology on Saudi students. Int. J. Inf. Technol. **13**(3), 943–950 (2021). https://doi.org/10.1007/s41870-020-00451-7
14. Alao, B.B., Gbolagade, O.L.: Coronavirus pandemic and business disruption: the consideration of accounting roles in business revival. Int. J. Acad. Multidiscip. Res. **4**(5), 108–115 (2020)
15. Newbold, S.C., Finnoff, D., Thunström, L., Ashworth, M., Shogren, J.F.: Effects of physical distancing to control COVID-19 on public health, the economy, and the environment. Environ. Resour. Econ. **76**(4), 705–729 (2020). https://doi.org/10.1007/s10640-020-00440-1
16. Tesar, M.: Towards a post-Covid-19 'new normality?' Physical and social distancing, the move to online and higher education. Policy Futures Educ. **18**(5), 556–559 (2020)
17. Aziz, R.C., et al.: Teaching and learning in higher education: E-learning as a tool. Int. J. Innov. Technol. Explor. Eng. **9**(1), 458–463 (2019)
18. Hashim, N.A.A.N., et al.: E-learning technology effectiveness in teaching and learning: analyzing the reliability and validity of instruments. In: IOP Conference Series: Materials Science and Engineering, vol. 993, no. 1 (2020)

Author Index

Printed in the United States
by Baker & Taylor Publisher Services